A Practical Guide to Remedial Reading

HAP GILLILAND
Eastern Montana College

The Charles E. Merrill
COMPREHENSIVE READING PROGRAM
Arthur W. Heilman
Consulting Editor

CHARLES E. MERRILL PUBLISHING COMPANY

A Bell & Howell Company

Columbus   Toronto   London   Sydney

Published by
CHARLES E. MERRILL PUBLISHING COMPANY
A Bell and Howell Company
Columbus, Ohio 43216

This book was set in Times Roman.
The production editors were Sharon Keck Thomason and
   Elizabeth A. Martin.
The cover was prepared by Larry Hamill.

Library of Congress Catalog Card Number: 77-93415

International Standard Book Number: 0-675-08359-1

Printed in the United States of America

1 2 3 4 5 6 7 8 9 10/ 85 84 83 82 81 80 79 78

Other Titles in Merrill Comprehensive Reading Program
Arthur W. Heilman, *Consulting Editor*

BURRON	*Basic Concepts in Reading Instruction, Second Edition*
EKWALL	*Psychological Factors in Teaching Reading*
FORGAN	*Teaching Content Area Reading Skills*
HEILMAN	*Smuggling Language into the Teaching of Reading, Second Edition*
HILLERICH	*Reading Fundamentals for Preschool and Primary Children*
MCINTYRE	*Reading Strategies and Enrichment Activities for Grades 4–9*
MANGRUM	*Developing Competencies in Teaching Reading*
MAY	*To Help Children Read, Second Edition*
PFLAUM-CONNOR	*The Development of Language and Reading in Young Children, Second Edition*
SHEPHERD	*Comprehensive High School Reading Methods, Second Edition*
STRAIN	*Accountability in Reading Instruction*
WEIMER	*Reading Readiness Inventory*

Other Texts of Interest

EKWALL	*Locating and Correcting Reading Difficulties, Second Edition*
GEYER	*Programmed Reading Diagnosis for Teachers*
JORDAN	*Dyslexia in the Classroom, Second Edition*
WEIMER	*Reading Readiness Inventory*
WOODS	*Analytical Reading Inventory*

Preface

Nearly every classroom contains some students whose reading level falls below their potential. This book was written for all who wish to aid those students. Because instruction in remedial reading must be based on a thorough understanding of each child's problems, diagnosis for determining the causes of the difficulties and the specific needs of each student is emphasized. Emphasis is also given to those children who are most likely to develop reading problems—those with learning disabilities.

Instructional Guides

A special feature of this book which is designed to help the teacher meet the individual needs of each remedial reading student is the inclusion throughout the book of Instructional Guides. These guides list problems which may be observed by the teacher, possible causes for these problems or methods of further diagnosis, and, finally, a variety of specific suggestions for instruction. When the teacher discovers that a child has a reading problem, she can turn to the Instructional Guide dealing with that particular problem and immediately find a list of specific suggestions for remediation.

Use of the Pronoun "She" to Denote the Teacher

Throughout this book, the pronoun "she" is used to represent the remedial reading teacher, while the pronoun "he" is used to refer to the student. This is not to be construed as an indication that reading teachers should be women; the pronoun is simply used for clarification. When a paragraph is concerned with the actions of both teacher and student, the meaning is clearer if different pronouns are used. Since in actual practice more remedial reading teachers are women and the majority of remedial reading students are boys, it is statistically accurate to use the male pronoun for the student and the female for the teacher.

Acknowledgment

The writer wishes to acknowledge the many ideas he has received from the teachers and student teachers in the Eastern Montana College Reading Clinic as well as the encouragement and assistance he has received from his family. These people have made this book possible.

Hap Gilliland

Contents

Instructional Guides

What Is Remedial Reading?

Jim is in the fourth grade in school. He is a whiz at arithmetic but has trouble with a second-grade reader.

Billy can sound out any word he encounters but has no idea what he has read.

Joe has spent eight years in school but is reading at second-grade level. He spoke no English until he started to school and can see no connection between the stories he finds in his basic reader and his experiences on the Navajo Reservation where he lives.

Mary lost her visual memory and her ability to read when she had typhoid fever. She is learning to read again by sounding out each word separately.

Johnny is "the brightest child in his room," but he "hates reading." He is a tough character who loves science and adventure (His own!) but refuses to have anything to do with "them girl stories" in the reading books.

These are students in a remedial reading class. Hardly a group of nice little carbon copies who will go along with whatever the teacher says; hardly a class for which *one* remedial reading method will work!

Are there more children like them? Yes, there are many more—but not like them! Each child is a unique individual with different problems, and each one needs a different program of instruction.

These children do have some things in common, however. The level at which each is reading is low in comparison to his general level of mental ability. In addition, each knows he has problems, and each hopes—secretly, perhaps—that the remedial reading teacher will have the answer to his problems.

What Is Remedial Reading Instruction?

A student is considered to be in need of remedial reading instruction if his reading level is less than three-fourths the reading expectancy level of a person of his age and mental ability. Since, for one or many reasons, these students have not learned to read as well as could be expected in the regular classroom, a different kind of reading instruction is needed. Remediation is for these students who have the potential to improve their reading skills through the remedial reading programs that have been established.

There is no one method of teaching remedial reading suitable for all students, or even for the majority of students. Indeed, the chief characteristic of remedial reading instruction is that it is individually planned to fit the special needs and abilities of the individual student.

In the average classroom, only about one-third of the class will be reading at grade level. Approximately one-third will be above grade level, and the other one-third will be below grade level. *However, not all of those who are reading below grade level are in need of remedial instruction.* The majority of the slow readers are simply low in ability. They are reading at a level commensurate with their mental capacity. Nonetheless, one-fourth to one-half of the poor readers in any classroom have the potential for much greater achievement and should receive special remedial instruction. In addition, a few of those who are considered average in reading should be considered candidates for special help because they have the capacity for much higher achievement.

Remedial reading instruction in the public schools typically is handled in any one of three places—the regular classroom, a special remedial reading class, or, for special cases, a reading clinic. Any instruction designed to help the poor reader reach his potential can be correctly described as remedial reading instruction; however, for clarification, the instruction is often differentiated through the terms designating where it is taught: *corrective reading*, if taught as a part of the regular classroom reading program; *remedial reading*, if taught by a special remedial reading teacher; and *clinical instruction*, if handled by a multi-disciplinary team of teachers and diagnosticians.

The Importance of Remedial Reading Instruction

Reading is the most universally used subject taught in the schools. While other subjects may be interrelated only slightly, the study of *all* these other subjects is dependent upon the reading skill of the pupil. Recent emphasis on reading instruction has resulted in improvement in the reading of school children. Comparison of the results of the national testing programs conducted by the National Assessment of Educational Progress show that in 1975, both nine- and seventeen-year-old children were reading better than their counterparts in 1971. According to Marie Eldridge, administrator of the National Center for Educational Statistics, "These results show that reading skills are improving at the elementary school level and in 'everyday' reading situations." [1]

The reading of black teenagers and of students from low income areas have both improved by five percentage points in four years, and 50,000 more nine-year-olds could read adequately in 1975 than four years earlier. Yet children's reading skills must improve even more if

---

[1] Marie D. Eldridge, quoted in *NAEP Newsletter,* Denver, National Assessment of Educational Progress, October 1976, p. 1.

they are to keep up with the additional demands placed on them. The reading expected of the student in almost every area of the curriculum is increasing by leaps and bounds, and good jobs are becoming increasingly rare for the person who leaves school with inadequate reading skills. Yet, according to a recent study by the University of Texas Adult Practical Literacy Research Project, 35 million adult Americans have reading skills that are too low to allow them to cope as functional consumers. These people cannot adequately fill out application forms for jobs or prepare income tax returns.

In spite of improvements made, the nation-wide testing of the National Assessment of Educational Progress indicated that only "89% of the 17-year-olds in the nation's schools are functionally literate. This means that nearly 11 percent are still unable to perform such tasks as reading a newspaper, a driver's license test, or even labels on medicine bottles and foods." [2] This number becomes much larger among disadvantaged students. Twenty-one percent of the 17-year-olds from disadvantaged urban areas and 42 percent of those who are black are still functionally illiterate. [3] If this number is to continue to decrease, adequate remedial reading instruction must be offered to every student who is not reaching his potential in reading.

On the average, it can be expected that at least one out of every ten students in a school will have some specific reading problems. Schools and teachers should plan to provide remedial instruction for about that number. In disadvantaged areas, it is not unusual for one-half the pupils to need help, and, in a few cases, this number reaches nearly 100 percent. Conversely, in a few rare cases, nearly every child in the school may be reading at or above his grade level. However, some of these students have the potential to do better and could profit by special help.

A student's inability to read adequately to meet his needs not only makes normal progress in all subjects almost impossible, but also may have disastrous effects on his self-concept, and his emotional well-being. The remedial reader is seldom a happy person. His feelings of inadequacy and insecurity make it very difficult for him to accept himself as being normal and intelligent. His problems are compounded by the fact that the development of an out-going, likable personality requires a sense of security and well-being, not a sense of failure.

A study made in one school system indicated that more than one-half of all school drop-outs were retarded by two or more class years in reading and that the number of drop-outs was greatly lessened when

Ruth Love, former director of Right to Read, quoted in *NAEP Newsletter,* Denver, National Assessment of Educational Progress, August 1976, p. 9.

[3] *NAEP Newsletter,* Denver, National Assessment of Educational Progress, February 1977, p. 1.

poor readers in high school were given remedial instruction. High school students who had been attending school only about one-half the time often had almost perfect attendance while receiving an hour each day of remedial reading instruction.

What Can Be Expected from Remedial Reading Instruction?

Remedial instruction *will* make the difference between success and failure for a great many pupils. However, the school which expects *any* program to work miracles will be disappointed. A student who has never been able to progress at the rate of the other children cannot be expected to progress at several times the average rate during the period of remedial instruction and then continue to progress at a better than average rate after the special help is discontinued.

Studies indicate that, prior to remedial instruction, the average student in remedial reading classes had been improving in reading at a rate of about one-half year for each year in school; that is, he had been progressing at about 50 percent of the average rate. In a period of sudden improvement, the average progress at the beginning of remedial instruction is 3.9 months of growth in reading for each month of remedial instruction. Although growth is usually greatest during the first two or three months of remedial instruction and somewhat slower to occur later on, the student does continue to progress at about 1.4 years of growth for each year of instruction, a rate which is faster than the average classroom rate. Progress in reading in the regular classroom after the termination of remedial instruction is, on the average, approximately three-fourths year for each year in school. That is, it is about halfway between the progress the student was making before remediation and the current progress of the rest of the class.

These studies point up the fact that, although the student can be expected to make good gains during specialized instruction and although his continued progress in the regular classroom will be much greater than it was before the remedial instruction, he still will continue to fall farther behind his classmates unless the school can follow up with the intensive additional help adequate to his needs.

The cooperation of the classroom teacher is essential to the success of the remedial program. The teacher should watch for any sign that a child is beginning to have difficulty in reading and give corrective help as soon as evidence of trouble appears, so that problems of a more serious nature may be prevented. If serious problems do develop, the child should be referred for remedial reading instruction as early as possible, thus, the time needed for treatment will be lessened, and the child will have a much better chance of eventually becoming a good reader.

When the students are dropped from the special remedial reading classes, the regular teacher should give them as much individual help of a corrective nature as possible and should call on the reading specialist for aid or suggestions if the student again begins dropping farther behind.

The Purpose of This Book

Since this book is intended as a practical guide for the teacher of children with reading problems, little space is devoted to theoretical background or to the psychological principles and the experimental research behind the suggested methods of teaching. These are touched upon only in a context in which they will help the teacher to understand the reasons for using certain methods or to select the methods most appropriate to the individual student.

The emphasis is on two areas—means of diagnosis of reading problems to determine the specific needs of the individual student and teaching methods to meet those individual needs.

To increase its usefulness to the teacher, information on methods is summarized in "Instructional Guides" throughout the book. The teacher needing help with a particular reading problem can turn to the guide dealing with that problem and find suggestions for remediation in that area. For quick reference, a list of the Instructional Guides follows the table of contents. The general topics are also included in the index. Many of the Instructional Guides are divided into three columns: observations (the clues which may indicate a need for remediation); possible causes (or means of diagnosis); and recommended procedures for remediation. Thus, this book is a reference volume in which the remedial reading teacher can quickly find a list of suggestions for meeting the needs of any student.

Summary

Instruction may be properly considered "remedial reading instruction" if it is designed to help the student whose reading level falls below his mental ability level.

In most school systems, this instruction is classified as corrective, remedial, or clinical, depending upon whether it takes place in the regular classroom, a special class separate from the regular class, or a special center under a multi-disciplinary team of specialists.

Although each student is unique and must have a special program of instruction designed for him to alleviate his own specific problems, there are some characteristics which are common to many remedial reading students. Many students also have learning disabilities or emotional problems, and there are several times more boys than girls with serious reading problems.

Approximately one of every ten students should have special remedial help in reading. While improved instruction is decreasing the number of students with serious reading problems, special help for those who need it becomes steadily more important as reading becomes more and more essential for academic or vocational success in any area.

Recommended Related Reading

Athey, Irene, "Developmental Processes and Reading Processes: Invalid Inferences from the former to the latter," in *Theoretical Models and Processes of Reading.* 2d ed., eds. Harry Singer and Robert Ruddell. International Reading Association, 1976, p. 730.

A discussion of the need for the reading teacher to be cognizant of developments in related areas to meet the changing needs of students.

Kennedy, Eddie C. "Learning About Remedial Reading," in *Classroom Approaches to Remedial Reading.* Itasca, Ill.: F. E. Peacock Publishers, Inc., 1971, pp. 1–17.

Discusses what are remedial and corrective reading and the teacher's role.

Spache, George D. "Defining the Basic Premises," in *Diagnosing and Correcting Reading Disabilities.* Boston, Mass.: Allyn and Bacon, 1976, pp. 3–13.

Discusses the basic concepts of remedial reading.

2

Basic Principles of
Remedial Reading

The most distinctive characteristic of remedial reading instruction is its individualization. Whether the student is actually taught individually or in a group, his program of instruction must be planned to fit *his* particular needs. Because reading instruction is designed for those students who have not achieved under a program of general instruction planned for the group, no one method of teaching, no matter how good, will be appropriate for all remedial students.

The remedial reading teacher, however, must be thoroughly familiar with basic methods of teaching reading. The teacher must know the skills taught in the basic program and must know which skills the student needs as background in order to learn others. Since the instruction for any one student will be concentrated on those skills in which he is deficient, the teacher must be able to use effectively a variety of methods for teaching each skill which might be applicable to any given student. Therefore, the remedial reading teacher first must be a good teacher of reading. In addition, the remedial teacher must be able to diagnose reading problems, understand children's differences in personality and learning methods, and be able and willing to adapt instruction to both. The teacher who has settled into a routine in the basic reading program sometimes finds it very difficult to adapt to the use of the great variety of methods needed in remedial teaching.

Remedial instruction is much more concentrated than the usual classroom instruction, for time in the remedial program is usually at a premium. Therefore, it is necessary to help the pupil to learn as many skills as possible in the limited time available. Although creative activities related to reading should be a part of the remedial program, the time used for these activities must be strictly limited. Many time-consuming activities which are a part of the developmental reading program must be eliminated and instruction limited to the specific reading needs of the student. A great deal of instruction must be telescoped into small periods of time, yet this must be done without putting undue pressure on the child. At the same time, a relaxed atmosphere is extremely important, as tension related to reading is often one of the chief causes of lack of achievement.

Certain general principles of diagnosis and treatment of reading disabilities apply to most cases of poor reading. Still, the instruction given to a thirty-year-old man will be very different from that given to a remedial reader in the second grade, just as the instruction for a student who lacks visual memory will not be the same as that for a person whose chief problem is severe emotional blocking. Nonetheless, the general principles will usually apply even though the application of these principles will be different for each individual student. Nine of these basic principles follow:

1. *Diagnose.* Determine the reading needs as well as the strengths and weaknesses of each student. Continue this diagnosis throughout all instruction.

2. *Individualize.* Teach each student differently according to his needs and by the methods through which he can learn most easily. Change this instruction as the student learns and his needs change.

3. *Start at an Easy Reading Level*—one which is well below the student's reading level so that he is virtually certain of success.

4. *Build the Student's Self-Concept.* Demonstrate his progress to him and help him develop confidence in his own ability to succeed.

5. *Motivate.* Build an interest and a desire to read in the student.

6. *Keep a relaxed atmosphere.* Develop a relationship between the students and the teacher in which reading can be fun for both.

7. *Use Variety in the Program.* Several types of activities should be included within the instructional period, and the instruction should be different from the reading program in which the student has previously participated.

8. *Build Word Recognition Skills.* All other skills are useless until the child can recognize the words.

9. *Use Specialized Methods.* With students who have special problems and specific learning disabilities, use methods adapted to the specific learning disabilities of the individual.

10. *Follow Up.* Use follow-up procedures to insure that the students are given the help they need after the period of special remedial reading instruction has ended.

Each of these principles is discussed in more detail in this chapter.

Diagnose

All remedial reading instruction must be planned to meet the specific needs of the individual student; therefore, thorough diagnosis is indispensable. Although exactly what is included in this diagnosis, what diagnostic instruments are used, who is involved in making the diagnosis, and when and where the diagnosis takes place will vary with the circumstances and the type of program, a thorough evaluation upon which instruction can be planned is essential.

In some cases, a complete diagnosis by an inter-disciplinary team of specialists of each student's reading and related problems is completed before any instruction is begun. In other cases, where all or most of the diagnosis is done by the remedial reading teacher, it may be necessary to do only enough testing for proper selection and grouping of students prior to teaching. The greater portion of the diagnosis may then be done largely as a matter of verifying leads obtained through observation and instructional procedures after instruction has begun.

Whether the diagnosis, in the main, takes place before or after the instruction begins, the following areas should be covered:

1. *Reading Level* is the most important single factor in diagnosis, since it is necessary to know the student's reading level in order to select students, to plan the appropriate type of instruction, and to choose materials which the child can read effectively.

2. *Intelligence.* Since students are placed in remedial reading classes because their potential for reading is higher than their present reading level, some information on the student's ability is needed for selection. This information also will aid the teacher in adapting the type of instruction to the needs of the individual student.

    Information on these two factors is needed for selection of students for the remedial reading program. The other areas listed below can be diagnosed either before instruction begins or as a part of the instructional procedure.

3. *Background and Interests.*

4. *Comprehension Skills Used in Reading Various Kinds of Material.*

5. *Vocabulary.*

6. *Word Analysis Skills and the Student's Ability to Apply Them to Word Recognition While Reading.*

7. *Physical Problems, including Vision, Hearing, and General Health.*

8. *Social and Emotional Problems.*

9. *Specific Learning Disabilities and Learning Modalities.*

10. *Speed and Study Skills of Students Who Are Reading above the Primary Level.*

In evaluating each area, both strengths and weaknesses should be noted. The discovery of strengths is nearly as important as the identification of weaknesses, since remediation often must be based on these strengths. For example, if a child is found to be poor in visual memory but strong in auditory skills, instruction will be more effective if the emphasis is placed on phonetic analysis than if it is on the building of a sight vocabulary.

The evaluative information must be organized and recorded in such a way that it can be a continuous guide to the teacher in planning instruction. Continued evaluation throughout the instruction is essential to determine the changing needs of the student and to adjust instruction accordingly.

Individualize

The greatest difference between remedial reading instruction and the usual developmental reading program is the amount of individualization required in remediation. Although individual differences are recognized and cared for in the developmental reading program, approximately the same basic skills are taught to all children in such programs, because every child must have an opportunity to learn these skills. Most remedial students have been thoroughly exposed to this basic reading program. However, while they may have a good understanding of some of the skills they have been taught, they may have little or no understanding of others. A student may not be able to apply certain skills although he makes good use of others. Therefore, every part of the remedial instruction must be based upon the particular needs of the individual student. The whole purpose of the thorough diagnosis described on pages 9 and 10 is to make this individualization possible.

The fact that each student's program is planned to meet his individual needs does not eliminate the possibility of grouping. In fact, group instruction is preferable for most pupils. However, the group must be kept small, and there must be a great deal of individualization within the group. Students with approximately the same reading level and similar problems should be grouped together if possible, regardless of the class from which they come. However, this is often not possible. A classroom teacher who has several remedial students in his or her class will probably want to release all of them for remedial instruction at the same time, although their reading skills may vary greatly. This simply means that there will need to be even more flexibility and individualization within the group. There will, however, still be some instruction for which the group can be together.

When it is possible to group according to needs, it is best to have a spread of no more than three grade levels in any one group. With a wider age spread than this, interests will be too divergent and motivation too difficult.

Most of the better programs place students in groups of one to six students, depending upon the individual needs and the severity of the problems of each student. Since individual needs will vary even within the small group, the teacher will often have no more than two or three students out of a group of six working together. The rest of the group may be working individually.

Such individualization requires thorough planning. Not only the teacher, but also each student must know exactly what should be accomplished during the period and understand why.

All instruction must be planned to meet the needs of the student as these needs have been determined through the diagnosis. This instruction must be based upon those skills which the student has already developed.

The teacher must be careful to avoid a tendency toward stereotyped remedial reading instruction, such as that found in those programs in which all students receive kinesthetic training, regardless of their needs, or in which all students use the same machine and work on speed, regardless of whether their comprehension and vocabulary are adequate. These programs are not based on the needs of each individual student.

In group work, it is particularly easy to assume that the skills learned by all the members of the group are identical and that, therefore, all group members are ready for the next step in the program. When, through group discussion, certain conclusions are reached, it is easy to assume that all members of the group have an understanding of those conclusions. But we *cannot* assume that because all received the same instruction, all have reached the same level of understanding.

Group instruction may be appropriate in the introduction of a skill area yet be very inappropriate as the students progress at different rates. A gifted child in the group may gain a thorough understanding of the skill and be able to apply it in a variety of situations while a slow learner is still trying to understand the basic concepts.

The teacher, then, must know the needs, the strengths, and the weaknesses of each individual and plan the remedial program to meet those needs. She must also continue to evaluate the student's changing needs throughout instruction and adjust the instructional procedures to meet those needs.

Start at an Easy Level

Remedial reading instruction *must* be started with material that is at a very easy reading level. In fact, it should begin with material, not at the student's instructional reading level, but from one to two grade levels *below this actual reading level.* This is necessary for five reasons:

1. Self-confidence can be developed only through a series of successes, and the child will make an effort only if he has some expectation of success.

2. The introduction of too many new words causes confusion and prevents the learning of any of them.

3. Acquisition of more advanced skills must be based on the simpler ones already acquired.

4. Skill comes from much reading, and this is not possible if the student must read difficult material.

5. Interest in reading can be developed only through material which the student can read easily.

Build the Student's Self-Concept

Most remedial readers have a very poor self-concept. Having met with continual frustration, not only in reading but in all subjects requiring reading, they may have almost completely lost confidence in their ability to learn as other students learn. Unless the teacher can rebuild the student's confidence in himself and convince him that he can achieve, he will not put forth the effort that is necessary for him to progress.

This means that the teacher must first convince the student that he can learn and is learning, and second, she must build the student's self-esteem and feeling of worthiness as an individual.

A student seldom realizes the amount of progress he is making until that progress is dramatized for him in some concrete way. He cannot remember not knowing a thing, because until he learned it, he was probably unaware of its existence. When allowed to go back over a comprehensive test given before and after a unit of work and to compare the answers, a student will make comments such as, "Do you mean to tell me I didn't *even* know *that!*" Concrete evidence of improvement is important to every child, but it is much more important to the remedial reader than to most other children.

Many types of charts and graphs can be devised for demonstrating to the student his improvement in reading. Graphs can be constructed to show improvement in comprehension, in reading speed, in word analysis rules which he has learned to apply in reading, in the number of letters for which he knows the sounds, and for nearly all the skills which he is trying to improve.

Charts and graphs showing a student's progress not only help the student's self-confidence, they also help the teacher to recognize that progress and to keep a positive attitude toward the child and his ability to learn.

Progress also can be demonstrated through the use of tape recordings of the student's reading which are made at intervals throughout the period of remediation.

Frequent praise is important in building a good self-concept. This does not mean that praise should be lavish, continuous, or given without being deserved. (The remedial student is quick to recognize insincerity.) It does mean that the teacher must recognize each thing that the child does well, each sincere effort that he makes, and motivate the child through praising the good rather than through criticizing the bad. In the usual classroom situation, criticism is meted out much more frequently than praise, and the remedial student has received much more than his share of criticism.

Because of teachers' critical attitudes toward the students' reading, most remedial students assume that their teachers dislike them. The remedial reading teacher must accept the student and help him to realize that he is a worthwhile person—that his value as a person has nothing to do with his reading ability. The teacher who genuinely likes students has a big advantage over the one who thinks of them only as responsibilities. The teacher's attitude should show that she respects the child as a person and expects the child's respect in return.

Letting the students tell their own experiences, recording them in writing, and using them as reading material also aids in building the self-concept of the students. It helps them to realize that their own experiences and creative ideas are important.

The poor self-concept of many remedial students is due not only to frustrations within the school but also to parental attitudes of perfectionism, inconsistency, and continual criticism. Parent conferences, in which there is a frank discussion of the child's problems and of the self-concept which he needs to develop, can be very helpful. Some reading clinics have experimented with classes in child psychologogy for parents of remedial reading students and have found them to be well accepted and very beneficial to the children.

Motivate

A teacher frequently hears a statement such as, "You've got to make him learn this!" Yet no one can make a child learn anything. Learning does not come from external pressure; it comes from an active effort to learn.

At times, a student may make an effort to learn simply because someone else wants him to learn—his teacher or his mother, perhaps.

For this reason, good rapport between the teacher and the pupil is important. However, unless the learner has a real interest, his effort is apt to be rather half-hearted and short-lived.

The remedial reading student may be motivated to learn through two kinds of interest: a sincere desire to learn to read and a deep interest in the material that is being read. The subject matter must be interesting to the student. Stories should be of a type that this particular student enjoys, and the pupil should be given an opportunity to help in the selection of his reading material. Most remedial readers, especially boys, like fast-moving adventure stories with plenty of action. The slow-starting story, with several pages of introductory material, is not suitable for this type of reader.

Non-fiction material should be either on subjects which are directly related to the student's life or in which he has a deep interest. This material may include camping information for the active scout, science material for the student who likes to experiment, or job information and application forms for the young adult. Opportunity for applying the information, such as building a model from the directions read, should be given whenever possible.

Not all reading material can be intrinsically motivating, however. Learning the basic sight words must be motivated by the student's understanding that over half of the reading that he will do at any level consists of these words. Learning letter sounds can be motivated only by the student's realization that this will make it possible for him to recognize the words he wants to read. The student cannot be expected to work hard to learn any skill unless he understands the reason why this skill will be important to him.

Keep a Relaxed Atmosphere

Many remedial students live with hostility, tension, and criticism. These may be their main blocks to learning. Finding that the reading room is a place where they need have no fears and will not be under tension may do more to promote progress than anything in the instruction itself.

A stern, authoritative attitude has no place in the remedial classroom. This does not mean that the teacher cannot be firm in standards of work and in expecting—and giving—respect. It does mean that the students can come with no fear of criticism or hostility.

Many teachers first beginning to work with remedial students feel that they must maintain an appearance that is all business and seriousness. When they learn to laugh with their students, to openly express their enjoyment of a story or a humorous incident in the classroom, they find that their students take a new interest in reading.

The good remedial reading teacher is also a counselor to her students: one to whom they can express their fears, their frustrations, and their dislikes. In a relaxed atmosphere the students can free themselves of their tensions and be ready to learn.

Use Variety in the Program

Since the remedial reader usually has a short attention span and is not highly motivated, he cannot be expected to stay with one activity for a long period of time or to maintain an interest in a monotonous program. He will become bored very easily. Therefore, the remedial reading program should be different from day to day, include a variety of activities during each instructional period, and be different from the regular classroom reading program.

Build Word Recognition Skills

All other reading instruction is useless unless the student can recognize the words to be read. The student who can identify a large vocabulary of words quickly and easily seldom has a great many problems in reading. Therefore, it is logical that most remedial students find that their greatest problem is word recognition. Thus, for the majority of students, a thorough program in word recognition skills is essential.

Since quick, easy recognition of the most commonly used words speeds up reading, makes it more enjoyable, and improves comprehension, practice on sight word vocabulary through much reading of easy material is helpful. Because the majority of remedial reading students find word recognition difficult, concentrated instruction in phonics and other word analysis skills is also usually necessary. However, the methods of teaching word recognition skills must be adjusted to the individual learning patterns of each individual student.

The program not only must supply the student with the word identification skills needed but also must make sure that he learns to apply these skills in his daily reading.

Use Specialized Methods

The remedial reading teacher must use specialized methods with students who have specific problems or learning disabilities, and this instruction must be individually planned to adjust to the particular learning problems of the individual student.

In general, the special instruction will attempt to do two things: first, strengthen areas in which the student is low in ability; second, find ways of teaching skills through other modalities in which the student is strong. For all remedial readers, but especially for those with specific learning disabilities, all instructions should be clear, concise, and brief. Control, teacher attitude, and expectations must be consistent. The sooner students with learning disabilities are identified and given special help, the better the chance of eventually helping them to be good students.

Many remedial reading students have poor visual memory. These students will need an extra emphasis on phonics—complete sounding out of many words. They may need kinesthetic teaching—tracing words printed on paper, sand, clay, raised letters, or stencils. They may be helped by the oral impress method—simultaneous reading with the teacher while the teacher follows the line of print with her finger, pointing to each word as it is spoken.

Students with poor visual-motor coordination and poor handwriting may need special small-muscle coordination exercises in drawing, writing, and stencil work.

The hyperactive child may need to work in a small enclosed area without distractions and to use materials that are designed to require activity of them.

The distractible child will need to work in a small space, with no distracting materials or bright colors in sight, where he can see no other activity. He will need to have only one piece of work in front of him at a time and to change activity even more frequently than others.

The child who repeats the same error over and over or who seems unable to change a pattern needs to work on another type of activity before coming back to the same material to correct his errors.

The student with poor auditory perception may need to go back to readiness materials with much auditory discrimination practice. Once he becomes a fairly proficient reader, he should work on rapid acquisition of thought from printed material without thinking sounds.

Repeated reversals of letters or word parts may indicate a need for special emphasis on directional attack—changing first letters without emphasis on the rest of the word, games that call attention to the first letter, alphabetizing, tracing letters which are commonly reversed.

The remedial reading teacher needs to be aware of any of these learning disabilities which may be present, be prepared to adjust the instruction accordingly, and, if necessary, to experiment with various methods in order to find a method that will help the particular student.

Follow-Up

If the remedial reading program is to bring lasting improvement in the reading of students, it should include a good follow-up program for aiding the students after their instruction in the program is concluded. Although students usually make good progress during a period of remedial instruction, this progress may not continue in the regular classroom when they are no longer receiving the special help. For this reason, there should be, if possible, a period of gradual adjustment during which the remedial reading teacher occasionally works with the student and has an opportunity to discuss problems and to counsel him. The remedial teacher and the classroom teacher should plan together a reading program that will continue to meet the student's needs and give him reading material in which he can succeed. Any indication of confusion, dropping back into old ways of reading, or loss of interest should bring about immediate help from the classroom teacher, and, if necessary, short returns to the remedial program.

If the remedial program is in a clinic which is not a part of the school system, some type of liaison program between the clinic and the classroom teacher should be established.

Summary

Complete individualization to meet the special needs of each student is the most significant feature of remedial reading instruction. This does not mean that each student must be taught separately, but it does mean that the program for each student will vary from that of the other students as much as is necessary to meet those needs which are discovered by a thorough diagnosis of the student's reading and related problems. Continued diagnosis will permit changes in the program as the needs of the student change.

The program must begin at a sufficiently easy level so that the student is virtually certain of success, and the student's self-concept must be built through successful reading and through help in seeing his own progress. The program must be varied, and methods and materials must be such that they will build an interest and a desire to learn. Word recognition skills must be built, since no other reading skills are of value until the student can recognize the words.

Students with specific learning disabilities require the use of specialized methods adapted to their special problems, and all students need some type of follow-up program to see that they continue to progress in the regular classroom reading program.

INSTRUCTIONAL GUIDE 2.1

The Basic Principles of Remedial Reading

1. *Diagnose*—Know each student's needs and problems.

2. *Individualize*—Plan the instruction to meet specific needs.

3. *Start at an Easy Level*—Let the student experience success.

4. *Build the Student's Self-Concept*—Dramatize his strengths.

5. *Motivate*—Build on interests and a desire to learn.

6. *Keep a Relaxed Atmosphere*—Make reading a pleasure.

7. *Use Variety in the Program*—Keep attention and interest high.

8. *Build Word Recognition Skills*—Form a basis for all other skills.

9. *Use Specialized Methods*—Adapt to learning disabilities.

10. *Follow Up*—See that growth in reading continues.

Recommended Related Reading

Bond, Guy L., and Miles Tinker. "Basic Principles of Remedial Instruction," in *Reading Difficulties—Their Diagnosis and Correction*. Des Moines, Iowa: Meredith Publishing Co., 1967, pp. 241–66.

A good discussion of basic methods and concepts.

Ekwall, Eldon E. "Some Important Operational Procedures," in *Diagnosis and Remediation of the Disabled Reader*. Boston, Mass.: Allyn & Bacon, Inc., 1976, pp. 22–49.

A good discussion of basic principles of remedial reading.

Schubert & Torgerson. "The Corrective Program in Reading," in *Improving the Reading Program*. 4th ed. Dubuque, Iowa: William C. Brown Co., 1976, pp. 200–212.

A very good chapter on basic methods of teaching remedial reading.

Spache, George D. "Strategies for Improving Remedial Reading," in *Meeting Individual Needs in Reading* by Helen K. Smith. International Reading Association, 1971, p. 53.

Suggestions for teaching remedial reading.

Venezky, Richard L., Dominic Massaro, and Rose-Marie Weber. "Modeling the Reading Process," in *Theoretical Models and Processes of Reading*, 2nd ed., Harry Singer and Robert Ruddell, eds. International Reading Association, 1976, p. 690.

A listing of areas in which research in reading is still needed.

3

Instructionally
Oriented
Diagnosis

Diagnosis as the Basis of Instruction

All remedial reading instruction is based upon the specific needs of the individual student. Therefore, thorough diagnosis of each student's needs is essential. However, diagnosis should be limited to only that which will improve instruction. Unessential testing will be eliminated if it is kept in mind throughout all planning and testing that *the only purpose of diagnosis of reading and related problems is to improve the instruction* to be given to each individual child and to facilitate his learning.

The testing schedule and the tests to be given will vary from one school to another. A complete diagnosis of all phases of the child's reading and related problems may be completed before instruction begins, or the pre-instruction diagnosis may be sufficient only for selection of the students to be admitted to the remedial reading program, with the additional testing integrated later into the instructional program. Regardless of how the diagnostic program is organized, some evaluation usually will be needed of each of the following areas:

1. Reading level

2. Intelligence

3. Background and interests

4. Vocabulary, comprehension, study skills, and speed

5. Word analysis skills

6. Physical, mental, social, and emotional problems

7. Specific learning disabilities and learning modalities

The obvious purpose of all testing is to obtain scores in each area. However, careful observation of the child during all testing will reveal much information about him, his reactions, and his reading skills which cannot be obtained from test scores. Observation of the way in which a child arrives at his answer, his reaction to directions from the teacher, and which particular questions he is able to answer may be more important than the actual score derived from the test.

The examiner, therefore, must be a good observer of children's reactions. She also must be able to establish a good rapport with the child. Otherwise, the test results may be completely invalid.

Testing usually begins with an achievement test which gives comparative scores in each area of reading. This should be an individual test, if possible, but a good group reading test can be used for preliminary screening, if additional testing will be done individually later. This preliminary testing will give an indication of the areas in which the student's reading is deficient.

As particular areas of weakness are discovered, still more information about the child's needs in these areas will be required. This additional information may be obtained by the use of diagnostic instruments designed to test specific skills, by informal tests designed by the teacher or diagnostician, or by careful observation while teaching in these particular areas. The object is to identify each specific strength and weakness so that instruction can be concentrated on the areas of greatest need. The purpose of testing is not only to find the specific skills in which the student needs help, but to determine the point at which instruction in this skill should begin.

The testing program should attempt to determine causes, insofar as this knowledge will aid in improving the child's reading. By knowing the kinds of reading instruction which have been used, fundamental skills which have and have not been taught, physical difficulties, home conditions which may have been upsetting, deficiencies in background for understanding, and emotional problems of the child, the teacher will be able to adapt reading instruction accordingly. Gaps in instruction may be filled in, and, if obstacles cannot be removed, an attempt can be made to compensate for them.

Determining the child's mental ability also will aid in adapting instruction. Attempting to reach goals which are above the mental capacity of the child not only may waste time but also may cause frustration and emotional problems. Goals set must be realistic for this particular student, so that they can be achieved successfully. On the other hand, setting expectations at too low a level can cause the child to be bored or satisfied with achievement which is inadequate for him.

As much information as possible should be obtained concerning the student's reading habits and his attitude toward reading as well as about his background for understanding what is read, for these factors must be taken into consideration in planning appropriate instruction. If, in the process of evaluation or teaching, emotional problems related to reading are evidenced, then some study of these problems may be necessary.

An effort should be made to identify any specific learning disability which may be preventing the student from learning to read easily. Such an effort may indicate which modes of instruction—auditory, visual, kinesthetic—will be most effective in working with the particular child.

Detailed diagnosis is time-consuming. And the time of neither the diagnostician nor the student should be wasted. Therefore, only those tests which will aid in the instruction of the child should be included. The reading teacher should also remember that a great deal of information on the student's reading will be gained through day-to-day instruction of the student. Some information such as the student's motivation and his deeper feelings about reading can only be obtained in this way.

Standardized tests and formal diagnosis are most effective for identifying general areas of weakness. Informal diagnosis, including teacher-made tests, interviews, discussions and day-to-day observation of reading are usually needed to pinpoint the specific skills to be taught and the best approaches to be used in teaching these skills.

Evaluation should always lead to specific recommendations for instruction. If there is little or no opportunity or desire to change instruction according to these recommendations, the diagnosis will be of little value. The value of testing, then, is in direct proportion to its usefulness in teaching.

A Team Approach to Diagnosis

If a complete diagnosis is to be carried out before instruction begins, then a team approach is advantageous. Shared opinions and verification of findings by more than one person increase the validity of the findings and the usefulness of the recommendations. This team approach should lead to a more complete and less biased treatment of the child.

The membership of the diagnostic team will vary according to the size of the school system or clinic, the type of problems most often being diagnosed, and whether or not the team is involved in instruction as well as diagnosis. The ideal team would include a reading specialist, a classroom teacher, a psychologist, and a counselor, with medical personnel and a speech therapist on call when needed.

If a team approach is used, it is important that the reading specialist who heads the team work with each member, relaying information and helping to determine the areas in which further testing is needed.

Ideally, before a final diagnosis is reached, a staff meeting is held so that each member of the team can share his findings with the others. Conclusions and recommendations can then be reached cooperatively. Differences of opinion should be expressed frankly, and a tentative plan for teaching should be developed.

The diagnostic program will be different in each school, and the schedule must be developed by the reading specialist to fit the needs of the particular program. Four examples of team diagnosis are described in the following sections. As these samples show, there is great variation in the personnel assisting with the diagnosis as well as in the testing included both before and as a part of instruction. In a large school system, the diagnosis may be carried out by a complete interdisciplinary team; in a small school, the team may be limited to the remedial reading teacher, the classroom teacher, and the principal.

The Child-Study Team Approach

Every special education program must have a screening program to identify and evaluate all children with physical, emotional, mental, or educational handicaps. Since this evaluation includes an assessment of intellectual, language, and communication skills, most children with reading problems will be identified through this screening procedure. The cooperation of the remedial reading teacher and the special education teachers will enable those children who have reading problems, but who do not belong in special education, to be referred to the reading teacher. Likewise, the reading teacher can refer children who need help in reading but whose potential for learning is too low for remedial reading instruction to the special education program. The reading teacher can serve on the child-study team for these children.

Since the most serious academic problems of many educationally handicapped children are in reading, it is essential that the teacher or resource teacher working with such children be trained as a reading specialist. If federal funds are used to support the program for learning disabled children, then the reading specialist who works with them must also be certified in learning disabilities. Since these programs overlap to a large extent, both the resource teacher and the reading specialist will usually be included on the child-study team for children with learning disabilities. This child-study team also includes the classroom teacher, and the principal or the principal's representative. If there are school psychologists or speech pathologists available to the school, they will complement the team. Parents should also be urged to be as active on the team as possible. This team determines whether or not other specialists such as the speech therapists, physicians, or psychiatrists are needed to complete the evaluation for any individual child.

In the child-study team approach, each member of the team evaluates the child and makes a written evaluation. Then the entire team meets together to discuss the implications of all this information, to decide whether or not the child is educationally handicapped, and to determine what type of educational program will best meet the needs of this child.

From the diagnostic information obtained by this team, an IEP (individualized education program) is written. This includes: baseline data (present levels of performance); goals for the year; short-term instructional objectives; and the criteria to be used for evaluating the child's achievement of the instructional objectives.

The child-study team approach is mandatory for all children being placed in any type of special education program. It is also a good model for a team approach to the diagnosis of any child to be placed in a remedial reading program. It involves thorough diagnosis and evaluation of each child. The end result is an individual plan based on the child's needs.

Diagnosis in a Small School

In a small school the testing of children for placement in a remedial reading program will be done largely by the remedial reading teacher. However, the interpretation of the test data and its application to the individual child is usually improved through discussion with the classroom teacher and sometimes with the principal or the parents.

As an example of the diagnosis in a small school, let us consider a small school on a Montana Indian reservation which has one classroom for each grade and hires one additional teacher for remedial reading. During the first week of school each year, the *California Reading Test* [1] is administered to all students by the classroom teachers. All upper-grade students whose scores are two years or more below their grade level as well as second- and third-grade students whose scores are one year below grade level are retested. For this second test, each student is given the *Stanford Diagnostic Achievement Test* appropriate to his reading level rather than the one appropriate to his grade.

All new students and those who have not taken it within the last three years are given the *Gilliland Learning Potential Examination,* and IQ scores are obtained, using the special norms for Indian students. Reading expectancy scores are obtained by the formula given in chapter 4 of this book. All pupils whose reading scores are less than two-thirds of their expectancy scores are placed on the list of potential remedial reading students. To this list are added any other pupils whose teachers feel that their potential is much higher than their actual achievement.

The remedial reading teacher then gives the *Test of Individual Needs in Reading* to every pupil on the list and discusses the reading program with all of the students who are candidates for the program. From those who wish to enter the program, she then selects those who she feels will profit most. The others are placed on a waiting list—to be admitted to the program as soon as space is available.

Additional diagnosis is conducted largely through observation and diagnostic teaching, but other tests may be given to individual students as the remedial reading teacher recognizes a need for them.

Diagnosis in a Large School System

In contrast to the situation just described is the reading program in a city of 65,000 people with twenty-six elementary schools and thirteen remedial reading teachers. Each teacher serves two schools, spending either the morning in one and the afternoon in the other or Monday and Wednesday in one and Tuesday and Thursday in the other. These

---

[1] Tests discussed throughout the text, along with their publishers, are listed in the appendixes.

arrangements are worked out between the reading teacher and the principal of each of the two schools. All remedial reading teachers have Friday free from classes for additional testing, preparation, record-keeping, parent conferences, etc.

Remedial students in this system are referred by the classroom teachers and the principal after the remedial teacher has discussed standards and selection criteria with the staff of each school. If more pupils are referred than can be handled, the reading teachers study their cumulative records, interview teachers, and do additional testing on pupils whose records are incomplete.

Pupils are then placed in remedial classes, usually with six pupils from the same grade level in each class. While pupils do free reading from library books, the reading teacher gives an informal reading inventory to each pupil and the *McKee Phonics Test* to each class as a group.

No additional testing is carried out except as the teacher sees a need for it, but the teacher has a variety of tests available to her, and pupils can be referred to the school nurse, school psychologist, or speech therapist for further testing or treatment at any time.

A Suburban School System

This school system is about the same size as that described above but it is in a suburb of a large city. Here, a central reading clinic has been established. Pupils are referred to this clinic by special education child study teams, classroom teachers, principals, physicians, psychiatrists, social workers, and by other professional people.

All pupils referred to the clinic are given a complete evaluation by a team of specialists consisting of a reading specialist, a learning disabilities specialist, a psychologist, a pediatrician, and a speech therapist.

Evaluation usually requires two half-day sessions, although this procedure may vary according to the information obtained on a particular student and as needed tests are omitted or added. All tests administered on the first day are individual. At the conclusion of each test, the examiner recommends any additional tests which she feels will be helpful. All testing is coordinated by the reading specialist.

The tests most frequently administered by this diagnostic team are:

Regularly scheduled tests—One in each of the following areas to each student:

Reading—Individual (oral reading and phonics test):

> *Test of Individual Needs in Reading*
> *Durrell Analysis of Reading Difficulty*
> *Spache Diagnostic Reading Scales*

Reading—Group (test of comprehension, vocabulary, speed study skills):

> *California Reading Test*
> *STS Diagnostic Reading Test*
> *Iowa Test of Basic Skills*
> *Stanford Diagnostic Reading Test*

Intelligence:

Wechsler Intelligence Scale for Children (individual)
Slosson Intelligence Test for Children (individual)
Gilliland Learning Potential Examination (group or individual)
Nonverbal Section, California Test of Mental Maturity (group)

Hearing:

> Audiometer

Vision:

> Telebinocular

Hand-Eye Coordination

Additional tests: As the examiners work with the children and get an indication of their needs, if their observations indicate that a child may have a learning disability or other problem, they may recommend that additional testing be done in a certain area. These additional tests commonly include any of the following:

> *California Personality Inventory*
> *Bender-Gestalt*
> *ITPA (Illinois Test of Psycholinguistic Abilities)*
> *Goldman-Fristoe-Woodcock Test of Auditory Discrimination*
> Visual memory test (from *Learning Potential Examination)*
> Stencil design test (from *Arthur Point Scale Performance Test)*

> *Memory for designs test*
> Visual span test
> Eye movement photographs
> Frostig tests

> *Mills Learning Methods Test*
> Speech articulation test
> Visual motor coordination tests

These tests may indicate a need for any of the following:

A complete physical examination
A neurological evaluation
Psychological testing using projective techniques (e.g., *Rorschach* or *Draw-A-Man)*

At the conclusion of all of the testing for an individual student, a staff conference is held. All those who assisted with the evaluation of this child's problems participate in this meeting, at which the results of all tests administered are discussed and recommendations for an instructional program suited to this child's needs are formulated. When possible, the child's parents, teacher, and principal sit in on this conference.

A small group of students with serious learning disabilities are assigned to the reading clinic for full-time instruction. A few others are referred to the mental health clinic or special-education programs. Most of the students receive a detailed recommended plan of instruction and remain in their own classrooms for their periods of remedial instruction.

Diagnostic Teaching

The remedial reading teacher should never feel that diagnosis has been completed once the instructional program begins. Diagnosis has also only begun. Diagnosis should be continuous throughout all teaching, since it is intended not as a summary of the *status quo* but as an aid to an on-going educational program. For those students making good progress, continual diagnosis is needed to adjust instruction to the student's new and changing needs. When the recommended procedures do not produce results, this should be cause for going over the findings to determine other possible courses which can be tried rather than for discouragement.

Diagnosis during instruction prevents a waste of time. Continual evaluation through tests and observation makes it possible to make full use of class time for teaching those skills most needed by the student. If you know the student's progress, you will not waste time reteaching those areas in which the student is already competent.

Tests given during instruction should be criterion-referenced. The usual standardized tests used to compare individuals are norm-referenced tests.

They survey many skills rather than evaluate mastery of any specific skills. They are designed to create a range of scores for comparison, and no child is expected to get a perfect score.

Criterion-referenced tests, on the other hand, are designed to assist the teacher in determining what instruction the student needs for reaching specific goals and when he has reached those goals.

Many basic reading texts now have criterion-referenced tests to accompany them. Many criterion-referenced tests not related to a specific basic reading text are also available. These tests may be used if they measure the specific skills which have been set as objectives for the particular student. As Grundin (1976, p. 203) says, "One of the greatest problems with norm-referenced value judgments lies in the determination of the criterion. If we talk about satisfactory reading skill, we must decide for what purpose or to whom it should be satisfactory."

Several things must be considered in testing to determine satisfactory achievement in a skill area. First, does the test test those skills which have been the objectives of instruction as determined by the student's needs? Second, are the skills measurable as distinct entities? Attempts to separately measure minute factors that are actually interrelated may result in instruction that is fragmented and not related to actual reading as a whole. As Holdaway (1976, p. 181) states, "We would not attempt to judge an orchestra simply by analyzing the qualities of each instrument, nor by auditioning each player." Third, is holding out for a certain level of achievement in one skill before teaching another delaying achievement? Harris and Smith (1976, p. 104) say that "the hierarchical arrangement of reading skills assumed by most criterion-referenced tests is questionable. While it's obvious that some skills must precede others, the ideal sequencing of reading skills is unknown and probably nonexistent. The idea that one skill must be mastered before the next is begun, a notion that criterion-referenced tests unavoidably reinforce, is inaccurate."

In spite of these problems, it is necessary to evaluate each student's achievement of skills in each area in which he receives instruction to determine how much instruction is needed. Although published tests can be used at times, the majority of this evaluation must be done using teacher-made tests and informal observation. Most of these informal methods are measures of achievement of certain tasks and are therefore criterion-referenced.

Remedial teaching is diagnostic teaching.   As a student is given instruction in a needed skill, the teacher is observing his reactions and progress to determine: (1) how much progress he is making in this skill and how much additional practice he needs in this step of instruction; (2) for what next step or for what related skill he is ready; (3) if the method of presentation is effective for this student, or whether a different approach might be more effective; (4) if other areas of weakness have been observed.

All diagnosis is tentative and subject to revision. Educational tests are not exact measurements which give infallible answers. They are samplings of a child's reactions on a particular day. He not only may react differently on a different day, but his reactions in an instructional setting may be quite different from his reactions in a testing situation. Although every effort is made to obtain as much information as possible during the original evaluation, the alert teacher may discover specific skills which are lacking, strengths which can aid the student's learning, or interests which will provide additional motivation. Such discoveries will lead to changes in the recommended instructional procedures.

Evaluation includes evaluation of learning methods. The original evaluation focuses largely on the child's strengths and deficiencies. The teaching which follows should include systematic trial of several approaches, each of which is judged on the basis of its success with this particular child. As the teacher observes the child in various learning situations, she can make judgments as to which methods she can use most effectively with this particular child.

Diagnosis must be continuous. Because learning is based upon that which has already been learned, the teacher must continue the process of diagnosis. The skills and information being taught will be the basis for future learning. Since it can never be assumed that any student has absorbed all the information that has been presented to him, the teacher must always be alert to determine the amount learned and the changing needs of the student.

Tests are instructional devices. If properly used, teacher-made tests to evaluate progress do not take time away from instruction. Rather, they are an effective means of teaching and review. In many areas, the fastest way of teaching facts is the "corrected test"—letting the student check his own test and evaluate and correct his own answers. Teacher-made tests should always be followed by discussion of the child's answers, correction of misunderstandings, and discussion of strong and weak points. The child should be allowed to use the test as a self-checking device by which he can examine and keep a record of his own progress.

Tests not only teach subject matter, they also teach self-concept—either good or bad. Pupils see them as contests which they either win or lose. If they are used in such a way that they are positive experiences, they can be rewarding to the child and give a feeling of success. They should be regarded as games of skill.

One important outcome of this type of testing may be a change in the student's attitude toward tests. If a student who has previously been thrown into a state of extreme emotional tension by every test (a situation which is quite common with remedial readers) can learn to enjoy taking tests (or at least accept them as something which he likes to do) because they give him information that will be helpful in choosing what he himself wants to do to further his own learning, then testing may be a very valuable part of remedial reading instruction.

Diagnostic teaching requires careful observation.   How does the student react to the teacher's questions? Does he like to analyze, discuss, and experiment or does he prefer to guess at answers quickly and expect to be told whether he is right or wrong? Does he jump to obvious conclusions or look for deeper meanings? Does he like to read aloud in the presence of others or does he try to avoid this situation? Does he want to try new things? Does he need a routine upon which he can depend? Can he carry out an assignment independently or does he need constant assistance?

The child should be observed in problem-solving situations in order to get an indication of *the procedures by which he arrives at his conclusions.* It is as important, for example, to know what process a child uses in attempting to identify a strange word as to know whether or not he identifies it correctly. This information cannot be obtained from a test score; it can only be acquired through observation of the child.

Observation of the learning process should put the *emphasis on the child's strengths* rather than on his weaknesses, on how he learns rather than on what has been learned. If possible, the remedial reading teacher should also observe the child in the regular classroom, as his reactions there may be quite different from his behavior in the remedial reading class and may shed some light on the causes of his problems.

Some institutions have found that even when a team approach is used, almost the entire diagnostic program can be based on diagnosis through instruction (Beery, 1968). The teacher begins by trying out different instructional methods and keeping records of the methods and materials used as well as the results obtained. The team members are available for consultation and discussion of progress. The entire team observes and takes part in the instruction of the students. Testing procedures are used when the team members feel that they are needed, but observations of the students are of greater importance than the test scores. Recommendations are tried out in short teaching sessions and revised through observation of results.

Observation may be made more effective by the use of *observation guides* or checklists which remind the teacher of areas to be observed. When checklists are used, the teacher should have a copy for each child and should rate him on each skill listed. A form such as the sample below may be developed by the teacher to cover those skills which are of concern at the time.

---

1 = Low	3 = Average	5 = High

Child's Insight into His Own Problems:

Very Little Insight			Much Insight	
1	2	3	4	5

Child's Ability to Use Skills Taught in Other Materials:

Little Use			Excellent Transfer	
1	2	3	4	5

Another method of continuing diagnosis is to list the traits down the left side of the sheet followed by a column for each child in the group. Comments or numerical ratings are listed in the column for the child observed. This type of form is easier to handle and to use to record information rapidly when several children are to be observed and the same group will be together each time. It is advantageous to record observations with a different color of pencil each week, noting the dates and color used on the sheet. This practice makes it possible to record continuing observations of the child on the same sheet and to show development of skills and changes in attitudes.

Space can be left at the bottom of the checksheet for summarizing the observations, under such titles as the following:

Areas of particular strength: _____

Areas of special weaknesses: _____

_____

Notable changes observed: _____

_____

    Checklists may deal with specific traits and abilities that might be observed, such as oral reading, word analysis, comprehension, vocabulary, speech, and emotional problems.

Correct interpretation of observations.   Interpretation is the most difficult part of diagnosis through observation. Reactions to instruction and understandings attained are extremely difficult to evaluate. A child's actions and statements can be observed and recorded, but this does not necessarily reveal the reasons for these actions. Especially in the observation of emotional reactions, there is reason for caution in interpretation. The child may be reacting as he appears to be, or his actions may be either a conscious or unconscious cover-up for a completely different inner feeling. Because of this fact, only tentative, general conclusions should be reached from one or two observations.

    Despite any drawbacks it may have, diagnosis through observation eliminates one of the chief problems in many remedial reading programs—the failure to translate the diagnostic data into action in teaching.

Recording and Applying Diagnostic Information

    Unless test results are used to plan individualized instruction to meet the needs of the pupil, the time and effort expended in diagnosis are wasted.

    It is important that the teacher keep complete and exact records of all evaluation, whether it occurs before or during instruction.

    In all cases, much evaluation will be through careful observation of the student during instructional periods. Information obtained in this way should be recorded daily at the end of every instructional period. No teacher can be expected to remember all the details of information obtained about each child in the remedial program. Only the exact daily recording of evaluative data makes it possible to thoroughly adjust instruction to the specific needs of each individual student.

The information obtained from the preinstruction diagnosis *should be summarized* on a graph or chart so that strengths and weaknesses can be noted easily and various skills compared. *Behavioral objectives should be developed,* based upon this record of diagnostic information, and recommendations for instruction should be aimed at meeting these objectives. These recommendations should be specific rather than broad and general.

Methods and materials should be selected which will meet specific needs. When possible, several alternative methods should be suggested to meet a particular goal so that they can be tried out and the most effective method for this individual child chosen.

Although methods chosen should *take into consideration both strengths and weaknesses,* the emphasis should be on strengths, for these can be utilized to make instruction more effective. At the same time, additional instruction will try to build up the weak areas.

While diagnosis began with broad, general, complex areas and gradually was narrowed down to specific information about small areas and specific skills, instruction should be handled in the reverse order. The child should not be expected to handle broad, general understandings or to state general principles until he has learned the detailed skills upon which the generalization is built. For example, in teaching comprehension skills, the teacher would not begin by asking the child to discuss the general theme of an article and its application to life. She would, instead, begin with reading to answer a specific question, reading for details or for sequence of events; gradually, she would build to the main idea of a paragraph and then to larger, more complex materials and ideas.

Following up on Recommendations

If the original diagnosis is a team project, the team members should be involved periodically in observing the child's reaction to the remedial reading program, evaluating his progress, and discussing possible changes or further recommendations. The job of the diagnostic team is not complete once instruction has begun. The team members should be involved as much as possible in the entire program, especially in determining the effectiveness of the instruction resulting from their recommendations for the child.

If the remedial reading teacher is the only person involved in the diagnosis and instruction, she should refer to her test results and objectives frequently to see that she has not overlooked any of the deficiencies which she originally outlined.

When a student is released from the program, a final report of his progress should be sent to his classroom teacher. This report should include information on progress in specific skills and make recommendations for additional help for the student and for follow-up procedures to make sure that skills are not lost and that new attitudes and interests are maintained.

If the remedial reading program is in the school which the student attends, the final report may be only a brief note to the classroom teacher regarding skills emphasized in the program, with an additional paragraph or two of recommendations. If the instruction is in a separate reading clinic, it may be necessary to send copies of the report to the school principal and the parents as well as the teacher. The length of the report will depend both upon the needs of the individual student and the needs of the school system.

Recommendations and reports of progress given to the classroom teacher should be based upon observation of the student during instruction to a greater extent than upon test scores. By the time the teacher has worked with the student daily over a period of time, has listened to him read, and watched him apply his skills, she knows much more about the student than she can learn from any test.

Continuing Follow-up Procedures after the Student Is Released from the Program

One of the greatest failings of most remedial reading programs is in working with the student and the classroom teacher after the student is no longer receiving remedial reading instruction. As Theodore Buerger has said, ". . . reading disability is, for the most part, a chronic condition needing long-term treatment. What is needed after a rather intensive remedial period is provision for supportive reading assistance during the follow-up period." [2]

The remedial reading teacher should talk frequently with the teachers of students who have been released from the program to determine whether or not the students have developed new problems. Occasional visits with the students themselves are even more helpful, for these talks may solve many problems. If it appears desirable, taking a student back into the program for even a few days may solve a particular problem

---

[2] Theodore Buerger, "A Follow-Up of Remedial Reading Instruction," *The Reading Teacher* 21 (January 1968): 333.

and give the student the boost he needs—both academically and emotionally.

The reading specialist also may be able to find reading material appropriate to the student's ability and interests that can be used for his reading in the regular classroom.

Ideally this follow-up program should continue through the remainder of the child's school years. The child who has had problems in elementary school usually again encounters difficulty in junior high and high school. Alerting the secondary school to this possibility and seeing that he gets help early when problems arise, may prevent his problems from again becoming serious. This requires cooperation between all levels of the school system, but this cooperation is worth developing if it prevents the failure of the high-school student.

Cautions in the Use of Diagnosis

Too often, both parents and teachers assume that test scores are exact measures and that diagnosis should give precise answers. Because this assumption may lead to the misuse of diagnostic results, several cautions should be kept in mind during all diagnosis.

First, an achievement test or a mental ability test is not an exact measure like a yardstick. The use of another instrument to test the same thing will not necessarily yield the same results. The test does not cover all areas of reading or of ability; it covers only a few of many possible areas and is only a small sampling of those areas which it does cover. Therefore, errors in testing are bound to occur.

Second, a reading achievement test score usually indicates the child's frustration level rather than his instructional level. Therefore, he cannot be taught at the level indicated by a group achievement test.

Third, there are many areas of reading which cannot be measured adequately with standardized tests. Some examples of these are the ability to use phonics on unknown words while reading, the ability to evaluate propaganda, and the ability to appreciate humorous material.

Fourth, a test is a measure of a student's reactions on a particular day at a particular time and under particular conditions. Many factors other than the skill being tested can influence the score. An intelligence test score, for example, is probably valid if the student—when the test is given—is feeling well, is not overly tense or emotionally upset, is not tired, wants to do his best, has good rapport with the examiner, has a good understanding of English, is taking a nonverbal test or one on which his reading ability is equal to that of the group on which the test was standardized, has no hearing or other physical problems which might affect the test, and comes from a cultural background similar to that of the group for whom the test was written and standardized.

Fifth, titles such as "dyslexic," "brain damaged," and "non-reader," "verbally handicapped," and "culturally deprived" can be misleading and can lead to stereotyping of pupils. In many schools, all pupils who have been given the same labels are given the same type of instruction, although their individual needs may be very different. The label may even become an excuse for the child's lack of achievement or for the teacher's lack of effort to teach him.

Sixth, complete diagnosis is time-consuming, and unless the recommendations resulting from the diagnosis are to be carried out in instruction, the time of both the diagnostician and the student is wasted. The amount of diagnosis that should be carried out will depend upon the degree to which the results will influence the instruction of the student.

Seventh, obtaining scores for each of a number of distinct skills does not necessarily result in the teacher's obtaining an overall picture of this student's reading. These parts of the jigsaw puzzle must be fitted together to form a clear picture of the related whole. In similar fashion, teaching isolated skills which the child lacks will not necessarily improve his reading. For example, teaching the rules for vowel sounds in phonics is usually of no benefit whatever unless the child also is helped to see the value of the use of these rules in independent reading and to integrate this knowledge into his habitual pattern of word attack.

Eighth, diagnosis must result not only in recorded information and recommended procedures but also in specific objectives which are understood and kept in mind to guide both teacher and student during remedial instruction.

Ninth, tests administered or scored by teachers who are careless or who have not had adequate instruction in test administration may not be valid. The remedial reading teacher should make sure that tests administered in the classroom are given according to the exact instructions and timing directions in the test manual and that they are scored correctly. All standardized tests must be administered by reading the instructions to the students exactly as they are printed in the manual, and timing on all timed sections must be exact. Otherwise, the results will be unreliable and, therefore, without value. The remedial reading teacher should not attempt to administer individual intelligence tests or projective techniques unless she has had special training in the use of these devices. The results of all tests should be interpreted by persons who have made a thorough study of the particular test and who understand its purposes and reliability.

Summary

The purpose of all diagnosis of children's reading problems is to make instruction more effective. This fact must be kept in mind throughout all testing and evaluation of testing, for thorough diagnosis makes it possible to plan an instructional program specifically geared to the individual student.

The diagnostic program should cover all phases of the child's reading and related problems. It should begin with evaluation in broad, general areas and be followed by more detailed testing to determine specific instructional needs in those areas in which the student is deficient.

The diagnosis should determine not only the child's present standing in each area tested but also the ways in which he learns best. The latter can sometimes best be determined through diagnostic teaching rather than standardized tests.

Diagnosis of reading problems is usually more valid and effective if a team approach to it is used. The team may vary from the reading teacher, the classroom teacher, and the principal in a small school to a complete inter-disciplinary team, including members from the educational, sociological, medical, and psychological fields. In either case, the team should be headed by a reading specialist who coordinates the work of the team members and sees that the diagnosis is oriented toward improved instruction for the individual student.

A thorough diagnosis of each child's reading and related problems may be made before remedial reading instruction begins, or the preinstructional diagnosis may cover only those factors necessary for selection and grouping of pupils, with the additional diagnosis being done as a part of the instructional program. Regardless of the type of testing program adopted, continuous evaluation is essential throughout the instructional program so that the instruction may be adapted to the changing skills and abilities of the student and to the methods by which he learns best.

The diagnosis will need to cover the following major areas of reading:

1. Reading level
2. Word analysis skills
3. Comprehension
4. Vocabulary
5. Study skills
6. Rate of reading

Diagnosis also should include the major areas which may affect reading achievement:

1. Intelligence

2. Background and interests

3. Vision

4. Hearing

5. Health

6. Social and emotional problems

7. Specific learning disabilities

Reports of the testing should include recommendations for instruction and should be readily available to both the remedial reading teacher and the regular classroom teacher.

Diagnosis should always be considered a tentative appraisal of a child's reactions at a particular time rather than an exact measure of the child's abilities. It should be used, not for labeling the child, but for planning an effective reading program adapted to the reading skills and the learning methods of the individual student.

Recommended Related Reading

Blanton, William E., and Roger Farr. *Measuring Reading Performance.* Newark, Del.: International Reading Association, 1974, 70 pp.

Covers a variety of means of evaluation of reading.

Brewer, William F. "Is Reading a Letter-by-Letter Process? A Discussion of Gough's Paper," in *Theoretical Models and Processes of Reading,* 2d ed., eds. Harry Singer and Robert B. Russell. Newark, Del.: International Reading Association, 1976, p. 536.

A theoretical model of the reading process emphasizing meaning and reasoning as the basis. May have implications for what to diagnose.

Ekwall, Eldon E. "Some Important Operational Procedures," in *Diagnosis and Remediation of the Disabled Reader.* Boston, Mass.: Allyn and Bacon, Inc., 1976, pp. 22–49.

Good coverage of diagnosis.

Franklin, Perry L. "Determining Student Ability to Read Subject Material," in *Teachers, Tangibles, Techniques,* ed. B. S. Schulwitz. Newark, Del.: International Reading Association, 1975, pp. 102–107.

Suggestions for diagnosis by the classroom teacher at the secondary level.

Gough, Philip B. "One Second of Reading," in *Theoretical Models and Processes of Reading*, 2d ed., eds. Harry Singer and Robert B. Ruddell. Newark, Del.: International Reading Association, 1976, pp. 509-35.

A description of a letter-by-letter theory of reading that may have implications in diagnosis and instruction.

Grundin, Hans U. "Evaluating Competence in Functional Reading," in *New Horizons in Reading*, ed. John E. Merritt. Newark, Del.: International Reading Association, 1976, pp. 198-207.

Discusses question: With what level of reading can we be satisfied?

Harris, Larry A., and Carl B. Smith. "Assessing Student Progress and Needs," in *Reading Instruction: Diagnostic Teaching in the Classroom*. New York: Holt, Rinehart, and Winston, 1976, pp. 98-128.

Describes overall plan of diagnosis and evaluation of progress.

Holdaway, Don. "Self Evaluation and Reading Development," in *New Horizons in Reading*, ed. John E. Merritt. Newark, Del.: International Reading Association, 1976, pp. 181-92.

Shows importance of letting student have a part in diagnosis.

Kennedy, Eddie C. "Constructing and Using Teacher-made Tests," in *Classroom Approaches to Remedial Reading*. Itasca, Ill.: F. E. Peacock Publishers, Inc., 1971, p. 18.

Information on advantages and disadvantages of teacher-made tests, suggestions for developing them, with examples.

Kochevar, Deloise E. "Individual Tests and Techniques that Bring Remediation in Reading," in *Individualized Remedial Reading Techniques for the Classroom Teacher*. New York: Parker Publishing Co., 1975, pp. 99-127.

Clear, concise discussion of the use of reading tests.

Mootowitz, Sue. "Are You the Key to your Reading Program—Building Your Own Reading Tests," *Instructor*, 80:7, March 1971, p. 52.

Good suggestions for making and using teacher-made tests.

Schubert & Torgerson. "Diagnosis in the Instructional Program," *Improving the Reading Program*, 4th ed. Dubuque, Ia.: William C. Brown Co., 1976, pp. 142-85.

Covers formal and informal methods of diagnosis.

Wilson, John A. R. "Successful Methods of Reading Diagnosis," in *Reading Rx: Better Teachers, Supervisors, Programs*, ed. Joseph S. Nemeth. Newark, Del.: International Reading Association, 1975, pp. 168-74.

Describes types of diagnosis and lists skills to be evaluated.

Wilson, Robert M. "Introduction to Diagnosis," in *Diagnostic and Remedial Reading for Classroom and Clinic*, 2d ed. Columbus, Oh.: Charles E. Merrill Publishing Co., 1972, pp. 21-43.

4

Mental Ability and the
Selection of Students

Whether they are to be placed in a remedial reading program outside the regular classroom or given special corrective help within the classroom, the students to receive specialized reading instruction must be selected carefully, so that the remedial reading program will be of greatest possible benefit both to the individual student and the school as a whole.

Students to be placed in a remedial reading program are generally chosen on the basis of the following five factors: (1) their mental ability is greater than their actual reading level; (2) the pupils desire help; (3) recommendations have been received from teachers; (4) the chronological age or grade of the child is important; and (5) the parents are willing to cooperate.

Before admitting a student to remedial reading instruction, it is essential that the teacher know whether or not the student is already reading at the level of his capacity. Even though his reading is below the average for his grade, he may already be reading at a level which is commensurate with his ability; therefore, he cannot be expected to profit a great deal from remedial instruction. Consequently, the remedial reading teacher must have a valid means of determining the reading expectancy for each student.

Research shows that children of almost any level of intelligence can learn the same reading skills. The difference is in the rate at which they learn these skills. This rate is known as their reading potential. That is, the student with a high level of intelligence has the potential to progress much more rapidly than the student with low intelligence. If we are to select those students who have the potential to progress more rapidly than they are now progressing, then we must have some way of measuring this reading potential.

There are two accepted means of determining whether a student is reading at his expected level. One is through measuring listening comprehension and comparing this with reading comprehension. The other is through comparing mental ability with reading ability.

Intelligence as a Measure of Reading Potential

The best measure of a student's potential progress in reading is his intelligence, but, in most cases, teacher judgment from observation alone will not provide sufficient evidence of the student's ability; as a result, some type of intelligence test usually will be needed.

Group Intelligence Tests

Giving all students in the school group intelligence tests may be sufficient for some pupils. Although a remedial student who is very bright may obtain a very low score on a group test, the opposite situation is not often true. Those students whose group intelligence test scores are well above their reading ability can be assumed to have the intelligence to profit from remedial instruction.

There are two types of group intelligence tests, verbal and nonverbal. Verbal intelligence tests, those which require the student to read the questions to be answered, should never be used in the remedial reading program because they cannot provide a distinction between the slow learner and the poor reader. The student with inadequate reading ability will make a low score on such a test regardless of his intellectual capacity. Even if the test requires no reading, the poor reader will be at a handicap if the items contained in it are samplings of information commonly learned through reading.

The *California Test of Mental Maturity,* the *Lorge-Thorndike Intelligence Test,* and the *Detroit Test of Learning Aptitudes* all have verbal and nonverbal sections which are usable with most remedial students. However, a low score on any group test should not be considered as a final indication of intelligence. If any teacher feels the student has the potential to do better or if the student comes from a cultural background different from that of the students for whom the test was written, that student should be retested individually.

Individual Mental Tests

The best and most useful intelligence tests available are such individual tests as the *WISC* and the *Stanford-Binet.* These tests should be used with all students whose scores on other tests are of doubtful validity and with as many other students as possible. However, it should be noted that they are time-consuming and must be administered by a person with special training in the use of individual mental tests.

The *WISC, Stanford-Binet,* and *ITPA* take approximately one hour each to administer and one to two additional hours to score and evaluate. This is an unreasonable amount of time to spend with every child in the program if all that is required is an IQ score; however, as with the individual reading tests, observations made while testing may be of much more value than the score itself. Information on the student's cooperation, self-criticism, attentiveness, perseverance, effort, activity, and ability to express his ideas all may be obtained during the testing period by the experienced examiner.

The Weschler Intelligence Scale for Children, or *WISC,* is probably the most accurate test of mental ability for most remedial reading students because its results are not greatly affected by reading ability. Although cultural background does influence scores in some cases, this influence is less significant than on most other tests, and the examiner usually can identify those areas which seem to have been influenced by the child's background.

Although the *WISC* can be used only with children between the ages of five and sixteen, the *Weschler Adult Intelligence Scale (WAIS)* is a similar test applicable to any person over sixteen years of age.

The *Revised Stanford-Binet Intelligence Scale* has been the standard of intelligence testing for many years and can be used for testing any person over the age of two years. It is probably the best test for children of preschool age and for mentally retarded adults.

The *Illinois Test of Psycholinguistic Abilities (ITPA),* though not an "intelligence test" as such, is a very important individual mental test, for it gives very specific information regarding particular abilities and aids in setting up remedial programs, especially programs for the child with learning disabilities.

There are a number of brief individual intelligence tests which, with a little practice, a teacher without the specialized training for the tests described above can administer. The *Slosson Intelligence Test (SIT)* for example, is based upon the *Stanford-Binet* but takes about twenty minutes to administer. A number of studies have reported high correlations between the *SIT* and both the *WISC* and the *Stanford-Binet.*

Since vocabulary is considered the one area which correlates most highly with total intelligence, several of the short individual tests are based entirely on the student's vocabulary. These tests are easy for the teacher to administer and are usable for general purposes. Three of these vocabulary-based tests are the *Peabody Picture Vocabulary Test,* the *Ammons Full-Range Picture Vocabulary Test,* and the *Quick Test.*

Problems Involved in Intelligence Testing

Every test mentioned in the preceding section favors certain socio-economic or cultural groups. Usually the test is geared to the upper middle-class suburban child, and since the test is usually a sampling of what this particular child has learned in comparison to what the children of the same age in the standardization group have learned, the child who has not had the opportunity to learn these things (the one with a different background) will be handicapped in taking the test. Most intelligence tests have little or no validity for the inner-city ghetto child, the reservation Indian child, the isolated rural child, or the child for whom English is the second language.

This fact is particularly true of the picture-vocabulary tests already mentioned. Before basing any judgments upon them, the teacher must consider carefully the child's background. If the child comes from a socioeconomic or cultural group which is less verbal than the middle-class or uses terminology which is different from that of middle-class suburban society, he may have a poorer, or different, vocabulary, regardless of his intelligence. These tests will also be invalid for any child whose mother tongue is a language other than English.

Before any test is used with disadvantaged students, a teacher who is thoroughly familiar with the background of these students should study the test carefully to determine the number of items on which this group may be handicapped. Since it is usually not possible to find any test on which a particular group of disadvantaged students is not handicapped to some extent, it becomes the task of the reading specialist to study the available tests and determine which test will have the lowest percentage of items which will be unreasonable for this particular group. This study also should give an indication as to what extent the results of the test used should be relied upon for this group of students.

Some attempts are being made to develop culture-free tests. However, it is difficult to develop items which will not be dependent to some extent upon the particular background of the student. For example, the *Learning Potential Examination* was especially developed for testing the nonreader, the rural child, and the American Indian. Although not recommended for general testing of urban children, it is probably the most valid test presently available for use with Indian students.

If the student dislikes the examiner, if he believes he will be better off with a poor score than a good one, if he is not feeling well, or if he is emotionally upset, he will not achieve test results which will be valid. Validity is also dependent upon the examiner's competency in administering, scoring, and interpreting the test. An intelligence test should never be considered an exact measure. A child does not "have" an IQ; rather, he exhibits a certain IQ on a particular test on a particular day. He cannot be expected to make exactly the same score on another test, or even on the same test, on another day.

All these factors should be considered in evaluating the results of an intelligence test, but they do not mean that intelligence tests are not important or valuable. They only mean that the teacher must be aware of the problems and not use tests as if they could measure the child's intelligence in the same way that a ruler can measure his height.

Determining Reading Potential

As has been stated previously, a student is considered a remedial reader if his reading expectancy, or reading potential, as indicated by his mental ability, his background, and his drive or desire to learn is higher than his actual reading level. Although it is not possible to measure factors such as motivation, it is possible to estimate the student's mental ability well enough to make a considered judgment as to whether or not he has the potential for enough improvement to invest the time and effort of the remedial reading teacher in a program for him.

A "Reading Potential" score can be obtained from knowledge of the child's IQ and his grade in school through the use of the following formula:

$$IQ + \frac{(IQ-100)}{100} \times \text{Grade in School} = \text{Reading Potential}$$

As an example of the use of this formula in determining a student's potential, the following calculations represent a student in the second month of fourth grade who has a tested IQ of 120.

$$IQ + \frac{(IQ-100)}{100} \times \text{Grade in School} = \text{Reading Potential}$$

$$120 + \frac{(120-100)}{100} \times 4.2 = \text{Reading Potential}$$

$$\frac{120 + 20 \times 4.2}{100} = \text{Reading Potential}$$

$$1.40 \times 4.2 = \text{Reading Potential}$$

$$5.88 = \text{Reading Potential}$$

From the formula, it can be seen that this child, if he were reading at his potential, should be able to read material appropriate to the eighth month of fifth grade.

Note that in the following example the plus in the formula becomes a minus since the student's IQ of 80 is less than 100:

$$\frac{80 + (80 - 100)}{100} \times \text{Grade in School} = \text{Reading Potential}$$

$$\frac{80 + (-20)}{100} \times 4.2 \qquad\qquad = \text{Reading Potential}$$

$$\frac{60}{100} \times 4.2 \qquad\qquad\qquad = \text{Reading Potential}$$

$$2.5 \qquad\qquad\qquad\qquad = \text{Reading Potential}$$

You can see that if the child in the second example were reading at his potential, he should be reading at the fifth month of second grade.

In effect, the IQ + (IQ − 100) simply serves to double the distance of the IQ from 100. Thus in the first example, IQ 120 becomes 140. In the second, IQ 80 becomes 60.

The 100 below the line simply serves to change the IQ score from a percentage to a decimal. IQ is actually a percentage of normal intelligence, or a decimal fraction from which the decimal has been removed. That is, IQ 80 means 80 percent, or .80 of average intelligence.

If you remember to write the IQ as a decimal, you can do as most reading clinicians do and simplify the formula to:

IQ + (IQ − 100) × Grade in School   = Reading Potential

or

(IQ + Deviation of IQ from 100) × Grade in School
                                     = Reading Potential

It is not necessary to memorize the formula at all if you simply remember to double the distance of the IQ from 100 and multiply by the grade in school.

The formula is based on the assumptions that a child begins to learn reading skills when he enters first grade and that his rate of progress is dependent upon his ability. If a child has a normal IQ of 100, he should make one year of progress for each year he is in school. Using the formula for a child in the second month of the fourth grade and an IQ of 100 yields:

$$\frac{100 + (100 - 100)}{100} \times 4.2 = \text{Reading Potential}$$

or

$$1.00 \times 4.2 \qquad\qquad = \text{Reading Potential}$$

Then, 4.2 = Reading Potential for this child. If the child has average intelligence (IQ 100), his reading potential is the same as his grade level.

A child who demonstrates an IQ below 50 is not considered to be educable. He cannot be expected to learn to read, regardless of the quality of the instruction he receives. If a child's IQ is above 50, he should be able to learn some reading. Therefore, an IQ of 50 is our starting point in determining reading potential. A child with an IQ of 50 should have a reading potential of zero. This is achieved through the IQ + (IQ − 100) factor in the formula, which simply serves to double the distance of the IQ from 100.

For a child in the second month of fourth grade and an IQ of 50, the formula would give us:

$$\frac{50 - 50}{100} \times 4.2 = 0$$

or

$$0 \times 4.2 = 0$$

Since his Reading Potential score is zero, no reading should be expected from this child.

For a student of the same age with an IQ of 75, we would expect half the progress in reading of a "normal" child, and the formula would be:

$$\frac{75 + (75 - 100)}{100} \times 4.2 = \text{Reading Potential}$$

$$.50 \times 4.2 = \text{a Reading Potential of 2.1}$$

This student should be reading at the level of the first month of the second grade.

Again, using the simplified system of doubling the distance of the IQ from 100 and multiplying it by the pupil's grade in school, we simply write the formula as:

(IQ + Deviation of IQ from 100) × Grade in School
$$= \text{Reading Potential}$$

I believe this formula is much more realistic than the much-used formula recommended by Bond and Tinker (1967):

Reading Expectancy = (Years in School × IQ) + 1.0

This formula and the revision recommended by Young (1976) expect too much of the student who is low in ability (one-half year of progress per year in school for the student with an IQ of 50) and too little of the gifted student. A student with an IQ of 150 should make at least two years progress in reading for each year in school.

Formula for Eligibility in Remedial Reading Programs

After obtaining a reading expectancy score, the teacher must still determine which students are to be considered to be in need of remedial reading instruction. Teacher recommendations, pupil motivation, and other factors may be as important in making this determination as test scores. However, most remedial reading teachers find it necessary to have a definite stated policy in order to control entrance and to counteract outside pressures, even though this policy may then be varied in the consideration of individual cases.

In the clinic which the writer directs, a pupil is considered eligible for remedial instruction if his reading level is less than two-thirds of his reading expectancy level. Using this as a guideline, a student with a reading expectancy of 6.0 would be accepted in remedial reading classes if his reading level was 4.0 or below. A student who should be reading in the middle of the second grade (2.5) would be considered for remedial instruction if his reading level was 1.8 or below.

Some schools start with this policy of two-thirds of reading expectancy for admission and, then, as the remedial program raises the general reading level of the school and fewer students need the help, raise the standard to three-fourths of reading expectancy to allow more students into the program.

Verification through Observation

Teacher opinion should always be considered in deciding which students might profit from remedial reading. Although not every child recommended by the teachers should be accepted, if a teacher who has worked closely with a child feels certain that his potential is much greater than that indicated by the tests, then that teacher's opinion may be more valid than the test results.

Observation of the child is always a good way of verifying test results. His reactions on the playground, his ability to manipulate objects (particularly his understanding of mechanical devices), his ability to solve nonacademic problems, his achievement in arithmetic, his knowledge from sources outside of school, his vocabulary, and his ability to discuss ideas are all clues to his intellectual ability. However, the teacher must be cautious about making quick judgments on the basis of any of these observations. The intelligence of the aggressive, talkative child is usually overestimated by the teacher, while that of the student from a different cultural background is usually underestimated. This is true especially if the student is from a cultural background in which he has been taught to answer only when he is certain of the answer, to speak only when it is important, and not to interfere with others in his own home. These observations should supplement, but not substitute for, the intelligence test.

Bright Students versus Slow Learners

In some remedial programs, all students who read below their grade level are accepted for remedial reading instruction, whether or not they are reading up to their ability level. This can have a very detrimental effect upon the program. When slow learners are placed in remedial classes, the teacher is forced to adjust the instructional procedures to the slower pace of these pupils. If any group instruction is used, this form of placement not only will delay the progress of the more able students but also may cause them to become bored or discouraged. The acceptance of an abundance of slow learners also may put a stigma on the program which will discourage the bright student from wanting to enter the program and receive the help which he needs.

In addition, the total benefit of the reading program to the school will be lessened if the teacher's time is used in giving individual or small-group instruction to slow students who are already reading at their potential and, therefore, do not have the ability to make great improvement.

This situation will not happen if the intelligence of all students is tested, their reading expectancy calculated, and only those whose reading is less than two-thirds of their potential admitted. A few slow learners, whose reading levels are even lower than their expectancy levels, can be expected to profit from the instruction and may be accepted, provided a significant number of bright underachievers are also included in the program. The majority of students in the remedial program will always be students of "average" ability whose reading level is below that expected for their grade.

Listening Comprehension

Another means of determining a student's potential ability in reading is by measuring his listening comprehension. It can be expected that if his comprehension is good when he listens to material that is read to him, he should be able to comprehend that same material if he can develop the word recognition skills to read it. Therefore, a comparison of his listening comprehension and his reading comprehension is another indication of whether or not the student's reading comprehension is commensurate with his ability.

The teacher can measure a student's listening comprehension in three ways: by using teacher-made tests with samples from basic readers, by using standardized reading tests as listening tests, and by using standardized listening tests.

Teacher-made Tests

A test of listening comprehension can be produced by using a selection from each level of a basic reader, such as the reader used for an Informal Reading Inventory, except that the passages do not need to be of the same length for this type of test. For each selection, the teacher writes about ten questions which cover as many kinds of comprehension skills as possible. The questions must be clear, logical, and based upon the comprehension skills which could be expected of a child reading at the level of the particular passage. Good suggestions for questions usually can be obtained from the teacher's manual for the basic reader from which the passage was selected.

In administering the test, the teacher begins with the passage at the student's present reading level. She reads the passage to the student, then the questions, and lets the student answer orally. If the student answers 70 percent or more of the questions correctly, she goes on to the next higher level passage. The highest level at which the student can answer 70 percent of the questions is considered his Reading Potential level. If two similar comprehension tests are used which cover parts of the same stories, one can be used as a reading comprehension test and the other as a listening comprehension test, thereby making it easy to compare the student's scores. The reading comprehension test also can be used as the Informal Reading Inventory for determining the student's reading level and instructional needs.

Reading Tests Used as Listening Tests

A standardized reading comprehension test can be read to the student instead of having him read the test. The answers, too, should be read aloud as he marks them, with the teacher being careful not to indicate by vocal expression which answer is correct. A good comparison of reading and listening comprehension can be obtained by using two forms of the same test.

This kind of test must be untimed, or one in which the students normally would have all the time they need to finish each section, if the scores are to be used as reading potential scores.

Whereas the teacher-made test must be administered individually, the standardized test can be given to students in a small group.

The *Metropolitan Reading Test* includes in its manual instructions and norms for "alternate administration" of the test as a listening test.

Standardized Tests of Listening Comprehension

Some tests are especially designed to measure reading potential. The *Durrell-Sullivan Reading Capacity Test*, for example, requires the student to associate words and paragraphs which are read by the teacher with pictures representing them. Spache's *Diagnostic Reading Scales* and the *Durrell Analysis of Reading Difficulty* both contain sections which evaluate listening comprehension. The *Learning Potential Examination* uses a combination of "symbolic representation" and "listening comprehension" to obtain a "predicted comprehension" score.

Any of the three types of listening comprehension tests can be used as a measure of the student's reading potential. The results should be compared with the reading potential scores obtained from a good intelligence test. Both scores should be considered in determining whether or not the candidate for a remedial reading program has the potential to profit from remedial reading instruction.

Other Considerations in the Selection of Students

Pupil Desire

Success in any learning endeavor depends upon a desire to learn. Although the teacher should be able to motivate some students who do not have any great desire for help, the presence of these students can deter the progress of others. Especially at the high-school level, students who could profit from remedial classes should be informed of the purpose of the program and should be accepted on the basis of their own choice.

Referrals

In remedial reading programs operated by school systems, referrals may be handled in two ways. In some cases, all students in a school are given achievement and group intelligence tests. From these scores, the remedial reading teacher chooses those students who appear to be good candidates for remedial reading. Teachers then refer additional students who they feel have the potential for reading improvement. Both groups of students are then given individual intelligence and oral reading tests and are discussed with their teachers so that the teachers express their opinions as to the suitability of the selections in consideration of their knowledge of the student's ability, attitude, emotional problems, etc. Teacher opinion should always be given serious consideration but should not be the sole criterion for selection.

In schools which do less group testing, remedial students are usually recommended by the teachers, with requests from parents and students also being given consideration. After all recommendations are received, the remedial reading teacher carries on a testing program for all those who have been recommended and, from this group, selects those to be included in the remedial reading program.

Group testing of all students in the school has some advantages in that students whose needs are not well known by the teachers are not likely to be overlooked. But regardless of which system is used, teachers should be well enough informed about the objectives and operation of the program to use good judgment in making referrals and asking for additional evaluations.

Reading clinics operated by colleges or as private enterprises, often accept all students on a referral or self-enrollment basis. Nonetheless, students for these programs should receive some evaluation before enrollment and should not be accepted for instruction if preliminary testing indicates that the student probably will not profit appreciably from the instruction.

Age

Although older children may make more rapid progress, the earlier a child's reading problems are detected and he is given appropriate remediation, the less retarded his reading will have become before it receives attention; therefore, the better the chance will be that the student will eventually reach his potential in reading and be able to achieve in other subjects. One investigator found that, of children who had been identified and given remedial instruction by the third grade, 70 percent regained their grade level in reading. Of those whose remedial reading instruction began in seventh grade, only 30 percent learned to read successfully in school, while less than 10 percent of those who began remedial instruction in high school reached the level at which they could read their textbooks successfully.

The recent research on dyslexia and brain damage points up the importance of discovering learning disabilities as soon as possible after the child enters school and beginning specialized remedial instruction early.

Children in the primary grades should not ordinarily be placed in remedial reading classes which meet during recesses or after school, as this may cause fatigue and resentment toward reading and usually will not be of great benefit. When classes for all ages of children in a remedial program are taught by the same teacher, primary children should receive their remedial instruction in the morning if this is possible.

Parent Cooperation

Parental interest in the remedial reading program is very important. Parents should be willing to attend conferences with the remedial reading teacher and carry out her recommendations, which may include examinations by ophthalmologists and other specialists or such changes in the home situation as the relieving of pressure regarding grades. Active opposition to the program by either of the parents or a tendency to downgrade the program may negate the efforts of the remedial teacher. Parental attitude, therefore, should be considered when choosing students.

Summary

Reading problems should be spotted and given help as soon as they begin, for the chance of curing reading problems through special help in the primary grades is very good. The older the child is when he is put into the remedial reading program, the less the chance that he will catch up with his age group in reading. This does not mean that only primary children should get help though. Each child should receive help when his reading problems are discovered, whether this happens in Grade 1 or in Grade 12.

A measure of intelligence is important in order to estimate the student's potential for learning to read as well as the intellectual level at which he should be functioning. Reliance on the usual group intelligence tests, however, may cause grave misunderstandings of the remedial student's ability. The poor reader is handicapped in taking the test, especially if it requires reading. If a student has low scores on a group intelligence test but does well in subjects not requiring reading or if his teachers feel that his capacity is greater than his scores would indicate, he should be considered for the remedial reading program and should, if possible, be given an individual intelligence test.

This procedure is not necessary for all students, as group test scores are adequate for those students who rate above average on the group tests.

For students from special cultural groups, tests should be selected with the student's particular background in mind.

If a valid intelligence score is available for the student, his Reading Potential level can be estimated by the use of the formula:

$$(IQ + \text{Deviation from } 100) \times \text{Grade in School} = \text{Reading Potential}$$

Potential reading ability also can be estimated through the use of tests of listening comprehension.

Students are usually considered eligible for special help if their reading level is less than two-thirds of their potential.

Finally, the student's age, his desire for help, and the cooperation of his parents also should be considered in selecting students for the remedial reading program.

Suggested Additional Readings

Bond, Guy L., and Miles A. Tinker. *Reading Difficulties—Their Diagnosis and Correction,* 3d ed. New York; Appleton-Century-Crofts, 1973, pp. 100–103.

Explanation of the Years in School formula for determining reading expectancy.

Culyer, Richard. "Predicting Reading Success" in *Translating Theory Into Practice.* North Carolina Council of the International Reading Association, 1972, pp. 35–39.

Discusses relative merits of check lists, readiness tests, teacher opinion, and mental ability tests in predicting success in reading.

Jensen, A. R. "How much can we boost IQ and Scholastic Achievement?" *Harvard Educational Review,* 39 (Wioter-Summer 1969): 1–123.

Shows that IQ is result of experience and early training.

Samuels, S. Jan, and Patricia R. Dahl. "Relationships Among IQ, Learning Ability, and Reading Achievement," in *Literacy for Diverse Learners,* Jerry

L. Johns, ed. Newark, Del.: International Reading Association, 1975, pp. 31–38.

Cites research to show that IQ determines only rate of learning, not level of reading that can be mastered if given time.

Kennedy, Eddie C. "Identifying Reading Disability," in *Classroom Approaches to Remedial Reading*. Itasca, Ill.: F. E. Peacock Publishers, 1971, pp. 73–95.

Lists many characteristics to consider in deciding whether or not to refer a student for remedial instruction.

Kochevar, Deloise E. "Developing A Strong Remedial Reading Foundation," pp. 17–26 and "Individualized Tests and Testing Techniques that Bring Remediation in Reading," pp. 99–128 in *Individualized Remedial Reading Techniques for the Classroom Teacher*. West Nyack, N.Y.: Parker Publishing Co., a Subsidiary of Prentice-Hall, 1975.

Varied information on testing in the reading program.

Young, Beverly S. "A Simple Formula for Predicting Reading Potential." *The Reading Teacher*. 29 (April 1976): 659–61.

Suggests a revision of the Bond and Tinker formula, substituting grade in school for years in school plus one.

5

Discovering and Alleviating Causes of Reading Problems

Common Causes of Poor Reading

Few serious reading problems are the result of a single cause; usually, a number of factors have combined to cause the reading disability, and there are nearly as many different combinations of causes as there are children with problems.

It is seldom possible to determine all the factors that have contributed to an individual's becoming a remedial reader, and it is not necessary that we do so before we can help him with his reading problems. It is, however, best to try to learn as much as possible about the causes of a student's problems, without unecessary waste of time or delay in beginning instruction, as there may be underlying causes which are still in operation and which may hinder remediation. Unless alleviated, these problems can prevent optimum growth in the student's reading skills.

Since reading problems are usually the result of a combination of causes, the teacher should not expect that elimination of one or more obvious causes will cure the disability.

Intelligence

A low level of intellectual ability is the most obvious cause of poor reading. The relationship of intelligence and reading was discussed quite thoroughly in the previous chapter, but it should be reiterated here that intelligence affects the speed, not the amount of reading that a child learns. Research shows that given adequate time, the child of low intelligence can learn all the reading skills that others learn. Although the child with a 75 IQ may take twice as long to learn reading skills as the average child, by the time he is in twelfth grade, he should be able to read at sixth grade level, with all the varied skills of the sixth grader.

Rejection of Reading by Boys

The mother of a remedial reader asked, "I'm expecting another child in June. Is there anything I can do to keep this one from having reading problems, too?" "Yes," the teacher answered, "Have a girl."

The preceding exchange may seem facetious, but, in actuality, the ratio of boys to girls who are identified as having serious problems in reading does vary from three to two in some schools, to ten to one in others, depending upon the community, its location, reading readiness instruction, individualization in the first grade, and upon the criteria for identifying a remedial reader. Many theories have been advanced as reasons for this greater number of boys than girls in remedial classes:

the fact that there are more genetic weaknesses in boys; differences in the rate of maturation, and, therefore, in readiness for reading; cultural differences and the difference in the early training and the expectations for boys and girls; differences in interests and motivation; the difference in the number of early head injuries among boys and girls; the difference in average size at birth; and differences in endrocrine balance. The actual reason is probably a combination of these and other factors, and most of these are factors about which the teacher can do nothing. However, there are differences in the interests of boys and girls and in the ways in which boys and girls can be motivated. These should be considered in planning instruction and are discussed in more detail in chapter 9.

Home Influences

One of the greatest influences on the child's reading is his home. The most obvious reading problems caused by the home are in the cases of physical abuse and neglect. The excessive use of drugs or liquor by the parents also causes many other problems which can affect a child's achievement. Hunger also obviously influences a child's ability to learn. Schools in poverty areas which have begun serving breakfasts to children when they arrive at school in the morning and lunches to those who need them have found an improvement in the reading of these children. Finally, the child who does not get sufficient sleep does not think as clearly or learn as well as his rested classmate.

The child who has been taught early that he should do a job simply because the job is there and needs to be done has a big advantage in the first grade over the one who expects to be motivated by external rewards.

In many homes, there is little understanding between parents and children. If the children do not understand the parents' reasons for their actions and feel that their parents do not understand them, there is usually little motivation for achievement.

Family attitude toward reading also influences motivation. In some families, there is high regard for reading, while in others, it is of no importance. If the parents are not interested and do not encourage the child, he has little reason for extended effort. In some families, reading may be considered a worthy activity only for girls, and this, naturally, will have a negative influence on boys.

The socioeconomic status of the parents influences their attitudes toward reading and the amount of reading material that will be available in their home. In some low-income communities, the child will see no examples—either in his home or neighborhood—of individuals for whom reading is a highly desirable activity.

Moving frequently has often been blamed for the poor achievement of some pupils who have been in several schools. Indeed, the resulting changes in methods and instructional areas missed often do cause a hardship for the child of below average intelligence or for the child of the migratory laborer who keeps his child out of school for long periods of time to help with the crops. However, studies show that while some students have lost out because of moving, many students of average and high intelligence who have been in several schools in several parts of the United States have gained more from the additional inspiration, motivation, and background than they have lost. However, while many have gained from mobility, others have lost. The chief characteristic of the mobile population appears to be the greater spread between the high and low achievers in the mobile population than among those who stay in one location (Gilliland, 1958).

Experiential Background

Lack of background for understanding the material can have a very detrimental effect upon the reading of children. Many basic reading texts are written for the upper middle-class urban child, and the child with a different background is unable to see any relationship between the stories which he is expected to read and his own experience. Even the suburban child may lack broad experience and find himself handicapped by an inadequate background of understanding. If the home background of the majority of students in a school is meager, the teachers usually try to compensate by giving the children experiences which will broaden their concepts or by replacing or supplementing the basic readers with materials appropriate to their backgrounds. However, if a child is forced to go to a school in which most of the children have had a much richer background of experience, the building of experience for him will be more difficult and too often will be completely neglected. It is important to remember that understanding of instructions and processes as well as the comprehension of material read is based upon experience which builds the mental background for ascertaining meaning.

Language Background

The child who speaks most fluently in a language other than English is at a disadvantage in learning to read, for he must learn English as he learns to read it, and this, naturally, slows down progress. If the child's parents speak both imperfect English and another language at home, the child may not be fluent in either language; therefore, it can be said that he does not have a language of thought. This child faces a much greater handicap than the one who is fluent in another language and must learn English.

In addition, some children whose only language is English speak a dialect which is so different from that of the teacher that the teacher and the child have difficulty understanding each other.

Speech Problems

Children with speech problems often have reading problems also. There are three main reasons for this. First, although some speech problems are the result of physical defects in the speech mechanism, many others are caused by the same factors that cause the reading problems. Many causes of problems in learning to read could, at an earlier age, have caused problems in developing normal speech. Second, ridicule or criticism by other children of his oral reading may cause emotional problems in reading. Third, inability to correctly pronounce certain sounds makes learning to decode those sounds difficult.

Ineffective Listening Skills

Good listening skills are important to learning reading skills for two reasons. First, reading instruction and the directions for related activities are given orally by the teacher. Second, the comprehension skills needed for understanding material being read are usually developed as listening comprehension skills first.

Cultural Differences

Many of the students with reading problems have developed those problems because their background of experience is so different from that of their teachers that communication is difficult. Because their cultural background and way of life is different, the books they are expected to read often have little meaning for them, and the motivational techniques used by the teacher are inappropriate for them. These students are at a disadvantage in the typical classroom and are, therefore, commonly called "the disadvantaged." They need an educational program adapted to their own background.

Emotional Problems

The reading teacher should be alert for signs of emotional problems, as they are a very common characteristic of children with reading disabilities. The child who is emotionally upset cannot concentrate on learning to read. However, it is often difficult to determine whether the emotional problem is the cause or the result of the reading problem. No matter which came first though, each can aggravate the other. Improving a child's self-concept and his emotional reaction to reading must often be the first step in remediating reading problems.

Physical Problems

General poor health lowers the vitality of the child and causes frequent absences from school. Each of these absences makes progress more difficult, as will rheumatic fever, asthma, malnutrition, or any other problem which lowers the child's energy level.

Although vision problems may slow reading rate and are often used as excuses for poor reading, usually only the most serious cases will actually prevent a child from learning to read.

Endocrine gland problems are not common, but for those children who have a glandular defect or deficiency, they may create severe problems. The most common of these problems among remedial readers is a thyroid deficiency which, if it is mild or moderate, often goes undetected for several years, thus having a cumulative effect upon the child's progress.

The more physically mature the child is, the less likely it is that physical problems will cause reading problems.

Lack of Motivation

Since motivation is necessary for achievement in any area, lack of motivation is an important cause of reading retardation, and its development is an important part of remedial instruction. In addition, since continued failure will greatly decrease the motivation of any child, most remedial readers are lacking in motivation.

Suggestions for improving motivation are included in chapter 9.

Learning Disabilities

Learning disabilities, such as poor visual memory, poor auditory perception, distractibility, and hyperactivity, are major causes of severe reading problems. Remediation for children with learning disabilities is discussed in chapter 12.

Poor Instruction

Some schools would like to blame all their reading failures on the outside influences already listed, but the simple truth is that many problems are caused, at least in part, by poor teaching techniques—by the failure of the teacher to adjust instruction to the needs of the child.

The national first-grade studies showed that no one method is more effective in teaching reading than all others and that probably 80 percent of the children or more will learn to read, regardless of the method of instruction. However, in every class there are some children who need the instruction adapted to their individual needs. Failure to know the needs of the children and to adjust to them results in many reading failures.

Two of the most common failings of the school are failure to determine the readiness of the child before beginning reading instruction and contributing to the development of tension through the use of material that is too difficult for the child.

Schubert and Torgerson (1976) discuss thirty-three classroom conditions and practices that tend to inhibit the learning of reading.

Symptoms of some of the common causes of reading problems are listed along with suggestions for alleviating them in Instructional Guide 5.1.

INSTRUCTIONAL GUIDE 5.1

Elimination of Common Causes of Reading Problems

Observation	Possible Causes	Recommendations
Rejection of Reading		
Lack of interest. Rejection of reading by boys.	Failure to apply techniques and materials which will motivate boys. Group pressures which cause boys to consider reading unmasculine. Treating reading as a mechanical process. Failure to develop good rapport and pleasant personal relationship between pupil and teacher.	Learn interests of children of his age and sex. Demonstrate an interest in every individual child. Demonstrate a contagious enthusiasm for reading. See Instructional Guide 9.1.
Home Influences		
Inability to concentrate. Lack of interest. Drowsiness.	Neglect. Physical abuse. Alcoholism.	Gain parental cooperation through conferences. Help parents to under-

INSTRUCTIONAL GUIDE 5.1 *(continued)*

Observation	Possible Causes	Recommendations
Lack of responsibility. Variation between and among skills.	Hunger. Insufficient sleep. Poor training. Family disputes. Lack of background. Mobility.	stand child's needs. Give experiences that improve child's background. Select materials which fit child's background.

Language Background

Limited vocabulary. Poor comprehension.	Teacher's language or dialect different from that spoken in the child's home.	Employ teacher or aide who speaks child's dialect. Use reading materials suited to child's vocabulary. Use language experience materials. Use vocabulary building.

Poor Instruction

Failure to learn normal reading skills, although no non-school causes are evident.	Use of material inappropriate to child's background. Overemphasis on exact oral reading. Overcriticism. Use of disparagement and criticism for motivation. Failure to check comprehension. Overcrowded classrooms. Failure to notice problems before they become serious. Use of only one-word recognition technique. Atmosphere of dislike toward children. Accepting low level of word recognition skills in beginning grades.	Develop pleasant atmosphere. Use materials appropriate to child's background and interests. Use easy material to kindle interest and self-confidence. Diagnose thoroughly and follow with instruction in specific skills needed.

INSTRUCTIONAL GUIDE 5.1 *(continued)*

Failure to provide a variety of reading materials.
Use of instructional material above the child's reading level.
Failure to individualize instruction.
Use of only the basic reader for instruction.

Lack of Readiness

Better recall of difficult words than of basic vocabulary.	Child was pushed into reading without readiness instruction or adequate evaluation to determine readiness.	Diagnose thoroughly and follow with instruction in specific skills needed.
Enjoyment of easy independent reading but dislike of group instruction.		
Unnatural voice.		
Repetitions.		

Determining Causes of Reading Problems through Interviews and School Records

In planning a remedial reading program for a child, the teacher must rely heavily upon test results for information regarding the child's needs in reading; however, such scores usually reveal little or nothing about the original causes of the reading problems or of the kinds of motivation which may be used to help him succeed.

Information on the child's home background, leisure-time activities, school history, and reaction to reading instruction as well as the family's reading habits and the parents' attitudes toward reading will aid in adapting instruction to the child's needs. Such information can be obtained through a study of school records, through inventories, and through interviews with the teacher, the parents, and the child. The majority of this information usually is gathered after the original screening for selection of students but before the additional diagnosis is begun.

Obtaining Information on Children Referred for Remediation

Whether the student is referred to the remedial reading program by the parents, the school, or some other agency, a referral form, giving the essential information needed for the selection of students, should be filled out by the child's teacher. This information also may provide clues to possible causes of the child's problems.

In developing a referral form, the remedial reading teacher should remember that classroom teachers are very busy people who often find it very difficult to find even a few minutes to answer a request for information. Therefore, the original referral form should contain a request for only essential information—the latest intelligence and reading test information and specific observations needed for planning the diagnosis and/or selection of pupils.

If the child has had medical or psychiatric care related to physical defects, learning disabilities, epilepsy, or emotional disturbances, the parents should be asked to sign a release which will permit the remedial reading teacher to obtain the child's medical records, for these may provide clues, both to the causes of his reading problems and to special considerations which may be necessary during instruction.

Obtaining Information through Cumulative Records

As soon as students have been selected for a remedial program through referral and preliminary testing, the remedial reading teacher should study the school's cumulative record for each child. That information which is pertinent to the remedial reading program can be transferred to a new cumulative record folder which is kept in a handy location where it can be referred to at any time during teaching or planning of instruction. The referral form, records of all tests administered, interview records, and the notes on observations and evaluations accumulated during instruction can be placed in this record. It is very helpful as a background for interpreting test scores and other diagnostic information and also offers many clues as to possible causes of reading problems and ways of adapting instruction to the child's needs.

Obtaining Information through Interviews

Interviews are superior to inventories as a means of gathering preliminary information about a student, for much information can be obtained through interviews which cannot be readily gained in any other way. Information on the child's background, his feelings, his plans, his attitudes and interests, and his desire to learn can be obtained through interviews with the child, his parents, and his classroom teacher. If all three of these sources are interviewed, information on the child's attitudes and feelings can be compared and significant differences noted. The interviews often reveal clues to the child's problems which should be followed up through further diagnosis.

Questions asked in interviews should always be *relevant to the child's reading* problems and to the making of recommendations for treatment. All information obtained through interviews as well as that obtained through questionnaires, tests, and cumulative records is for professional use only and must always be kept *absolutely confidential.*

Except in those cases where a comparison of opinions is desirable, the interviewer should ask for *no information which is available from other sources.* Information, such as birth dates, schools attended, etc., should be taken from school records, written inventories, etc. rather than in an interview.

The use of the interview as a question-and-answer session or as an opportunity to fill out a form may cause reasonable resentment, although a list of questions which the reading teacher plans to ask is useful as a guide while conducting the interview. However, these questions should be used only as a *guide* to conversation. Getting the other person to talk and to relate the things that are on his mind is more important than obtaining answers to specific questions. When questions must be asked which may seem "nosy" or embarrassing, their relevance to the child's reading problem should be explained.

One way to judge an interview is by who does the talking. If the remedial reading teacher talks half the time or more, she has probably conducted a poor interview.

Interviewing the Classroom Teacher. The best time for an interview with the classroom teacher is after the cumulative records have been studied but before the testing program begins. This makes it possible to ask questions not answered in the cumulative records but pertinent to diagnosis or instruction. It also gives the remedial teacher an opportunity to provide answers to questions about the diagnosis that is to be done and the remedial program in general. In addition, the classroom teacher often has valuable suggestions concerning her observations of disabilities or other characteristics which will aid the remedial teacher.

This conference is also an opportunity for the remedial reading teacher to make it clear that the purpose of both the diagnosis and any instruction which follows is to aid the objectives of the classroom teacher. Even though the remedial reading teacher may, for a while, do the majority of the reading instruction for this child, the responsibility for the total education of the child is still with the classroom teacher. Thus, the teacher should realize that this is a team effort to help the child in every way possible and that the remedial reading instruction is aimed at supporting and aiding her work in the regular classroom.

The conference with the classroom teacher is a good time to agree on a scheduled time for testing the child. The remedial reading teacher also may wish to schedule a time to observe the child in his regular classroom.

Interviewing the Parents.   An interview with the child's parents before or shortly after beginning instruction can do much to help make the instruction in reading successful. In cases in which the parents enroll the child for testing and instruction, a convenient time for the interview may be when the parents bring the child for the testing. There is an advantage in having the interview at this time in that the parents cannot expect the conference to be a report on the child at such an early point, and, therefore, the teacher's objective of gaining information can be achieved more easily. It should be made very clear from the start that the purpose of the conference is for the teacher and parents to find ways in which each can give the maximum help to the child.

A preview of the available information about the child should make it possible for the teacher to be prepared with items that the parents may be asked to "tell me about . . ."

The conference should also give the parents an opportunity to obtain answers to their questions about the program. This should relieve any anxiety or misapprehensions which they may have. If the parents have confidence that the remedial program will help the child, they will be less likely to put any excess pressures on the child at home; thus, they can make it possible for him to learn more easily.

Additional conferences during instruction may improve communication and result in added cooperation and aid from the parents.

Interviewing the Student.   An interview with the student at the beginning of instruction is the basic technique for discovering his interests and his attitudes toward reading. The remedial reading teacher in the public school will find it worthwhile to call in each of the prospective students above fourth-grade level for a short interview while preliminary selections are being made. In this interview, the purposes of the program can be explained to the student and an idea of his feelings can be ascertained. The teacher may be able to determine whether or not the student recognizes his problems and to determine his feelings about them and about reading in general. During the interview, the teacher should try to get an indication of whether or not the child will take some responsibility for his own improvement. The teacher should remember that the older the child, the more important is his desire for aid. An effort should be made to put the child at ease at the beginning of the session. The teacher must show a friendly interest, not a critical attitude.

Whether the instruction is to be group or individual, one of the best topics for the first interview is a discussion of interests. This discussion will serve the dual purpose of giving the teacher information on the type of reading material which will interest each student and indicating to the child the teacher's personal concern for him and his interests.

It is usually best to jot down in advance some of the questions that may be used with most of the students as well as specific ones related to particular students. However, care must be taken that the purpose of the discussion does not appear to be the answering of a set of questions.

Determining Readiness for Reading

Many reading problems can be traced to the child having been pushed into reading before he had the necessary skills to learn to read. This is particularly true of children whose cultural background does not include the exposure to reading, writing, and oral language activities of the typical middle-class urban home. The ability to see small differences in words necessary for word recognition and the ability to reproduce words on paper, are developed through a great deal of handling of reading, writing, and drawing materials under the helpful supervision of parents. A child's interest in reading is developed through being exposed to reading materials, seeing others read, and having others read to him. The auditory discrimination necessary for learning phonics and the child's ability to think and express his ideas fluently in English are developed through family conversation, games involving speech, parents' interest in the pronunciation of words, and the encouragement to talk.

The child who has had these skills thoroughly developed through family interaction, through parents' interest in school-like activities, and through a wealth of materials is ready to begin reading when he enters first grade. Many children, however, have had few if any of these influences. If these children are pushed into reading before these skills are developed, they usually fail to learn to read. Unless the teacher recognizes the reasons for this failure and develops these skills through the types of activities other children have in their homes, this may be the first of a long succession of failures for the child.

A child who has not developed these skills may be referred to the remedial reading teacher at the first-, second-, or even the third-grade level, and the reading teacher may find that she must help the child develop the readiness skills before any instruction in other reading skills can be effective.

The reading teacher can aid many children in avoiding these problems if she can help the school develop a pre-kindergarten screening program which will delay for a year those children who are sure to have difficulty because of immaturity and lack of readiness. This will also make it possible for her to give immediate additional aid to those who still have inadequate readiness skills when they enter school.

Some of the child's readiness skills can be evaluated through standardized tests. Other skills require informal diagnosis. Observation, with the aid of checklists of the skills to be observed, is a common method of informal diagnosis.

Auditory and Visual Discrimination

Two factors which greatly affect a child's readiness for reading are his auditory discrimination and his visual discrimination. Unless he can distinguish small differences between words, both those which he sees, and those which he hears, he will be unsuccessful in learning word analysis skills. Therefore, the reading teacher must be prepared to evaluate the child's auditory and visual discrimination as possible causes of his reading problems.

Two good tests of Auditory Discrimination are:
Wepman Test of Auditory Discrimination
Goldman-Fristoe-Woodcock Test of Auditory Discrimination
A test intended specifically as a test of visual discrimination is the *Frostig Developmental Test of Visual Perception*. Some reading readiness tests intended for first grade use also include auditory discrimination, and most include tests of visual discrimination. Some of the commonly used readiness tests which include sections for evaluating auditory or visual discrimination are:

Clymer-Barrett Prereading Battery. Evaluates discrimination of beginning and ending sounds, word matching, letter name knowledge, form completion, and sentence copying.

Contemporary School Readiness Test. Evaluates visual discrimination, auditory discrimination, writing name, knowledge of colors, background information, numbers, readiness for handwriting, and visual memory of words.

Gates-MacGinitie Readiness Skills Test. Includes auditory discrimination, visual discrimination, listening comprehension, following directions, letter recognition, visual-motor coordination, auditory blending, and word recognition.

Harrison-Stroud Reading Readiness Profile. Evaluates visual discrimination, auditory discrimination, using symbols, context clues, and letter names.

Macmillan Reading Readiness Test. Tests visual discrimination, auditory discrimination, vocabulary, letter names, and visual-motor skills.

Metropolitan Readiness Test. Includes visual discrimination, word meaning, listening, alphabet knowledge, numbers, and drawing a man.

Murphy-Durrell Reading Readiness Analysis. Evaluates auditory discrimination, visual discrimination, letter name knowledge, and learning rate.

Identifying Oral Language Deficiencies

Fluency in oral language is a prerequisite for learning to read and write. Listening vocabulary, ability to think of words to express ideas, fluency in self-expression, and ability to understand changes in language structure are all important to developing comprehension in reading.

Vocabulary Level

Before a child can identify an unknown word through a combination of phonics and context, it must be in his listening vocabulary, that is, those words he can recognize and understand when he hears them. The *Peabody Picture Vocabulary Test* and the *Quick Test* are both intelligence tests, but because both are based entirely on vocabulary they are good tests of vocabulary level. The child is shown four pictures. The examiner reads a word from the vocabulary list and the child chooses the picture which relates to that word.

Oral Language Facility

The child's comprehension of what he reads depends upon his comprehension of oral language. Understanding of oral language depends, not only on his knowledge of the vocabulary used, but his understanding of sentence structure. Many inner city, disadvantaged, culturally different, and bilingual children cannot express their ideas fluently in English or understand complex sentence structure. Their vocabulary and knowledge of linguistic structure may be limited to that which is necessary to understand and express concrete ideas in simple declarative sentences.

The remedial reading teacher should be prepared to evaluate the child's facility in the use of oral language. If it is inadequate for learning to read with comprehension, the teacher should be able to prescribe practice to develop this facility.

Word fluency.   To determine the child's facility with words, ask him to name all the words he can think of in two minutes that begin with the same sound as *dog.* Count the words. Is he able to think of a variety of words easily or does he use only one kind such as nouns? The way he arrives at the words he says may also be significant. Does he think of words independently or does he rely on items that he can see around him?

Oral language fluency.   An idea of a child's ability to express his ideas verbally can be obtained by showing him a series of pictures and asking him to "Tell me about this picture."

Using this method, Loban made a study of the oral language fluency of Caucasian and Negro children in Oakland, California. He found that the language fluency of the majority of black children entering first grade was inadequate for beginning reading instruction.[1] In a similar study of the oral language of Northern Cheyenne and Crow children in Montana, Simpson found that these Indian first graders used less than 40 percent of the oral language of the Oakland children in Loban's study. She concludes that

> "These children should become much more proficient in oral English usage before being introduced to beginning reading instruction. Attention needs to be given to activities and oral language exercises which will help the children develop linguistic readiness for reading . . . more school time should be spent in opportunities for children to interact with language.[2]

Simpson recommends a combined language experience and children's literature approach to beginning reading to emphasize language development. Children not fluent in English should first hear much language, then use language to express their thoughts and experiences, then produce language for themselves to read. After they read what they produce

---

[1] Walter Loban, *Problems in Oral English, Kindergarten Through Grade Nine,* NCTE Research Report No. 5 (Champaign, Illinois: National Council of Teachers of English, 1966).

[2] Simpson, Audrey K. *Oral English Usuage of Six-year-old Crow and Northern Cheyenne Reservation Indian Children, A Descriptive Study,* Unpublished Doctoral Thesis, University of Maine, Orono, 1975, p. 144.

for each other, then they are ready to start learning to read the language others produce for them.

Spontaneous expression. By recording spontaneous conversation, the teacher can analyze it to see if children are using only factual declarative sentences or whether they use variety in sentence structure, verb tense, adjectives, and clauses.

Ideational fluency. Dorothy Lampard [3] suggests the following method of determining a child's facility in calling up a variety of ideas about a given topic (his fluency in idea development): Ask the child to name, as fast as possible, all the words for "round things" that he can think of. Allow two minutes. Count the words, but also watch his methods. Does he rely on things he can see? Does one word suggest another, as apple-orange?

Transformation of sentences. Give the child a sentence and ask him to change it to a question; to a negative sentence.

Ability to recall lengthened constructions. Have the pupil repeat a sentence after you, then add to the sentence and have him repeat it. Continue as long as he can remember the sentence. For example:

I saw a dog.

I saw a dog running down the street.

I saw a dog running down the street chasing a cat.

I saw a dog running down the street chasing a cat with a yellow face.

Do the same except make the additions to the left (before the sentence).

Do the same with embedded constructions (inserted within the sentence). For example:

The house is old.

The red house is old.

The red house on the hill is old.

The red house under the tree on the hill is old.

For practice, all of these can be made into group games by having each child in turn repeat the sentence and add his own ideas to it.

---

[3] This and the following two suggestions were made by Dorothy Lampard at the 1968 Annual International Conference of the Rocky Mountain Reading Specialists Association.

Considering Cultural Differences

Any student whose background, motivations, and interests are quite different from those of the middle-class suburban American is at a disadvantage in our schools which are taught by middle-class teachers with middle-class values. Children who commonly have difficulty because the school has not adjusted to their needs include the child from the inner-city and ghetto areas, the American Indian, the Mexican-American, the Oriental, the foreign-born child or child of foreign-born parents, and the child from any other minority group whose cultural or ethnic background is noticeably different from that of the mainstream child.

Culturally different and disadvantaged students commonly have problems in learning to read because of lack of experiential background, deficiency in oral language expression, a poor English vocabulary, previous lack of school-type discipline and motivation, and a negative self-image. The student's home may include many individuals of varying relationships, including older people who expect him to accept the traditional concepts of his people; consequently, he frequently rejects middle-class values, including the drive to compete that runs through society.

Many schools fail to recognize the needs of these children and make no changes to adapt either to their cultural background or to their language problems. Bilingual children need special help with vocabulary and idiomatic expressions, while those with dialects quite different from standard English need special help with phonics. The teacher should be careful not to intimate that the child's dialect is "inferior." If standard English is emphasized, it should be taught as a second, but equally useful, language.

The teacher needs to study the culture of the children in order to know how to teach them and must know what kinds of motivation will or will not work. Without this knowledge, she may use methods which will offend the students and make them refuse to learn.

The building of self-confidence and motivation is more essential with the disadvantaged than with other students because they have often been convinced that they cannot succeed and that teachers do not like them.

Short, high interest, quick-starting books are even more important for these students than for others. Whenever possible, reading should be related to the student's culture and values, his interest areas, and his experiential background. Ethnic books should be examined carefully for evidence of prejudice on the part of the writers.

Some of the best materials are those developed in the classroom, such as experience stories, stories written for younger children by older ones, class or community newspapers, community history, accounts of favorite family and folk stories, filmstrips produced by the students, and information on local occupations.

Instructional Guide 5.2 summarizes some of the common problems encountered in teaching remedial reading to disadvantaged and culturally different students, along with giving possible solutions.

Teaching remedial reading to these children requires adaptation of the general principles used in teaching reading to all remedial students and application of them to the particular cultural background of the child.

Emotional Maladjustment

Emotional maladjustment is both a cause and a result of failure in learning to read. Most students with serious reading problems have a very poor self-concept and a large percentage have personality problems, but it is difficult to tell in which cases the reading difficulty was caused originally by emotional problems and in which cases the emotional problems resulted from the reading problems. Regardless of the original cause, though, the reading teacher must attack the emotional problem through a successful reading program and also must look for other causes of emotional disturbance that may be preventing progress.

In most cases of emotionally upset children, the reading teacher must first convince the child that he has the ability to learn to read. In some cases, this is the teacher's most difficult task. Poor motivation and personality maladjustments are also often concomitants of emotional problems and offer additional challenges to the reading teacher.

Detection of Emotional Problems

Poor readers can be found with all levels of adjustment, so the teacher should be hesitant about attributing reading problems to emotional problems unless she can pinpoint distinct evidence of maladjustment. Even then, she must be aware that the emotional problem may be alleviated by good instruction in reading.

The best evaluation of emotional problems related to reading takes place through careful observation rather than testing. However, some personality inventories can be useful in suggesting possible problems for which the reading teacher should be alert.

INSTRUCTIONAL GUIDE 5.2

Teaching Disadvantaged and Culturally Different Children

Observations	Recommendations
Lack of motivation to read. Lack of effort. Lack of personal involvement.	Show respect for him and his ideas. Praise him sincerely. Recognize him when he does well. Give him frequent compliments. Use short lessons. Develop short-term goals. Emphasize to the child daily that he has been successful. Close every lesson with a demonstration of success. Read practical materials, such as *TV Guide* and occupational information. Ask for his ideas and use them in the lessons. Allow him to set his goals. Show him the reason for what he is asked to do. Help him to build a positive self-image. Test him regularly for appropriate level of instruction. Give him a sense of responsibility for his own learning. Use books at a level that he can read silently with comprehension and enjoyment. Give him responsibility for keeping records dramatizing his progress. Choose reading materials with concrete concepts.
Poor self-concept.	Use all of the above techniques. Believe in him and talk him up. Give him the experience of success *every* day. Praise him sincerely.
Belief that his people cannot succeed.	Use all of the preceding techniques. Emphasize the strong points of his culture. Do not try to make him over into a middle-class child.

Observations	*Recommendations*
No desire to compete.	Let students help each other. Emphasize cooperation and mutual help. Demonstrate self-improvement without comparison with other students.
Lack of concern for time.	Keep schedule as flexible as possible. Apply as little pressure as possible. Recognize home conflicts which may cause delays. Play games having to do with time.
Student sees no need for remedial reading. Student has no desire to practice.	Develop short-term, immediate goals. Teach him how to take tests, how to fill out forms, how to behave in an interview. Read information on various jobs, on dealing with "red tape," and on manipulation. Set drills to music or beat a drum during drills.
Student can read but prefers not to because the neighborhood "gang" does not approve.	Find materials that stress his viewpoint. Role play his own situation. Use experience stories of his own problems. Show respect for his opinions.
Bilingual child. Child's mother tongue is not English.	Teach him to read in mother tongue first. Use books written especially for his cultural group. Use language experience. Discuss comprehension questions in his native language.
Comprehension and phonics problems caused by dialect differences.	Use material with sentence structure similar to the child's. Teach sounds of letters as pronounced in the child's dialect. Let him pronounce all words in his dialect. Use experience stories with the child's

Observations	Recommendations
	sentence structure, but with standard spelling.
	Let him write captions for cartoons.
Poor auditory learning.	Play listening games.
	Use visual methods.
	Emphasize visual skills.
	Teach words through visual-kinesthetic methods.
	Let him express himself through art.
	Use vocabulary-building games.
	Use his ability as an imitator.
	Use oral impress.
	Use choral reading.
Failure to observe.	Plan ahead for him to tell what he saw on the way to school the next day.
	Play observation games.
	Take short field trips in the neighborhood so he can observe and describe what he has seen.
	Discuss the things he has observed every day.
	Study cartoons and photographs.
Lack of background to understand stories.	Use books written especially for his cultural group.
	Use self-created materials.
	Help him to relate story incidents to his own life.
	Apply his reading to real-life situations.
	Use films to build background and follow them with discussion.
	Build background through reading much material on the same subject.
	Take field trips—but don't go overboard or build the desire for unobtainable life situations.
	Do not emphasize what he lacks.
	Allow much free conversation, sharing, and relating of experiences.

Observations	*Recommendations*
Child has trouble remembering sight words.	Remember that he cannot remember what does not have meaning for him. Discuss the words—their different meanings. Use the words in interesting or humorous sentences. Use kinesthetic practice. Use all of the items listed below.
Poor vocabulary. Oral language deficiency.	Use discussion of word meanings.
Knowledge of only one meaning for each word.	Check comprehension carefully and correct misconceptions, discussing reasons for them. Explain in advance the meanings of words and phrases that may cause difficulty. Provide a guide with synonyms and explanations for each page of a book. Play word games emphasizing multiple meanings. Use intensive emphasis on oral language development. Interest him in study of word origins, starting with his own name and words from his own language or dialect. Use word comparison. Study word roots, prefixes, and suffixes. Keep books at an easy level. Use many books at one level and read as many as are needed. Use language experience.
Lack of verbal skills. Inability to express ideas well orally.	Use role playing. Use socio-drama. Use creative dramatics. Handle objects, while talking about them. Discuss ideas and experiences freely. Play games requiring the use of complete sentences. (Make not rejecting his language part of the game.)

Observations	*Recommendations*
Inability to understand idiomatic expressions.	Play word games. Use language games. All of the above. Use self-made materials. Act out real and literal meanings of words and expressions. Use a guide showing drawings with relevant meanings for each page of reading material. Use relevant reading material.
Reticence to speak in class. Inability to express answers orally.	Allow enough time for the child to think and then draw or write the answer after giving a question; accept his statement as it is. Use questions that have no wrong answers. Use role playing. Use the chalkboard for questions and individual slates for answers. Dramatize stories. Read plays.
Restlessness.	Take advantage of his enjoyment of an activity. Let him run machines. Play active word games. Read about sports and active lives.
Discipline problems.	Build pride in his own group and in him as an individual and as a representative of that group.
Belligerence.	Be humble. He will usually be grateful to those who sincerely help him.
Home environment lacks paper, scissors, paste, play-dough, pencils, crayons, and other manipulative play materials. Lack of visual discrimination developed through pictures, etc.	Introduce reading slowly. Use form boards and puzzles. (Start simply by using a triangle, square, circle, etc. Progress to harder jig-saw puzzles.) Use many picture books. Point out small differences in letters and printed symbols. Practice differentiation often.

Observations	*Recommendations*
	Introduce symbols in slow sequence, with sufficient exercises to enable the child to remember them.
	Develop readiness, not before reading, but as reading progresses.
Concern over weaknesses of culture: narrow traditionalism of community, antiintellectualism of family.	Stress strengths: cooperativeness, concern about each other, physical bravery.
Broken, overcrowded homes.	Stress strengths: advantages of extended family; less sibling rivalry; strong family ties; aid to each other; security; strengths of his cultural group.
	Encourage children's enjoyment of each other's company.
Lack of routine and study time.	Stress strengths: informality, lack of tension, warm humor.
Lack of desire to compete.	Stress strengths: benefits of cooperation, lack of strain and tension.
	Use games, music, sports, humor, and concrete objects for high motivation
Lack of discipline.	Stress strengths: freedom from self-blame, feelings of guilt, loss of love, and parental overprotection.
	Develop ability to express anger verbally.
Lack of physical possessions.	Stress strengths: enjoyment of self-created activities, lack of "keep with the Joneses" pressures.
	Encourage generosity.
	Emphasize freedom from tensions of competitive society.
Lack of abstract thinking.	Use problem-centered approach.
Limited verbal expression.	Stress strengths: high non-verbal fluency and originality.
	Encourage high creativity in music, dance, and other physical activities.
	Use language rich in imagery.
	Encourage adeptness in visual art activities.

Personality inventories.   Personality inventories, generally speaking, do not have high enough validity to warrant their use in the regular school testing program. Their results are difficult to interpret. However, in a reading clinic, they can serve a very useful purpose in lending clues to possible causes of emotional problems and thereby act as guides to observation.

The *California Test of Personality* gives a good indication of the student's general emotional adjustment, as well as a useful classification of possible areas of difficulty. The *Vineland Scale of Social Maturity* also reveals useful clues. Some psychologists also use both the *Draw-A-Person* and the *Bender-Gestalt* tests for this purpose. One should remember though that the validity of these and other personality tests depends largely upon the rapport between the examiner and the student and the student's desire to answer the questions honestly. The results should be interpreted in this light.

Observation.   The teacher can tell much about the child's emotional well-being through observation. For example, throughout all instructions, the teacher should be alert for signs of tension, such as rigidity of body and arms, a high unnatural voice, or an apologetic attitude. These are signs of tension, which is often the result of criticism by teachers or parents or ridicule by classmates. Tension causes some children to be almost totally unable to reason. Unless the teacher can help these children to relax, they will probably make little or no progress in word analysis or inferential reading.

Poor self-concept resulting from continual failure or comparison with other students can be noted in the student's lack of self-confidence, insecurity, and overdependence upon approval. Moodiness, irritability, and behavior which is infantile, overly agressive, or negativistic are indications of more serious emotional problems.

Although the aggressive child may be a problem in the classroom, he is usually easy to work with and makes good progress with individual instruction. However, the child who has become withdrawn may be seriously maladjusted and should be referred for further evaluation, if this is possible.

The alert teacher can spot many symptoms of emotional problems while working with her students. Guide 5-4 on page 91 may also be helpful to the teacher as a reminder of probable causes and possible treatment for children who show signs of emotional maladjustment. A checksheet, such as that in Instructional Guide 5.3, may be helpful to the teacher as a reminder of those areas to be observed and as a simple means of recording observations. In using this checksheet, the teacher circles a number between one and seven to rate the child on each characteristic.

INSTRUCTIONAL GUIDE 5.3

Evaluation of Emotional Adjustment

Self-Confidence

| 1 | 2 | 3 | 4 | 5 | 6 | 7 |

very lacking in self-confidence .... appears very self-confident

Tension

| 1 | 2 | 3 | 4 | 5 | 6 | 7 |

appears very tense .... appears very relaxed

Cooperation with Teacher

| 1 | 2 | 3 | 4 | 5 | 6 | 7 |

antagonistic .... very cooperative

Attitude

| 1 | 2 | 3 | 4 | 5 | 6 | 7 |

grouchy, complaining .... cheerful, happy, cooperative

Cooperation with Students

1   2   3   4   5   6   7

disturbs others .... respects others

1   2   3   4   5   6   7

must work alone .... can work with one other child .... works well with group

Concentration

1   2   3   4   5   6   7

extremely short attention .... mind wanders .... daydreams .... good until tired   excellent concentration

Activity

1   2   3   4   5   6   7

hyperactive .... cannot sit still .... squirmer .... no pointless movement

Shyness

1   2   3   4   5   6   7

will not read aloud .... hesitates, appears shy, embarrassed .... reads when asked .... frequently asks to read

Does He Ask for Help?

1   3   5   7   6   4   2

seldom asks .... asks when he needs it .... asks continuously

Discussions

1   3   5   7   6   4   2

refuses to speak .... takes part confidently .... talks excessively .... monopolizes

Referral.   The remedial reading teacher should not expect to diagnose or treat serious maladjustments. If serious emotional disturbance or any type of psychosis is suspected, the student should be referred to other agencies for evaluation. If a psychologist works with the reading programs, she can either make the diagnosis or determine to what agency the student should be referred. In small school districts which do not have psychological services, the child should be referred to a mental health clinic, social worker, or a psychiatrist directly.

Treatment of Emotional Problems

Occasionally a child with such serious emotional problems that psychiatric treatment is essential before reading instruction can be effective will be referred to a remedial reading program. However, in most cases, good remedial reading instruction from an understanding teacher not only will improve the child's reading but also will help his self-concept and relieve much of the emotional tension related to his reading.

In an atmosphere free of the irritations and critical attitudes which have caused his tensions, the disturbed child will usually make progress in his reading, and this progress will improve his attitude still more. Even in this situation, the teacher must expect some emotional upsets until the child becomes adjusted to the class. When these situations arise, the small-group situation usually makes it possible to handle them with a calm attitude and a reassuring hand on the shoulder that lets the child know the teacher cares.

Just as his inability to learn to read magnifies the child's emotional problems and the emotional problems in turn decrease the child's ability to concentrate on learning to read, so, also, improvement in reading decreases the child's emotional tensions, and this, in turn, increases his ability to learn.

At the same time that the teacher is helping to remove one cause of emotional maladjustment by improving the student's reading, she should be watching for clues to other causes of emotional disturbance. If she finds such causes, she should either alleviate them the best that she can or get the child any additional help that is needed. The teacher should study the characteristics listed in Instructional Guide 5.4 and be alert for symptoms of emotional disturbance.

Physical Problems Related to Reading Disabilities

The child who has no obvious health problems but whose health in general is poor may have less than a normal amount of energy and, therefore, be inattentive or unable to put forth the effort needed for normal progress in reading. If he has had a prolonged illness or frequent

INSTRUCTIONAL GUIDE 5.4

*Symptoms of Poor Self-Concept and Emotional
Maladjustment Affecting Progress in Reading*

Observation	Possible Causes	Recommendations
Tension		
Hands and body rigid. Grim expression. High, unnatural voice when reading. Headaches. Stomachache at reading time or at same time daily. Excessive blinking of eyes. Tics. Stuttering or stammering.	Tension or anxiety. Criticism or ridicule when reading aloud. Anxiety.	Use calm, quiet manner. Encourage the child. Use silent reading for the most part until he builds self-confidence. Have him practice thoroughly and then read aloud in a small group. Work on causes, not symptoms; attention to symptoms makes them worse.
Insecurity		
Insecure. Irritable; moody Overly sensitive. Quick-tempered. Tense. Shy. Infantile in behavior.	Criticism of oral reading. Attitudes of teachers, parents, classmates. Rejection. Tension. Unfair comparisons. Sibling rivalry.	Use all of the above. Engage in no criticism whatsoever. Use behavior modification techniques. Build child's self-concept. Use materials such as SRA's *Distar.* Give him extra attention. Use physical contact. Be consistent in treatment. Accept the child.
Overly Aggressive Behavior		
Striking or kicking other children. Noisy. Insisting on attention. Compensatory obnoxious behavior.	Insecurity. Dictatorial treatment in school or home. Bullying or abuse by other children. Criticism from classmates.	Use same recommendations as those listed for insecurity and withdrawn behavior. Use democratic planning; let him have a choice of activities. Show him he is wanted.

Observation	Possible Causes	Recommendations
		Determine if there are abusive actions toward him and try to eliminate them. Teach individually or in small groups. Teach in a relaxed atmosphere. Be unemotional in discipline.
Withdrawn Behavior		
Stays out of activities. Daydreams.	Possible serious emotional disturbance. All of the causes listed under "Insecurity."	Use impress method. Use all of the recommendations listed under "Negativistic Behavior." Examine the child with projective techniques. Refer him for psychological evaluation.
Negativistic Behavior		
Making little or no effort to read. Unconsciously rejecting reading. Failing intentionally. Indifference. Failure to read except when required to do so. Antagonism toward reading.	Resentment toward parent or teacher. Desire for gang approval. Lack of encouragement. Fear of making mistakes. Way of punishing adults. Lack of material appropriate to age or interests. Reading at time which eliminates more desirable activity. Reflection of attitude of family. Lack of social or emotional readiness. Poor vision or hearing. Physical or emotional fatigue.	Use all of the above recommendations. Use low vocabulary material written for children older than this student. Alternate reading with him. Use experience stories. Determine his interests and locate appropriate material for them. Use choral reading. Relate materials to out of school activities. Check his vision and hearing. Rearrange time schedule if necessary. Check with the family on interests, on materials available in the home, etc.

Read interesting material to him.

Encourage him.

Build his feelings of security.

Give him successful experiences in other areas (hiking, crafts).

Build rapport.

Arrange for a physical examination.

See Chapter Nine for more suggestions.

---

minor illnesses which have kept him out of school, he may have been unable to keep up with his group and, because the reading material was then too hard for him, have dropped farther and farther behind. The teacher also should be alert for symptoms of lack of proper nutrition and of fatigue due to lack of sleep, as these too can contribute to reading problems.

Glandular problems often go undetected through the elementary school years, yet hypothyroidism has been linked to reading problems. The child who is low in thyroid usually remains overweight even with a very low intake of food and is low in energy for either physical or mental tasks, though he is seldom irritible or disagreeable. If she spots these symptoms, the teacher cannot be sure of the cause, but she can suggest an examination.

Hearing

Slight hearing losses do not necessarily cause difficulty in learning to read; however, it is not possible to determine how much a hearing loss will affect any particular individual's reading achievement. All students entering the remedial program should be screened with an audiometer if this is possible. The teacher should also be alert for such symptoms of hearing problems as turning the head to one side when listening, apparent inattention, or frequently asking to have instructions repeated. Instructional Guide 5.5 on page 96 lists common symptoms of hearing problems and includes suggestions for adjusting to the hard-of-hearing child in the reading program.

Vision

Reading problems may be related to poor visual acuity. In addition, many severe reading problems are caused, at least in part, by poor visual perception and poor visual memory. These problems are discussed in detail in chapter 12. "Poor vision," as the term ordinarily is used, means poor visual acuity, or poor ability of the eyes to obtain a clear image. Hamilton found that the average number of elementary school children with visual problems was 21.4 percent.[4] At the age of four years, 4.2 percent manifested visual problems. This increased to 36.7 percent at age 13 then decreased to 21 percent by age 17.

This incidence of children with defects in visual acuity is only slightly higher among poor readers than among good readers. Poor sight does not necessarily cause reading problems. Whether visual defects will hinder the learning of reading depends both upon the type of defect and the presence of other problems. Because vision is seldom the sole cause of poor reading, parents should never be led to believe that getting glasses for their child will, of itself, make him a better reader.

Some of the common symptoms of poor vision for which the teacher should watch are: holding the book farther from or closer to the eyes than normal, losing the place frequently, and having a shorter attention span when reading than during other activities. Eye strain may cause the child to rub his eyes, become tense when reading, or develop headaches.

If possible, vision screening should be a part of the preliminary diagnosis of every remedial reading student. An instrument such as the Keystone Telebinocular, which detects a variety of visual defects, should be used. The Snellen Eye Chart does not provide adequate vision screening for the remedial reading program. Although the chart will help to identify the child who is nearsighted, it will not detect the problems which are more likely to cause difficulty, such as farsightedness and poor fusion.

If the Snellen chart is the only available testing instrument, the teacher should also have on hand some easy reading material printed in very small type which she can have the child read to help her determine whether or not he has difficulty reading fine print. This, however, is only a make-shift screening device. The teacher who does not have good vision screening instruments will have to rely mostly on observation of the child while he is reading. Any cases of suspected visual defects should be referred for a professional examination.

---

[4] J. E. Hamilton, "Vision Anomalies of School Children," *American Journal of Optometry and Physiological Optics,* 51 (1974): 482–86.

A new electronic eye examination called VER, or Visually Evoked Response, has promise for diagnosing many visual defects much earlier than was possible in the past. It is possible that as more of these electronic instruments become available to the optical profession, many problems, such as poor convergence, may be discovered and corrected while the child is very young—before he begins to learn to read.

Children who have glasses which correct their vision need no special treatment in the reading program, although those whose vision is not correctable may need books with larger print or special arrangements made just for them. If the child is nearsighted, he should be seated very near the chalkboard when it is being used or he will probably not see it well enough to profit from the instruction. Those who are farsighted will find it easier and more enjoyable to read from material projected with the overhead projector, controlled reader, tachistoscope, or other projectors than they will from books.

Instructional Guide 5.5 lists some of the common clues which may indicate a visual defect, along with some defects which may cause them.

Eye Movement

When any person reads, he moves his eyes across the page in a series of stops, with quick movement from one stop to the next, rather than in a steady movement. He sees only during those stops or fixations, not during the interfixation movements. The eyes of the very good reader move forward in fairly evenly spaced fixations, with few backward movements, or reversals, other than the return sweep at the end of each line of print.

The *opthalmograph*, or eye movement camera, produces an exact recording of a child's eye movement on film so that the reading teacher can study it in detail. The eye movement photo not only measures the student's exact reading speed and number of fixations and regressions but also sometimes reveals other problems, such as poor coordination of the eyes in reading or lack of word recognition skills. The ophthalmograph is, however, a more expensive instrument than most schools can afford.

The reading teacher can get a good idea of the student's eye movement through observation, although she cannot get an exact count of the number of regressions through just watching. To observe the child's eye movement, the teacher should have the child hold his book up between himself and the teacher so that she can just see his eyes over the top of the book as he reads silently.

It is not difficult to determine whether or not an individual has a great many regressions in his eye movement when reading. However, it is generally agreed that good or poor eye movement patterns are the result rather than the cause of good or poor reading.

Except in the case of extremely poor directional attack, it usually is not necessary to attempt to improve eye movement. Improvement in the student's word recognition, comprehension, and speed will result in improved eye movement patterns.

In cases of very slow reading with extremely poor directional attack, a card moved back and forth across the page, following the words the student is reading so that he cannot look back at the beginning of the line, is sometimes beneficial. The Controlled Reader and other similar directional control devices also are intended to promote better forward movement of the eyes while reading.

INSTRUCTIONAL GUIDE 5.5

Vision, Hearing, and Health

Observations	Possible Causes	Suggested Treatment
Glandular Imbalance		
Overweight. Slow-acting mentally and physically.	Possible underactive thyroid.	Refer to physician.
Underweight. Overactive. Irritable. Eating too much.	Possible overactive thyroid.	Refer to physician.
Hearing		
Turning one ear toward speaker. Watching teacher's face instead of book. Frequently asking for repetition. Inattention. Speaking in monotone or unnatural voice. Omitting endings from words.	Defective hearing. Accident. Illness. Obstruction in ear. Nerve impairment. Infection in inner ear. Damage to eardrum or middle ear.	Check with audiometer, watch tick test, whisper test. Refer for medical help. Seat near front and center of room (about second seat back is best for lip reading). Seat to one side with good ear closest to teacher if loss is in one ear.

Observations	Possible Causes	Suggested Treatment
Omitting *s*, *k*, *t* sounds from words. Confusing similar words. Following directions given orally poorly. Having difficulty with phonics. Having earaches. Opening mouth when listening. Asking others what teacher has said. Working and playing alone. Failing to follow instructions.		Enunciate clearly. Always face children when speaking so child can see lips. Train child in lip reading, if this is possible. Emphasize context and visual recognition of words rather than phonics. Use kinesthetic instruction. Have child repeat instructions.
Inability to distinguish between similar letter sounds.	Poor auditory discrimination. Possible learning disability. Lack of habit of attention to sounds. See Instructional Guide 12.4, "Auditory discrimination."	Teach discrimination with reading readiness materials. Emphasize visual learning. Test by reading pairs of similar words; have the child tell if the words are the same or different.
Frequent misunderstanding of words.	Poor auditory comprehension.	See Instructional Guide 12.4, "Auditory Comprehension."
Difficulty remembering and following series of oral instructions.	Poor auditory sequential memory.	See Instructional Guide 12.4, "Auditory Sequential Memory."

Vision

Frowning, looking with strained expression. Moving head when reading. Rubbing eyes frequently. Styes and granulated lids.	Visual defect.	Check vision. Refer to eye specialist.

Observations	Possible Causes	Suggested Treatment
Holding book close to face. Inattention during use of chalkboard. Stumbling when walking. Squinting when looking at distant object. Complaining of not seeing the chalkboard. Good near-point vision on Telebinocular.	Nearsighted. Inability to see well at a distance.	Can be checked with Snellen Eye Chart. Seat as near as possible to chalkboard. (This disability usually does not affect reading.)
Holding book far away from or very near to him. Exhibiting tension during silent reading. Headaches. Short attention span. Good far-point vision on **Snellen** chart.	Farsighted. Inability to see book clearly.	Check with Telebinocular or Eames Eye Test. Refer for eye examination. Use projected materials. Use only large-print books if child does not have glasses.
Poor scores on eye tests at both near and far point.	Astigmatism. Defect in lens of eye.	Refer to eye specialist. Use sight-saving (large-print) books if condition is not correctable.
Turning head to one side or sitting in an unnatural position when reading. Losing place when reading. Eyes appearing to turn in or out. Moving head when reading. Eye tests show poor fusion, lateral posture, or vertical posture.	Strabismus. Lacking coordination of eye muscles. Eyes do not focus on same spot easily. May suppress vision in one eye.	Check with Telebinocular, using regular test and special paragraphs for binocular reading. Refer to eye specialist. Help, if possible, with visual training. Give no special treatment unless recommended by a physician.
Inability to recognize small differences in words.	Poor visual discrimination.	See Instructional Guide 12.5, "Visual Perception."
Difficulty in copying symbols.	Poor visual imagery.	See Instructional Guide 12.5, "Visual Imagery."

Observations	Possible Causes	Suggested Treatment
Ability to spell phonetically but inability to remember sight words.	Poor visual memory.	See Instructional Guide 12.5, "Visual Memory."
Inability to distinguish important from unimportant features.	Figure-ground constancy problem.	See Instructional Guide 12.5, "Figure Ground."
Having difficulty getting meaning from what he sees.	Poor visual conceptualization.	See Instructional Guide 12.5, "Visual Conceptualization."
Eye Movement		
Having many regressions in eye movement. Having many fixations in eye movement.	Slow speed. Poor word recognition. Material is too difficult for him.	Build speed with easy material. Build speed of sight word recognition with flash cards and tachistoscope. Check word analysis skills. Move card along line covering words being read. Set accelerator at an angle. Use projected directional attack materials.

Summary

A child seldom develops a reading problem from one cause alone. Most reading problems are the result of multiple causes. If teachers are alert to the possible causes, they can spot many of them before the problems become serious. Also, if they can determine some of the causes of the problems of remedial reading students and eliminate them, this will, in itself, alleviate many of the reading problems.

Some of the common causes of reading problems are: poor home conditions, such as poverty, want, abuse, and lack of motivating factors; lack of background for understanding what is read; lack of adequate understanding of the English language; emotional problems; social maladjustment; physical problems, such as poor vision, poor hearing, or generally poor health; speech articulation problems; low mental ability; learning disabilities; and inadequate instruction in the school.

Information about a child's home, his background of experience, his past school achievement, and his interests is helpful in diagnosing his reading problems and planning appropriate remedial instruction. As much of this information as possible should be taken from the cumulative records of the school.

Interviews with the child's classroom teacher, his parents, and the pupil himself will reveal much information not available from other sources. Lists of questions or subjects for discussion may aid the remedial reading teacher in conducting these interviews, but they should be used only as guides to getting conversation started. The emphasis should be upon the child and the remedial teacher's interest in helping him, not on filling out a form. All interviews should be approached as an opportunity for the participants to discuss ways in which each of them can help the child reach his goals in reading.

Students whose cultural background is noticeably different from that of the dominant society are at a disadvantage in learning, unless the school has adapted to their needs. They should be given reading materials which they can comprehend and which enhance their self-concept and pride in their own background. Mutual help rather than competition should be used for motivation, and adjustment should be made to dialect or language differences.

Teachers often find that their poor readers "have a short attention span," "are day dreamers," or "are seldom relaxed." These are a few of the many symptoms of emotional tension which are common in remedial students. Some students have brought to school with them emotional tensions which have made it almost impossible for them to learn to read. However, even the well-adjusted child usually begins to develop signs of emotional upset if he is continually faced with frustration in the reading task. Regardless of whether the emotional problem or the reading problem came first, each usually enhances the other. Good, objective teaching of reading which is planned to meet the student's individual needs and uses material at the student's success level in a pleasant, relaxed atmosphere is the best therapy for most of these problems.

Except in extreme cases, physical problems are not the sole cause of reading disabilities. However, poor vision, inadequate hearing, endocrine imbalance, fatigue, lack of energy, and generally poor health resulting in irregular attendance are often contributing causes which further retard the progress of the already poor reader. The remedial reading teacher should be on the alert for symptoms of any of these problems and, if she detects any, should refer the child to the medical profession for appropriate professional diagnosis.

Recommended Related Reading

Alm, Richard S. "Causes of Reluctance," in *Remedial Reading—An Anthology of Sources,* Leo M. Schelland and Paul C. Burns, eds. Boston: Allyn & Bacon, 1968, pp. 95–105.

Discusses reasons for children's lack of effort to learn to read.

Cooper, David, Lee Ann Cooper, Nancy Roser, Larry Harris, and Carl B. Smith. "Gather Relevant Background Information," in *Decision Making for the Diagnostic Teacher—A Laboratory Manual.* New York: Holt, Rinehart, & Winston, 1972, pp. 7–34.

Case study of an individual child including a variety of sources of information and suggestions for planning a program of remediation.

Ekwall, Eldon E. "Reasons for Failure in Reading," in *Diagnosis and Remediation of the Disabled Reader.* Boston: Allyn & Bacon, 1976, pp. 1–20.

Thorough coverage of a variety of causes of reading problems.

_____. "Relaying Information, Record Keeping, and Writing Case Reports in Remedial Reading," in *Diagnosis and Remediation of the Disabled Reader.* Boston: Allyn & Bacon, 1976, pp. 359–85.

Includes samples of various kinds of reports and report forms.

Gilliland, Hap. "Diagnosis Through Interviews, Inventories, and School Records," in *An Individualized Instructional Program in Corrective and Remedial Reading.* Billings, Mont.: Montana Reading Publications, 1966, pp. 5:1–5:34.

Contains guides for interviews with parents, teacher, and pupil, and suggestions for collection of additional information.

_____. *The Relationship of Pupil Mobility to Achievement.* Chicago: University Microfilms, 1958.

Research which indicates that moving from one school to another may handicap the low ability student but is more likely to improve the achievement of the average and high ability student.

Johnson, Dale D. "Cross-Cultural Perspectives on Sex Differences in Reading," *The Reading Teacher,* vol. 29, no. 8, May 1976, pp. 747–52.

A comparative study of the proportion of boys and girls having reading problems in four countries.

Kennedy, Eddie C. "Supplying the Reading Needs of Disadvantaged Students," in *Classroom Approaches to Remedial Reading.* Champaign, Ill.: F. E. Peacock Publishers, 1971, p. 413.

Lists some of the strengths of many "disadvantaged" students which can be utilized in teaching them to read. Also gives characteristic weaknesses and suggestions for diagnosis and remediation.

McNeil, John. "Sex Differences in Effectiveness of Teaching Machines versus Women Teachers for Teaching Reading," in *Improvement of Reading Through Classroom Practice,* ed. J. Allen Figurel. Newark, Del.: International Reading Association, 1964, pp. 296–97.

Report of experiment which indicates that sex differences in reading are due to teacher attitudes.

Naiden, Norma. "Ratio of Boys to Girls among Disabled Readers," *The Reading Teacher,* vol. 29, no. 5, February 1976, pp. 439–42.

Gives statistics on the proportion of boys and girls needing remedial reading instruction and possible causes for the differences.

Schubert, Delwin, and Theodore Torgerson. "Classroom Conditions and Practices That Tend to Inhibit Learning" and "Noneducational Hazards to Learning," in *Improving the Reading Program,* 4th ed. Dubuque, Ia.: Wm. C. Brown Company, 1976, pp. 36–68.

Thorough coverage of many causes of reading problems.

Strickland, Dorothy S. "Expanding Language Power of Young Black Children: A Literature Approach," in *Better Reading in Urban Schools,* ed. J. Allen Figurel. Newark, Del.: International Reading Association, 1972, pp. 9–17.

Describes a program for improving the understanding of spoken standard English through the use of good literature, thereby improving the student's ability to learn to read.

Wilson, Robert M. "Noneducational Diagnosis," in *Diagnostic and Remedial Reading for Classroom and Clinic,* 2nd ed. Columbus, Oh.: Charles E. Merrill Publishing Company, 1972, pp. 41–82.

Discusses common causes of reading problems and their identification.

Determining
the Student's
Reading Level

The most important requirement in the success of any remedial reading program is to be certain that every student is reading material in which he can be successful. Use of easy reading material is essential for five reasons.

First, self-confidence can come only from a series of successes. Before a child can succeed, he must have a desire to try, and before he will want to try, he must have some reason to believe that success is a possibility. Most remedial readers have little or no confidence in their own ability to succeed in reading. They usually have faced daily failure over a long period of time before coming into the program, and there is little reason for them to believe that if they just try again, they will succeed this time. Discouragement resulting from continuous failure usually has built an attitude of fear and anxiety in relation to reading. This anxiety can be replaced with self-confidence only through much reading at a level at which the student is virtually certain of success.

Second, material which is too difficult for the individual child prevents learning. For example, if the vocabulary load is too difficult, the student will not learn more; he will learn less. To place the same problem in a different context we might note that a person who enters a room in which thirty persons are sitting and is introduced to all thirty probably will remember none of their names—unless he has a remarkable memory. If, instead, he is introduced to four or five persons and has an opportunity to hear each of their names several times before leaving, he probably will remember all of them. A student who is introduced to thirty words which he does not know is in a similar situation unless he has a remarkable memory for words (and if he had such a memory, he would not be a remedial reader). He probably will be unable to remember any of the thirty words. However, if he is introduced to only four or five words at a time and these words are repeated, analyzed, and reviewed, he may be able to learn all of them. For this reason, the actual number of words learned will be greater when the material is easy than when it is more difficult. A record should be kept of each unknown word that the student encounters, and additional practice should be given on those words. If a student encounters five or six words which are unknown to him, during each day's reading lesson, the reading material is at the level appropriate for him to make the optimum improvement.

Third, reading skills should be taught in sequence. Just as a student would be unable to learn multiplication if he had no understanding of the principles of addition, he will be able to learn the more advanced skills in reading effectively only after he has an understanding of the basic skills upon which they are built. Therefore, instruction in reading must start at a level at which the child can read efficiently.

Fourth, skill in reading—including comprehension, speed, and understanding of vocabulary—comes from much reading. The child who is reading very slowly and struggling with word recognition cannot read much material. If he is reading material which he can handle easily, he will cover much more material and get much more practice on the basic words, thus speeding up his sight word recognition. He will be able to concentrate on the meaning of the material and will increase both his comprehension and his understanding of vocabulary. He also will be able to increase his speed of reading, as speed can only be developed while reading easy material. Even the very good adult reader, whose other reading skills are excellent, must use easy material to develop speed.

Fifth, interest in reading can only be developed with material that the student can read easily. Only when he is released from the tension of struggling with word recognition can the child be relaxed enough and get enough meaning from his reading to be able to enjoy the experience. This enjoyment of reading gives him the desire to learn which is essential to the success of remedial instruction. This enjoyment of reading is also the one factor which will eventually encourage him to read outside of class because he wants to do so, and as has been noted previously, the student who does much reading on his own is the one who gets enough practice to make rapid improvement.

If, after a time, the remedial student acquires enough self-confidence so that reading some material of greater difficulty does not discourage him, the teacher can increase the difficulty of some of the material used for instruction, although the major portion of his reading should remain at an easy reading level. As confidence develops, the level of material used should be varied according to the purpose for which it is used. For example, for practice in using word analysis skills, the material should be at the student's basic reading level (with two to five unknown words out of each hundred) in order to give him plenty of practice in analyzing words in context. However, most of the material for developing comprehension should remain about a year below the student's basic reading level; recreational reading should be even lower.

Since the success of remedial instruction depends in large measure upon choosing the right level of material for the student, the first task of the remedial reading teacher is to determine the student's reading level and the readability of the available materials for the individual student.

The Reading Levels to Be Identified

A student does not read at the same level in all types of material. To some extent, the difficulty of material that a child can read will depend upon his interest, his background for the subject about which he is reading, the type of material, the clarity of the writing, and the environment in which he is doing his reading. A student with a great interest in one area may have developed a vocabulary of specialized words in that area and, therefore, be able to read more difficult material in that area than in others. He also can comprehend more difficult material in those subject areas in which he has an interest and an adequate background. However, in general, each child is limited in the level of material which he can read by his broad-area word recognition vocabulary. Valid information on this reading level, therefore, is essential to the proper choice of reading material and to the successful instruction of any student. To identify more easily the level of material in which a pupil should read for different purposes, several levels should be identified for each child. The generally accepted terminology for each of these includes the following levels:

The recreational reading level.   This is the level at which the student can read for enjoyment, understanding, and appreciation. At this level, he should be able to read without assistance and with very little concern for word recognition or comprehension problems. This is the level at which all remedial reading instruction should begin. It will also be used for the majority of the instruction throughout the remedial program.

The instructional reading level.   This is the level at which the pupil can read successfully when working with and aided by the teacher. Because it is difficult to build the necessary self-confidence and interest at this level, reading at this level is used in remedial reading only for instruction in specific skills—mainly for practice in the use of word analysis.

The frustration reading level.   This is the level at which the child's reading breaks down and he becomes frustrated and discouraged. An excellent student who is greatly interested in a particular subject may wade through a small amount of material at this level, but such material should *never* be used for instruction in reading.

Oral Reading Tests

An individual oral reading test is a more exact measure of reading level than any of the other tests available. Therefore, every child in a remedial reading program should be given such a test as the chief method of determining the level at which he reads.

The oral reading test is essentially a test of word recognition. The score or grade level assigned is based upon the number of words at each grade level which the pupil does or does not recognize while reading. This score, however, is not usually the same as the score obtained from the vocabulary section of a standardized test or from reading the words from a word list test, as each of these tests measures different skills. The oral reading test is a measurement of the ability of the student to recognize words in context when he is reading in a connected discourse. It is, therefore, a measurement of those skills needed to read independently.

The chief reason for the use of the oral reading test is to determine the exact levels at which the student should read, both for independent and instructional purposes. However, it is also a diagnostic instrument, as it provides a systematic method of observation. The experienced teacher uses it to learn much about the child's reading habits—good and bad—his word analysis skills, and the possible reasons for his comprehension problems. Vocal and facial expressions as well as bodily movements while reading also may give indications of the child's interests and attitudes.

There are two main types of oral reading tests: the informal oral reading inventory developed by the teacher from samples from basic readers and the standardized oral reading test. Which should be used in a particular reading program will depend upon the particular skills to be evaluated and the individual preferences of the examiner.

The Informal Reading Inventory

The Informal Reading Inventory is a very effective tool for determining the exact reading level of the student. An advantage it has over other tests is that the remedial reading teacher can use it to evaluate the student's ability to read those particular books which will be encountered in the classroom. In addition, the teacher can apply the same techniques in day-to-day evaluation of the child's reading, thus helping the child to see more clearly his own needs.

Constructing the inventory. To construct an Informal Oral Reading Inventory, the teacher should select passages from each book of a basic reader series from the primer to the eighth-grade level. These passages should be either 100 or 200 words in length. (Passages of 200 words add to the accuracy of measurement but also double the time required for administration of the inventory.) These passages should be as typical of the vocabulary of the whole reader as possible. Poetry included in basic readers usually contains more difficult words than the other portions of the book. Science material also has a different vocabulary. Selections of fictional narration are preferable because the vocabulary level in these is usually more closely controlled than in other materials. The passage should be taken from near the middle of the reader, as the review material at the beginning of the reader is often at an easier reading level than the rest of the book.

If possible, the passages should be cut from old copies of the readers and glued onto sheets of tagboard which are numbered to indicate the grade level. If this cannot be done, the children may be asked to read from the books themselves, but this procedure has two disadvantages. First, the material is too bulky to be stored in the teacher's desk where it is always readily available. Second, it is much more obvious to the pupils that they are being tested in a number of books. This is frustrating to some pupils, especially if they recognize the books in which they are reading as being low-level readers. If the passages cannot be cut out, they may be typed. The only disadvantages in this practice are that the typed material is of a different size from that in the book and is sometimes not quite as easy for the children to read as the printed material in the book.

Comprehension questions should be written to cover each of the passages. These should contain no catch questions and, usually, no questions which require "yes" or "no" answers. Completion questions or those to be answered with a word or phrase are good for use on these tests, for they should check on whether or not the student comprehends the main idea and important supporting details. Questions about sequence and inference are also good. Questions on details unimportant to the understanding of the selection should be avoided. The questions should be revised as experience with them indicates which ones are least helpful in diagnosis.

Dittoed copies should be made of each selection and the accompanying questions. It is on these copies that the teacher records the child's oral reading errors and his answers to the comprehension questions.

Administering the test.   In administering the Informal Reading Inventory, the teacher should start with a selection which is about two years below the child's estimated recreational reading level. Beginning at an easy level gives the child confidence and decreases tension. The teacher hands the card to the student and asks him to read it aloud. As he reads, the teacher records all of his errors on her copy of the material which he is reading.

Recording Unknown Words: Each word the child does not recognize should be underlined on the teacher's copy. If the child does not recognize a word after a hesitation of appboximately five seconds, the teacher should tell him the word and count it as an unknown word. If, however, the child has pronounced the beginning sound of the word or otherwise indicated that he is attempting to sound it out, he should be given adequate time to do so without interference. He should not be given help in analyzing the word phonetically unless he specifically asks for it. If he asks for help in sounding out the word or asks what the word is, the word should be counted as unknown. If he says the wrong word, he should not be corrected, but the word should be counted as unknown. On the other hand, if he discovers his mistake through the context and corrects it, the word should be counted in the scoring as only one-half an unknown word.

There may be instances in which a word is skipped or another word with a similar meaning is substituted, and the teacher does not know whether the child actually knows the word or not. If, for example, the student is reading along quite fluently and rapidly and then skips a small, simple word like "the" or "on," he may be seeing and thinking the word without saying it aloud. This is a common characteristic of adults and upper-grade students who are rapid silent readers. In this case, the miscue would be recorded by circling the word to indicate that it was skipped. It can then be considered in analyzing patterns of "errors" but not counted as an unknown word. The substitution of synonyms and of simple words like "a" for "the" is also more often a sign of rapid thought-getting than of poor word recognition. However, if longer, more difficult words are skipped or substituted, it is more probable that the student does not know the word, and the examiner must observe the error in relation to the way in which the student reads the rest of the material at the same level. This is usually not difficult for the teacher who is experienced in the use of the Informal Reading Inventory. In any case in which there is doubt about whether the student knows the word, the examiner should allow the student to finish reading the selection without interruption and then point to the word in the student's copy and say, "What was this word?"

It is important to differentiate between words which are understood but mispronounced and those which are sounded out incorrectly and not really recognized and understood. This is complicated somewhat in cases in which the child has a speech defect or a distinct dialect, especially if the dialect is unfamiliar to the examiner. The examiner must be careful not to count as an unknown word one which is recognized by the child and pronounced according to his usual speech patterns. Rosen and Ames (1972), Baratz (1969), and others have shown that black students consistently change words to fit their dialect. This is particularly true of the past tense of verbs and of possessives and plurals of nouns which do not take the same form as in standard English. Crow,

Athapascan, and other Indian children more at home in their own language than in English often use past, present, and future tenses interchangeably and confuse pronoun gender. If these changes, which are adaptations to their daily language usage are identified by the examiner as unknown words, the result will be assigning to the student a reading level score below his actual reading level. Cunningham (1975) has shown that teachers are more inclined to mark words read in black dialect as errors than other miscues which do not change meaning. If the teacher does not know the dialect spoken by her pupils, she must learn enough about that dialect so she will know which apparent changes made by the child in reading are dialectal differences and which may be unknown words.

Miscues in reading may also be the result of mentally predicting sentence structure or meaning. When the student changes the words or the order of the words in the sentence in order to make it make sense to him, the teacher must recognize this fact and not identify and record these miscues as unknown words.

In testing oral reading, whenever the child miscues (changes the word from that which is written), the word as the child says it should be written above the word for which it was substituted on the examiner's copy. This procedure allows the examiner to go back later and analyze the types of errors that have occurred. Often the words substituted will fit into a definite pattern. For example, the word which the child says and the word for which it was substituted may be similar in any of several ways. They may be similar in general configuration, as *lay* for *buy;* in meaning, as *bunny* for *rabbit;* in beginning sounds; or in ending sounds. These patterns are clues to the way in which the child perceives a word and to habits that may need correction.

Recording Repetitions: Each time a child repeats a word or phrase before going on, an *R* should be placed above that word or phrase.

Recording Other Errors: The examiner should also record errors other than those of word recognition and repetition, and should note other characteristics of the student's oral reading. This information will aid in determining the specific instruction needed by this particular student. It is for this purpose that the examiner needs a copy of the inventory for each student who is to be tested. On this copy, the examiner should take copious notes on every aspect of the child's oral reading. Notes taken during oral reading should include information on phrasing, vocal expression, fluency, and use of punctuation; substitutions, repetitions, hesitations, and other evidence of poor sight vocabulary; and signs of tension, embarrassment, indifference, attitude toward the reading situation, and interest in reading.

Additional and more thorough evaluation can be aided by tape recording the student as he takes the oral reading test. This makes it possible for the examiner to go back and recheck the student's reading while scoring the test. Tape recording the test is especially valuable to the beginning remedial teacher or clinician who is trying to improve his skill in evaluating oral reading.

Addidional suggestions for diagnosis through oral reading and for developing skill in evaluating oral reading are included in Chapter 8. Instructional Guide 8.3 on page 146 lists items to be observed, possible causes of problems, and many recommendations for treatment of problems detected through oral reading.

Instructional Guide 5.1 on page 67 lists a number of symptoms of tension and emotional problems which may be detected during the oral reading test.

Checking Comprehension.   After each selection has been read orally by the child, the examiner should ask the student the comprehension questions that she has prepared. Except where the child's answers are of some length, she should record what he says verbatim. In addition to determining the number and percentage of correct answers, the examiner will want to note whether the child answers the questions at length or in single words, whether he answers exactly or uses vague statements, and whether or not he appears to be guessing.

Determining Reading Level·   If the child's reading reveals fewer than five unknown words at a particular level, the examiner should ask him to read the selection at the next higher level. The student should continue to read at successively higher levels until he reaches a level at which he fails to recognize five or more out of each 100 words. This is his frustration level, and he should not be asked to attempt to read at a level higher than this.

The student has now completed the Inventory; the teacher is now ready to go back over all the material, clarify her notes, and add additional comments. She should again count the number of unknown words on each page, making sure that each one is classified correctly. This word count is used to determine the student's reading levels.

The instructional reading level is the highest level at which the student found *fewer than five* unknown words per 100 running words of context. To determine this level, the examiner locates the first selection in which the student made five or more word recognition errors. The instructional level is the next level below this.

Some authorities include the level at which the student makes five errors in the instructional level, but this is because they include in their count all words which were skipped as well as those which the child corrected himself. Betts (1946), Johnson and Kress (1965), and many others consider the level at which the student makes from five to ten word recognition errors as a questionable area between the instructional and frustration levels. If the person's comprehension is better than 70 percent at this level, it could be considered within the instructional level. This is valid only if all omissions and repetitions are included with the unknown words in counting word recognition errors. Ekwall's (1974) experiments showed that if all repetitions were counted, the mean number of word recognition errors at which children showed physical signs of anxiety was 8.9 per 100 words. If repetitions are not included, then the standard of five or more unknown words per 100 should be adhered to as the indication of the frustration level.

At the instructional level, the child should be able to answer at least 75 percent of the comprehension questions. The questions serve as a check for both examiner and student. If several students drop below this level, the teacher should check the questions to be sure they are reasonable for children at this reading level. If one child falls below this level while most of his peers are above, this child should be given reading instruction at a lower level, with emphasis on comprehension rather than word recognition.

The instructional level is used for such instruction as practice in word identification techniques while working directly with the teacher.

The recreational or independent reading level is the highest level at which the student makes *no more than one* word recognition error per 100 words and has 90 percent or better comprehension. This level is usually one grade level below the instructional level, but for remedial students, it may be two levels below.

These levels will be verified during the child's reading, partially by the number of unknown words but to a greater extent by whether or not the student can read easily and enjoy what he is doing at this level. For example, his reading at the recreational level should be well phrased, rhythmical, and natural and should not cause symptoms of tension. A child usually will not select reading as a recreational activity if it is hard work. This independent reading level should be used for all unsupervised reading—whether instructional or recreational. As Ekwall says:

> To lower the standards would very often place children in material much too difficult for them to read. Or perhaps we have been guilty of this in the past, thus accounting for part of the fact that we often teach children *how* to read but we may also be teaching them to *hate* to read. (1976, p. 665.)

The frustration level is the level at which the student finds five or more unknown words out of each 100 words. At this level, his reading breaks down, his comprehension is less than 75 percent; he becomes tense, restless, or fidgety. He may read in an unnatural voice or appear to be reading word by word.

Although this inventory is one of the most accurate measures of the child's reading levels, it is made on the basis of a short passage and should be verified by the teacher on the longer passages used in instruction. Teacher judgment should also include oral reading fluency.

At this level, the load of unknown words is so great that it is impossible for the child to learn them, and he usually makes little or no progress in learning to read. He should not be expected to read at this level for any purpose, although, unfortunately, this is the level at which a great many remedial students are expected to read in their regular classrooms.

Ekwall (1976) monitored the reading of children with a polygraph, an instrument designed to detect the experiencing of anxiety. He found that students

> when they became frustrated, exhibited the same signs as someone afraid of a crowd about to get up to give a speech before a large audience, or of someone shaken by an automobile accident. Is it any wonder that students do not choose to read difficult material unless forced to? Can you imagine a situation in which every time you were forced to read you experienced the feelings of a person after an automobile accident?

Could you learn new skills while faced with this kind of anxiety? Neither can your students.

Standardized Oral Reading Tests

Several good standardized oral reading tests are available from test publishers. Most of these tests are similar in construction and in administration to the Informal Reading Inventory.

The published test has a number of advantages over the teacher-constructed inventory.

1. The exact level of each passage in the standardized inventory is known, while it is difficult for a teacher to know whether or not the passages she has selected for the informal inventory are typical of the vocabulary difficulty of the book as a whole from which they come.

2. The published test is more convenient to use because it is already printed—usually in booklet form, is ready to use, and can be used in a manner more like a normal reading lesson.

3. By obtaining a copy of the test for each child to be evaluated, the teacher will find it easier to make and keep a permanent record of each child's reading problems.

4. If comprehension questions accompany the oral reading material, they have usually been well constructed by a reading specialist to aid in analyzing the particular skills needed by the student.

On the other hand, the teacher-made inventory also has its advantages:

1. The teacher who makes her own inventory is more familiar with the material in it and with the comprehension questions she writes than she would be with a published test. She may, therefore, do a more effective job of noting minor errors and in recording information on her own inventory.

2. If the test is to be used for placing children in the basic reading program in the regular classroom, the informal inventory can be made from the basic reading materials to be used in the classroom, thereby making the results a more valid measure of each child's ability to read these particular materials.

It should be noted that both of these advantages apply to the regular classroom rather than to the remedial reading program.

The organization of the reading selections is similar in most of the published oral reading tests. However, not all published tests include comprehension questions. Some of these tests can be used initially as a group silent reading comprehension test to indicate at what level individual oral reading should begin. Some of the tests also include tests of word analysis skills or word lists for further checking of sight vocabulary.

The examiner should recognize that no one oral reading test is an exact measure of reading ability of a student above the seventh- or eighth-grade level. If a student has learned the word analysis skills taught through the eighth-grade level adequately, he should be able to recognize any word which is in his listening vocabulary. Therefore, reading level above the elementary grades depends more upon understanding of the meaning of words and such abilities as interpretation of material than upon word recognition. Oral reading tests, then, are for use in elementary grades and with older students who are reading at elementary levels.

Several of the available standardized individual oral reading tests are the following:

Durrell, Donald D. *Analysis of Reading Difficulty*

Gates, Arthur I. *Gates Oral Reading Test*

Gilliland, Hap. *Test of Individual Needs in Reading*

Gillmore, John V. *Gillmore Oral Reading Test*

Gray, William S. *Gray Oral Reading Test*

Spache, George D. *Diagnostic Reading Scales*

Complete publishing information on these and other tests is listed in Appendix A.

Using the Results of the Oral Reading Test

In the remedial reading class.   The results of the oral reading test will be the chief basis for the selection of the materials to be used in the instruction of each student in the remedial reading program. The observations of the kinds of errors made by the student, his method of word attack, and the fluency with which he reads will form the basis for additional testing and for helping to determine those skills in which he needs instruction.

The results of the oral reading test should not be considered final. They should be verified through observation and rechecked whenever the student reads aloud. It is necessary to remember that the student's reading level will vary with different kinds of material and different interest areas. Also, as the student progresses in his reading ability, the level of the material used will need to be readjusted accordingly.

Whenever a student begins to read new material—particularly for recreational purposes—it is advisable to have him read a portion aloud. In this way, the same standards originally used for determining his recreational and instructional reading levels can be used to determine whether or not this particular material is appropriate for his use.

It is often profitable, particularly with more mature students, to discuss with the student the results of the oral reading test, especially in terms of the types of errors made. This helps the student set objectives for himself and increases his motivation to work on his problems.

In the regular classroom.   The Informal Reading Inventory or a standardized oral reading test should be used in every classroom before students are exposed to basic readers or other graded reading materials. This testing can be done in an average time of less than five minutes per student, while the rest of the class is doing free reading from self-selected materials. For this purpose and at this time, informal oral reading is the only test necessary. Comprehension and word analysis skills can be checked later. The results of this test will also be more valuable than any standardized achievement test for selecting the students who should be recommended for remedial instruction.

Vocabulary Tests

A vocabulary test, which consists of a graded word list, is a quick way of estimating the reading level of a student. Though not as exact as the oral reading inventory, it can be administered quickly and is another good way of verifying the results of other tests.

Basic reader lists.   The teacher's manual for most series of basic readers includes a list of the new words introduced in that book. To construct a test from such a list, the teacher simply writes down every fifth or seventh word from the list of new words, until she has compiled a list of twenty words. These words should be typed in columns, with one column of twenty words for each basic reader.

To administer the test, the teacher points to the column which is about two levels below the student's probable reading level and asks the student to read the list of words. If he misses five or fewer words on one list, he goes on to the next level until he comes to a level at which he misses more than five words. The last level at which the student finds five or fewer unknown words in the list of twenty is his approximate reading level.

Achievement Tests

Standardized reading achievement tests have an important role to play in the diagnosis of reading problems and in the selection of students for the remedial reading program. They are also useful in comparing the reading achievement of different students for grouping purposes. They are not, however, intended as measures of the level at which each student can read. The achievement test is not standardized on the basis of the difficulty level of the material which the child can read, and most are never analyzed by the publisher on that basis. Therefore, the accompanying manuals do not include any norms or conversion tables for determining the basal reader levels of the child's reading. The score on the achievement test is usually six months to two years above the child's actual instructional reading level. The assumption that this score indicates the level of material the child should read is responsible for a great many students having been given required reading material that is actually at their frustration level.

The Cloze Test

A cloze test is constructed by deleting every fifth word from the material to be read, beginning with the second sentence, and replacing these words with lines of uniform length. All punctuation is left as it was in the original. The reader attempts to fill in each blank with the exact word which has been deleted.

The cloze test provides an effective means of verifying the results of the oral reading test for students in the second grade and above.

A cloze test for determination of a student's reading grade level is constructed in a manner similar to that of the Informal Reading Inventory, in the sense that samples are taken from each reader level from first through eighth grade. These samples, however, should be of 250 to 300 words each in length, and the material should be typed.

The student is given the passages from two grade levels below to two grade levels above his estimated reading level and then is asked to fill in the blanks with the words which he thinks were deleted. In scoring, only words which exactly match the deleted words are counted as correct.

The instructional level is the highest level at which the student gets 40 to 60 percent of the words correct. The frustration level is the level at which the student has less than 40 percent of the words correct.

The cloze test has one advantage over other comprehension tests in that it permits many more answers in proportion to the number of words read than the number of comprehension questions that could be used. Also, the reader has only to read and comprehend the passage on which he is being tested, whereas on other comprehension tests, his problems may be in reading and understanding the questions. The cloze test, however, is a better measure of a student's ability to read and comprehend a particular selection than of his general reading level.

Teacher Judgment

Many facets of a child's reading cannot be measured by standardized tests of any kind. It is the close observation and considered judgment of the examiner while doing the testing that verifies the results and aids in interpreting the test scores.

With experience, an alert teacher will learn to note many small clues to the student's reading problems and instructional needs. Most classroom teachers, however, tend to overrate their pupils' reading ability. In a study of 123 classroom teachers who averaged eleven years of experience each, Millsap (1962) found that teachers in Grades 1 to 6 were correct only 70 percent of the time in determining whether or not their pupils could read their materials. Seventh and eighth grade teachers were right 51 percent of the time, and secondary teachers 43 percent of the time. Tharp (1960) also found that teachers tend to overrate their student's reading ability; other investigators have had similar findings.

Determining the Readability of Materials

Determining the level of material which the student should read is of no real value unless the teacher knows the difficulty level of the reading materials available. Materials published specifically for use in teaching remedial reading usually are written at a specified vocabulary level, and the publisher usually identifies these levels in the catalogues which list the books. If the teacher has books in her library which are published by Follett, Harr Wagner, Montana Council for Indian Education, Garrard, or any other publisher which specializes in publishing materials for remedial reading and does not know the difficulty level of these books, she should write to the publisher and ask for the brochures which list the readability of the materials.

The publishers of some trade books also check readability carefully and specify the reading level. However, more than 50 percent of the trade book publishers do not measure readability in any way. The only designations they make for their books indicate "the age of children for whom they are written"—another way of saying "the interest level."

Any book which probably will be used frequently and for which the teacher does not know the difficulty level should be analyzed to determine its readability.

Determining the Readability of Trade Books.

There are many readability formulas, and for the majority of trade books, most of them will give similar results. The simplest and easiest formulas to use are based upon sentence and word length; these formulas are appropriate for most trade books. The formula developed by Ed

Fry uses a simple graph and is one of the most commonly used formulas at the present time.

The formula described in Instructional Guide 6.1 requires approximately the same information. It is a quick formula to use, is published in a brochure along with the *All Purpose Readability Formula*, and is reprinted here by permission of Montana Reading Publications.

It should be emphasized that the formula in Instructional Guide 6.1 is appropriate only for trade books, such as those usually found on the shelves of children's libraries and book stores. It is convenient because it does not require the looking up of words on any word list.

This formula is not intended to classify books specifically written for science material or for the disadvantaged or remedial reader. High-interest, low-vocabulary books intended for the remedial student are written with an easy vocabulary so they can be read by the student with poor word recognition skills. However, since they also are written to appeal to the older student, they may have the longer sentences and more complicated sentence structure which will appeal to those students. A formula such as one described above, which is based largely upon sentence length, may rate those books as being more difficult than their actual vocabulary level would indicate.

Determining the Readability of Remedial Reading Books

Formulas for determining the readability of books, especially those written for remedial readers, should be based upon the difficulty of the vocabulary used. Several of these formulas are available. The "Spache Formula" can be found in *Good Reading for Poor Readers* by George Spache; the "Garrard Formula" developed by Edward Dolch can be obtained from the Garrard Publishing Company of Champaign, Illinois. The *All-Purpose Readability Formula* can be obtained for fifteen cents from Montana Reading Publications, Stapleton Building, Billings, Montana. All three of these formulas compare the vocabulary of the material being evaluated with a list of the most commonly used words.

If the remedial reading library contains many books which are not designated for grade level, it may not be possible for the teacher to evaluate all of them for readability. If only a tentative estimate can be made on some, then it is imperative that when a student chooses one of these for recreational reading, the teacher check his ability to read it without frustration by having him read a passage aloud, using the same standards as in the informal reading inventory.

In using any reading formula, remember that vocabulary or sentence length are not the only items that make reading difficult or easy. The

INSTRUCTIONAL GUIDE 6.1

A Quick Estimate of Readability

To determine the reading level of the material:

1. *Count 100 words:*

   Starting with the middle page of the book, count the number of words in the first complete sentence at the top of each page until you have counted 100 words. Put a slash mark (/) after the one hundredth word. The rest of the process is carried out most easily if the beginning and end of each of these sentences is also marked lightly with pencil.

2. *Count the number of syllables:*

   Count the number of syllables in the 100 words. To do this, put a check mark above the second, third, and fourth syllables of all words having more than one syllable. Count the number of check marks and add 100 to your total.

3. *Mark Column 1, syllables, of the graph on the following page:*

   Circle the number of syllables per 100 words as determined above.

4. *Count the sentences:*

   A count of the number of sentences contained in the 100 words will yield a whole number and a fraction.

5. *Mark Column 3, Sentences, of the graph on the following page:*

   Circle the number of sentences, or if the sentences occur between the numbers given, obtain the location by interpolation.

6. *Determine the approximate readability level:*

   Draw a line between the two circled numbers. The spot at which that line crosses the center column of the graph indicates the approximate readability level of the material.

7. *Repeat the process:*

   Repeat the process at another point in the book to verify the results. Some books vary greatly from one part to another in their difficulty.

Syllables	Reading Level	Sentences
166	College	3.8
160	12	4.0
154	11	4.2
148	10	4.6
142	9	5.0
138	8	5.4
134	7	5.8
130	6.5	6.2
128	6.0	6.6
127	5.5	7.0
126	5.0	7.4
125	4.5	7.8
124	4.0	8.2
123	3.5	8.6
122	3.0	10
121	2.5	12
120	2.0	14
118	1.5	16
116	First Reader	18
114	Middle Primer	20
112	Primer	23
110	Pre-Primer	26

author's ability to express his or her ideas clearly, as well as the nature of the ideas being expressed, the sentence structure used, and many other factors affect readability. As Hansell (1976) says,

> "Formulas may indeed measure symptoms, but the deeper causes of language difficulty have yet to be identified. If and when they are identified, the problem of measuring language complexity remains."

For the present, vocabulary difficulty is the most exact measure of readability. It is also the most important readability factor for remedial students. For most of them, their ability to read is hampered most by their poor word recognition.

Summary

It is essential that the remedial reading teacher know the exact reading levels of every student, since the learning of a remedial student can be almost completely blocked by the use of material at his frustration level. The most accurate means of determining the level of book which any child can read is the individual oral reading test. There are several good oral reading tests on the market, and they also can be constructed by the teacher from a series of basic readers. The results of the individual Oral Reading Inventory may be verified through any one of the following methods. The score on a standardized achievement test can be used if one year is subtracted from the score, since the majority of achievement tests overrate the student's reading level by a little more than one year; a cloze test will evaluate the student's ability to read with good comprehension in a particular book; a vocabulary list, if properly constructed, also will give a good estimate of the student's reading level.

Comprehension questions, unless standardized on a large group of students, are not a measure of reading level but can be used as an estimate of whether or not the student has adequate understanding at the level determined by other tests.

After the student's reading level has been determined, this level must be matched with high-interest material written at the student's recreational reading level.

Publishers of books written specifically for remedial reading instruction usually furnish the teacher with information on the reading difficulty level of the books. For other books, the readability can be determined by the use of a readability formula.

At the beginning of remedial reading instruction, all reading should be at the student's recreational reading level. Later, some material at the instructional level can be used for practice in the application of word analysis and study skills. However, all independent reading should remain at the student's recreational reading level.

Instructional Guide 6.2 summarizes the means of determining the student's instructional, independent, and frustration reading levels through the use of each of the methods described in this chapter.

Recommended Related Reading

Baratz, J. C. "Teaching Reading in an Urban Negro School System," in *Teaching Black Children to Read,* eds. J. Baratz and R. Shuy, Washington, D.C.: Center for Applied Linguistics, 1969, pp. 92–116.

Contains many ideas on evaluating the oral reading of Black students.

Betts, Emmett A. *Foundations of Reading Instruction with Emphasis on Differentiated Guidance.* New York: American Book Company, 1946.

The first thorough description of the Informal Reading Inventory, upon which all others have been based.

INSTRUCTIONAL GUIDE 6.2

Determining the Student's Reading Level

Reading Level	Individual Oral Reading Test	Cloze Test	Standardized Achievement Test	Graded Word List	Comprehension Questions
Frustration Level	Lowest level with five or more unknown words per 100 words.	Lowest level with 37 percent or fewer blanks filled in correctly.	Grade placement level from norms.	Lowest level with six or more unknown words per twenty words.	Less than 70 percent comprehension. Uncertain of answers.
Instructional Level	Highest level with four or fewer unknown words per 100 words.	Highest level with 38 percent or more correct.	One year below test norms.	Highest level with five or fewer unknown words per twenty words.	Must have 70 percent or better comprehension.
Independent or Recreational Level	Highest level with no more than one unknown word per 100 words or two years below instructional level, whichever is higher.	Highest level with 75 percent correct or two years below instructional level, whichever is higher.	Two to three years below norms.	Highest level with no more than one unknown word per twenty, or two years below instructional level, whichever is higher.	Usually 80 percent comprehension or better. Considers his own understanding adequate.

Burmeister, Lou E. "A Chart for the New Spache Formula," *The Reading Teacher.* vol. 29, no. 4. January 1976, pp. 384–85.

A chart that makes the Spache readability formula easier to use.

Cunningham, Patricia M. "An Inquiry Into Teachers' Attitudes Toward Black-Dialect-Specific and Non-Dialect-Specific Reading Miscues," in *Reading: Convention and Inquiry,* eds. George H. McNinch and Wallace D. Miller, Clemson, S.C.: National Reading Conference, 1975, pp. 162–68.

Research which shows that teachers are more apt to correct children for miscues which are black dialect than for other miscues which do not change meaning.

Ekwall, Eldon E. "Informal Reading Inventories, The Instructional Level." *The Reading Teacher,* vol. 29, nô. 7. April 1976, pp. 662–65.

A good explanation of the reasons for the standards used in determining frustration and instructional reading levels in informal reading inventories.

_____. "Should Repetitions be Counted as Errors?" *The Reading Teacher,* vol. 27, no. 4. January 1974, pp. 365–67.

Polygraph study to determine the exact reading level at which children show physical signs of frustration.

Forese, Victor. "Cloze Readability versus the Dale-Chall Formula," in *Teachers, Tangibles, Techniques,* ed. B. S. Schulwitz. Newark, Del.: International Reading Association, 1975, pp. 23–30.

A research report which indicates that the cloze test is a good measure of a student's ability to read a particular reading selection.

Fry, Edward. "A Readability Formula that Saves Time." *Journal of Reading,* vol. 11, April 1968, pp. 513–16.

The Fry Readability formula and how to use it.

Guidry, Lloyd and D. Frances Knight. "Comparative Readability: Four Formulas and Newberry Books," *Journal of Reading* 19 (April 1976): 552.

Compares the results of the Lorge, Flesh, Dale-Chall, and Fry readability formulas and suggests adjustments that make them more nearly equal.

Hansell, T. Stevenson. "Readability, Syntactic Transformation, and Generative Semantics," *Journal of Reading* 19 (April 1976): 557–61.

Research and discussion of the various factors that affect a student's ability to comprehend written material.

Harris, Larry A. and Carl B. Smith. "Assessing Student Progress and Needs," in *Reading Instruction,* New York: Holt, Rinehart, and Winston, 1976, pp. 98–128.

Discusses informal reading inventories, cloze tests, and various formal and informal means of diagnosis.

Johnson, Marjorie Seddon and Roy A. Kress. *Informal Reading Inventories.* Newark, Del.: International Reading Association, 1965.

A thorough discussion of, and guide to, developing informal reading inventories.

Kibby, Michael W. "The Proper Study of Readability: A Reaction to Carver's 'Measuring Prose Difficulty Using the Rauding Scale,' " *Reading Research Quarterly* 11, pp. 686–705.

Criticizes a readability formula which attempts to use concept difficulty and style as well as vocabulary level in determining readability.

Kochevar, Deloise E. "Individual Tests and Testing Techniques that Bring Remediation in Reading" in *Individualized Remedial Reading Techniques for the Classroom Teacher.* West Nyack, N.Y.: Parker Publishing Co., 1975, pp. 99–127.

Discusses IQ, perception, readiness, reading, and achievement tests, and their application in the reading program.

Kretschmer, Joseph C. "Updating the Fry Readability Formula," *The Reading Teacher* 29 (March 1976): 541.

A correction procedure that makes the Fry Formula more accurate.

Paradis, Edward, Robert Tierney, and Joe Peterson. "A Systematic Examination of the Reliability of the Cloze Procedure," in *Reading: Convention and Inquiry,* eds. George H. McNinch and Wallace D. Miller. Clemson, S.C.: National Reading Conference, 1975, p. 273.

Abstract of a research study to determine the reliability of the cloze test.

Pearson, P. David. "The Effects of Grammatical Complexity on Children's Comprehension, Recall, and Conception of Certain Semantic Relations," in *Theoretical Models and Processes of Reading,* 2d ed., eds. Harry Singer and Robert B. Ruddell. Newark, Del.: International Reading Association, 1976, p. 67.

Research on readability which indicates that shortening sentence length does not increase readability.

Rosen, Carl L. and Wilbur S. Ames. "Influence of Nonstandard Dialect on Oral Reading Behavior of Fourth Grade Black Children Under Two Stimuli Conditions," in *Better Reading in Urban Schools,* ed. J. Allen Figurel. Newark, Del.: International Reading Association, 1972, pp. 45–55.

A study of the consistency with which Black children change standard English into Black dialect when reading connected prose passages orally.

Spache, George D. "The Spache Readability Formula," *Good Reading for Poor Readers.* Champaign, Ill.: Garrard Publishing Co., 1974, pp. 195–207.

The Spache formula and how to use it.

7

Organizing Instruction

Organization of remedial reading instruction must include planning for both the overall remedial program in the school and the specific instruction for each child in the program. Naturally, the plan for each individual student will depend, to some extent, upon the overall objectives of the remedial reading program. Is the criterion for success a change in attitude toward reading, an increase in the frequency and the extent of reading outside of the program, growth in comprehension, greater ability to read and study in other subjects, or improvement on a test of reading skills?

Relationship to the School as a Whole

In some schools, all program planning is left in the hands of the remedial reading teacher, while in others, the overall goals are established almost entirely by the administration. The situation is probably best when administrator, classroom teachers, and remedial reading teacher discuss such questions as:

How will the remedial reading program help the entire reading program of the school?

What plans should be made for long-range evaluation of the school's total reading program?

How will the diagnostic information accumulated in the remedial program be used to strengthen the developmental program?

What specific objectives in reading will be established for the remedial reader?

On what basis will students be grouped—by needs, reading level, interests, projects, or the classrooms from which they are taken?

How will the entire staff be involved?

How will parents be involved?

What attempt will be made to discover and remedy problems before they become serious enough to require referral to the remedial reading program? Will the remedial reading teacher help the classroom teacher with these problems? If so, what time will be allotted for her to do this?

How will skills taught in the remedial reading program be integrated into the regular classroom instruction?

How will the remedial reading teacher follow up on students who are no longer in the program?

How will student progress be evaluated? Will some other report be necessary in lieu of grades?

The answers to all of these questions will influence the remedial reading teacher's planning of her own program.

The Student's Schedule

The scheduling of students for remedial reading requires good relationships and cooperation among the remedial reading teachers and the regular classroom teachers, for, when not handled carefully, scheduling can cause animosity and decrease both the level of cooperation of the classroom teacher and the effectiveness of the remedial reading program. The reading teacher should be thoroughly familiar with the daily program in the regular classroom and work with the classroom teacher in developing schedules for remedial reading pupils. Cooperation is important, particularly since compromises on the part of both individuals are often necessary. Although problems may arise, they most likely will not be serious if each teacher is more concerned about the welfare of the student and meeting his needs than about her own convenience.

Classes should be scheduled at such a time that they will not deprive the child of an activity which is important to him or in which he is particularly successful. Taking him away from recess, physical education, art, or any other activity which gives him enjoyment may make him resentful of the program and destroy his interest in reading. In addition, taking him from the class in which he is successful will deprive him of the one thing he needs most, a feeling of success and self-confidence. How can time be found for remedial reading instruction for a child who already takes longer to do his work than other children? It must be done *by eliminating the tasks in which he will not be successful anyway.* Memorizing a group of spelling words that are too hard for him, staring at a workbook in which he cannot correctly fill in the blanks, and other classroom activities from which the remedial student gets little benefit can be eliminated from his schedule to make time for remedial reading.

Remedial reading instruction should not be held fewer than three times per week, and daily sessions are much better. The longer the time between instructional sessions, the greater the amount of repetition and reteaching that is necessary. Primary-grade children should meet for thirty minutes every day. Instruction may last for an hour at the high-school level, if the activities within that hour are varied properly.

A limit of six students should be set for any remedial reading class. In classes for students with serious problems, the group will need to be smaller, and some students may require some individual instruction. Except for children with serious learning disabilities, a small group is usually preferable to individual instruction, although the actual instruction for the children within the group will often need to be individualized.

Regardless of the homogeneity of the groups, some individual instruction must be given to every student. This means that all students must be given instruction in how to work independently or in small groups without the teacher's direct supervision, while the teacher works with others.

The length of time each student should stay in the program should be decided individually on the basis of each child's needs, motivation, and progress. The greatest gains are usually made in the third through the eighth weeks of instruction. Students who do not have serious problems but need help with skills can be placed in the program for between eight to twelve weeks and then returned to the classroom in order to leave room for others who need the same type of program. However, others will have gained only enough self-confidence in that time so that they can *begin* to make growth in reading skills. Dropping these students from the program may destroy all that has been accomplished. Most students will probably need to remain in the remedial reading program for a full year, and a few with learning disabilities will need several years of specialized help.

Each child should be brought to the level at which he can read classroom textbook material appropriate to his mental ability adequately in as short a time as possible so that he can be returned to the regular classroom reading program and help given to other students.

The remedial reading teacher should maintain a waiting list of students who have been referred to the program and of those who have told the teacher they wish to be admitted. As students are returned to their regular classroom reading programs or transfer from the school, students from the waiting list can be admitted.

The Teacher's Schedule

The remedial reading teacher should have adequate time allotted within the regular school day for planning of classes, preparation of materials, counseling of individual students, diagnosis and follow-up sessions, and meetings with classroom teachers and parents. The remedial teacher needs more time for planning, record-keeping, and organizing and preparing materials than does the regular classroom teacher because much greater individualization and variety of both materials and methods is required. Since the purpose of remedial classes is to give each student instruction individually planned to meet his specific needs, failing to give the teacher an opportunity to plan this individualized instruction defeats the purpose of the program.

Many schools allot two-thirds of the remedial reading teacher's time for working with pupils and one-third for planning, conferring individually with students, meeting with teachers and parents, and handling other responsibilities. Others allow only one-half of her time for actual instruction because of a preference that the teacher devote extra time to working in assisting classroom teachers to adapt instruction to children with learning disabilities or serious reading problems, to locate material to meet special needs of specific children, and to identify reading problems.

All classes ordinarily should be held in the remedial reading classroom. This room should have adequate space for storage of all remedial reading materials so that they are readily available and for learning centers with projectors and tape recorders set up and ready for use.

At least ten minutes should be allowed between each group so that the teacher can prepare materials and have them ready when the next class arrives.

In schools with open classrooms, team-teaching, or individualized instruction, it is sometimes advantageous for the remedial reading teacher to go to the classroom to work with the children, so that she becomes a regular member of the team during the hour she works with that class. However, if materials cannot be kept in the open classroom, it may be more efficient to have the students go to the remedial reading room than to carry materials to the classroom every day.

Basing Instruction on Student Needs

Planning for remedial reading necessitates individual planning for each student with his particular needs in mind. Such thorough planning, with specific objectives for each student, is essential to good instruction. It consists largely of pulling together all the information on the child and, from this information, determining the objectives of teaching and then making decisions as to how these objectives can be reached.

The first step in planning is to draw together all the information on each child, gathering it from preliminary testing and from the teacher, parents, and school records. From this information, a list of specific needs can be formulated.

This list of needs should include: (1) the reading level of the student; that is, the level of material he should read, both for independent recreational reading, for instruction, and for practice in the use of word analysis skills; (2) the particular word analysis skills in which he needs instruction and the point at which his instruction should begin; (3) his comprehension skills level; (4) his study skills; (5) his rate of reading; and (6) any clues to possible learning disabilities, emotional problems, or other characteristics which might influence the type of activities through which his learning might be enhanced or hindered.

Writing Behavioral Objectives

After the child's specific needs have been listed and after his level of performance in each of the areas of reading has been assessed, the teacher is ready to decide on her specific objectives in teaching this particular child. These objectives should be written down so that she can keep them in mind throughout all planning and instruction. Objectives should be written in behavioral terms and should delineate exactly what performance will be expected of the child when instruction has been completed.

A behavioral objective has three parts. It specifies the conditions under which a behavior is to occur; it describes the type of behavior which is to occur as a result of the planned instruction; and it defines the level of performance that will be accepted. These three parts may be illustrated with the following objective: Given a paragraph containing unknown words including the long *e* sound (the conditions), the students will identify these words and pronounce them correctly (the behavior) 90 percent of the time (the acceptable performance).

The statement of an objective is truly meaningful only if it is so specific as to tell what the student will be able to do after he has been given a particular experience. However, the teacher should be careful that this restriction does not cause her to overemphasize the cognitive processes and the development of skills which can be measured and to underemphasize the affective goals, the understandings, and appreciations which the students can gain. The fact that an affective goal, such as the development of an enjoyment of reading, is difficult to measure does not mean that it is unimportant. The teacher should list these affective objectives, even though she may not be able to be as specific in detailing the level of performance.

Lesson Planning

After information on each student has been recorded, the students' instructional periods scheduled, and specific objectives for each student determined, the teacher is ready to begin planning instruction for each group of students.

The First Week

Usually it is not possible to plan more than the first two or three days in detail before instruction begins because a great deal is learned about the students during the first instructional periods. This is especially true if the teacher has not had an interview with the student and discussed his interests before instruction begins.

The first few minutes of the first session usually should be spent getting better acquainted with the students, and if the students come from different schools or different classrooms and do not know each other, getting them acquainted with each other. Most of this session can be spent profitably in discussing interests and out-of-school activities.

Short stories written at the recreational reading level of the students may be placed where they will be available during this first session so that each student may choose one he would like to read. The stories should be well below the students' instructional reading level so that they will have no difficulty reading them and should contain much action and adventure.

During the second session, it is advantageous to have each student do some oral reading so that the teacher can be sure that the material selected is at the proper level for each student. If any unknown words are found during this reading, a word box can be started. Reading these words with the tachistoscope the following day may add interest as well as variety.

It is particularly important that the first week contain enough variety and arouse enough interest so that the students will begin the program with enthusiasm and anticipation of an enjoyable session during each day to come. Word games may be helpful in this effort. It is also absolutely essential that instruction begin at the student's success level and that he experience success every single day, especially in the beginning of instruction.

As much of the student's learning as possible should be based upon his strengths rather than his weaknesses. This is particularly important

during beginning instruction because it permits the student to be successful from the very start.

Not only should instruction begin with strengths, but the teacher
also should bring out the child's strengths and his good qualities constantly throughout all instruction. She should give him constant encouragement which is never spoiled by criticism. The teacher should also
be constantly alert for ways to make learning fun, for a child remembers
that which he enjoys much longer than that which is unpleasant to him.

The Weekly Plan

After the first week, it is usually possible to plan a week's program
in advance for most of the groups, provided the teacher is flexible enough
to change plans if new needs or interests are discovered during the course
of the week.

Teaching should be done in such a way that the students are aware
of the purposes of the various activities. They should have an opportunity
to express their opinions and make suggestions, and, whenever possible,
their suggestions should be incorporated into the lesson plans.

The plans must be so organized that no student will spend the entire
period at one activity. Usually a twenty-minute limit should be set for
any one type of activity. If the session is thirty minutes long, this means
there should be at least two different types of activity planned for each
day; there should be three if one of the activities is the review of words
from the word box or some other activity that takes only four or five
minutes. If the class session lasts for an hour, there should be at least
four activities planned, as at least one will take fewer than twenty minutes.

One of the activities each day should be concentrated practice in
reading. Instruction in phonetic analysis, various comprehension skills,
vocabulary, study skills, and so on are important, but only because they
are to be put into practice in reading. The student will gain in his ability
to read only if he practices reading. This practice should include frequent
free reading, selected by the student.

Individual lesson plans.   Gary Robinson is a remedial reading teacher
in a junior high which has seven periods each day. Mr. Robinson teaches
remedial reading during the first five class periods, with six students
in his class each hour. He uses the last two periods for planning, individual
conferences, meeting with other teachers, evaluating students who are
on his waiting list to enter his program, etc. His program is completely
individualized.

Mike Williams is in Mr. Robinson's third period class. When the
bell rings at the end of the second period, Mike hurries from his science

class to the remedial reading room, for he knows he will not have to wait for the rest of the class but can begin reading as soon as he gets there. When he arrives, there are already two other students at the file getting their folders. He takes his folder from the file, opens it, and finds the list which he planned yesterday with Mr. Robinson:

Review words in word box.

Read aloud with tape, *Reading Skill Builder 4*, Part 3, beginning on page 27. Answer the questions and write a paragraph explaining the reason for your answer to the last question.

With Dwight Brown, read Controlled Reader film 3 (4) 17.

Answer comprehension questions on the film with 90 percent accuracy.

Read for pleasure: "Autumn Victory," in *Teen Age Tales*, Book B.

Mike gets his word box and goes through the cards, reading the word on the front of each, then turning it over and reading the sentence on the back to check his accuracy (see Chapter 10). When he finishes, he gets the *Reading Skill Builder* and the cassette tape on which the same story is recorded. He puts the cassette in the tape player and reads the story along with the tape, pointing to the words as they are spoken. While reading, he stops the tape and writes three words that he does not know on cards from his word box. When the story is finished, he answers five questions with single-word answers and then writes a two-sentence explanation of the last answer.

Meanwhile, Mr. Robinson is working with Dwight Brown, so Mike gets the Controlled Reader film and threads the projector. He is reading the word list that precedes the story when Dwight moves over beside him to read the story along with him. After reading the story, they answer the comprehension questions and then discuss two of the questions on which they disagree. After they check their answers, Dwight goes back to his other assignments, and Mike begins reading from *Teen Age Tales*.

He has been reading for a few moments when Mr. Robinson sits down beside him, glances over the work he has done, and asks him how he likes the story he is reading. Mike tells about a particularly exciting incident, and Mr. Robinson asks him to read that part aloud, which he does. They discuss the story for a minute; they then go over the words for the word box, adding the three that Mike had written earlier and one that Mr. Robinson had written down while Mike was reading aloud. They analyze these words phonetically, write sentences to go with them, and then put all of them in the word box. Mike also files away, in his alphabetical file, four other words from the word box on which he needs no further review.

Three of the new words have common prefixes which Mike did not recognize, so Mr. Robinson promises to find some material on prefixes and work with him on this point tomorrow. They discuss the other activities to be carried out the next day, record them in Mike's folder, and then Mike goes back to his story for the rest of the period.

Group lesson plans.   Sandra Williams works with students from the first through the sixth grades in a small elementary school where she groups her students according to reading level and type of problems. Class sessions vary from thirty to fifty minutes for the different groups. Figure 1 presents her lesson plan for one group of fifth- and sixth-grade students who come to her at 10:30 A.M., immediately after they return from morning recess.

Sandra divides the sheet on which she writes her lesson plan into four columns. She uses the first column for her lesson plan for this group for Monday and the third column for the plan for Tuesday, leaving the second and fourth columns blank so she can write her evaluations beside her plans. Since she works with each group four days per week, she uses two sheets of paper for each week's lesson plan.

It should be noted that her students sometimes work together and sometimes work independently but that when they all need the same instruction, she groups them together. When only one needs instruction in a certain area, she gives individual instruction while the others work independently or help each other.

Daily Evaluations

Only by recording her observations and evaluations daily can the teacher really meet the needs of each individual student. For example, according to Sandra Williams' lesson plan, all four students have had instruction in the way in which prefixes change the meaning of words and on the meanings of certain prefixes. Two of the students, Carla and Bruce, do not need more instruction on these prefixes, so they are doing recreational reading on Monday while the teacher is working with Jim and Juan. In her evaluation of Monday's lesson, the teacher notes that Juan has no difficulty with the use of these prefixes but that Jim still needs additional help. Therefore, on Tuesday, Jim completes a similar exercise. Since each of the four is working individually at this time and Ms. Williams needs to help the others as well as Jim, she has Bruce, who has a good understanding of prefixes, work with Jim until she is

FIGURE 1

Lesson Plan and Evaluation

10:30 Bruce Brown, Jim Bear Crane, Juan Martinez, Carla Schultz

Monday—Plan	Evaluation
Students will work in pairs. Bruce and Juan will check each other on words in the word box. Carla and Jim will use the Language Master to check their words.	Don't put Jim & Carla together for machines. Carla monopolizes the machine because Jim is too shy to interfere. Jim needs to run machines because he is good at it and gains security this way.
Boys will read "Autumn Victory" silently and answer ten comprehensive questions with 90 percent accuracy. Carla will dictate a language experience story about her trip this weekend and read it with 100 percent accuracy.	Carla's experience story was good. Read with 3 errors, then re-read correctly. (Type before tomorrow.) Bruce 100%, Jim 90%, Juan 60% at first. Juan found and explained errors on three questions, so raised to 90%. Needs work on sequence of events.
Students will complete work sheet with prefixes with 90 percent accuracy.	All made 100%. 2 made the worksheet too easy, but 2 think it helped Jim. He needed the success.
Carla and Bruce will read for enjoyment in their recreational reading books. Jim and Juan will define with 80 percent accuracy ten words starting with "non" and "in." They will spend the rest of the time playing "word domino."	The boys got all the words defined, but Juan did most of it. Jim still doesn't understand how to get the meaning from English prefixes, although he no longer leaves them off when he reads. No time for game. Bruce was restless so discussed his book— poor choice. Find one on cars.

Tuesday—Plan	*Evaluation*
Class will use overhead projector as tachistoscope to practice words from all four word boxes. Students will read aloud simultaneously and then write the words with 100 percent accuracy.	Carla & Jim 100% - no more practice time needed. Juan missed 4 words, Bruce 10 - three from his box. He needs kinesthetic practice on these. Has missed each one 3 times in a row. Don't put him with others on Tac. next time.
Jim will define orally a new list of ten prefix words with 80 percent accuracy. Bruce will help Jim until I'm free and then read "Hot Rod Thunder" for fun. Carla will read an experience story with 100 percent accuracy. Juan will read "Ghost Rock Mystery" and list events in the order of their occurrence.	Bruce likes new book. Asked to take it home. Juan listed events, correctly. Carla read experience story without error. Went outside to practice reading it aloud so she can read it to the boys Wed. Jim finally defined 8 of 10 words. Now understands prefixes "non" and "in" fairly well. Needs work on others.
Carla, Bruce, and Juan will listen to Listening Skill Builder Number 3 from tape and will answer questions with 80 percent accuracy. Jim— neurological impress with "Cheyenne Legends of Creation."	Bruce got 90% right, Juan 80%. Carla was still practicing her story. Jim kept with me better today. Is reading with fewer pauses.
All four will play the game "prefix rummy."	Other 3 were all helping Jim recognize which prefixes went together because of similar meaning, so he won the game. It helped Jim and was a good experience for all.

free to work with him. Later, all four play a game which gives Jim some of the additional help that he needs, while at the same time providing a review for the others and maintaining their interest in the use of prefixes.

Ms. Williams has also noted Bruce's apparent lack of interest in his story, discussed it with him, and jotted it down in her evaluation column. The next day she has a story in his interest area for him to read. She has also noted the type of errors that Juan made in his comprehension questions on Monday and, consequently, gives him practice in this particular skill the following day.

This is an example of a teacher who observes her students carefully and evaluates their work daily. Her evaluations are made on the basis of the objectives which she has set for each student's achievement. When a student does not reach the level of mastery which she considers necessary, she gives him additional instruction to bring him to that level. When he has reached the level prescribed, she does not bore him or waste his time with additional unneeded instruction. His only additional practice in this area will be maintenance practice, which will be given in an interesting way to be sure he will not forget what he has learned.

Daily evaluation of remedial reading students should include observation and evaluation of: the student's reading and his achievement of objectives, the student's learning methods and reactions, and the effectiveness of teaching methods and materials.

By frequent evaluation of the student's reading and accomplishment of behavioral objectives, instruction can progress in logical order from the known to the unknown.

By noting which learning activities are most effective with individual students, the teacher can vary the instruction to give each student the help which will be most effective for him.

By listening carefully, and being willing to listen to the children, the teacher can pick up much information about their interests, their likes, and their dislikes which will be useful in choosing materials and motivating learning. She may also gather information on home situations or out-of-school problems which may be affecting the children's achievement.

By carefully evaluating the effectiveness of her own teaching, the teacher can improve continually as a teacher and adapt her instructional methods to the students she teaches. It is this kind of evaluation which marks the difference between the teacher who through three years of teaching experience has become a highly effective professional and the one who after twenty years is still an amateur because she has had only one year of experience—repeated twenty times.

Maintaining Gains Made During Instruction

Maintaining gains which the students make is a major problem in remedial reading instruction. Remedial reading students frequently make tremendous gains in skills at the beginning of instruction, but these gains may not be continued. In fact, even those skills which have been successfully learned may be forgotten all too soon.

One of the reasons for difficulty in maintaining gains made in remedial reading is the teacher's desire to teach the student as much as possible in the limited time available. Because she wants for him to derive as much benefit from the time as possible, she teaches a skill, and as soon as the student shows that he can handle this task, she rushes on to the other skills which he needs to learn. With new skills and ideas crowding in, the student forgets those he has just learned.

Although this concentrated program is necessary, the answer is not to be satisfied with less, but to teach with long-term gains in mind. There are several ways of promoting this maintenance of skills.

First, the instructor should teach for overlearning by giving extra practice on each skill beyond that which is necessary for learning the skill. This does not mean a repetition of the type of drill that the student sees as unnecessary and boring since he already knows the skill; rather, it means finding new and different ways of emphasizing the same skill.

Second, the teacher should apply the skill in as many ways and in as many different settings as possible. Showing the student that he can use the skill in various ways assures carry-over from instruction to application in the student's daily reading. This application, in turn, improves retention.

Third, review is essential. The teacher should apply the skill periodically, thereby not allowing the student to forget the skill when moving on to other instruction. For good retention, the practice of the skill should be frequent at first, with practice sessions spaced farther apart later on in the instructional period.

Fourth, the teacher and program should progress to higher skills which require the use of this skill. The instruction in the higher skill and the practice related to it will act as practice for retention of the skill upon which it is based.

Fifth, the teacher should continually evaluate the retention of previously taught skills.

Sixth, oral reading should be frequent enough and of enough variety so the teacher can check the student's application of the skills which have been taught through it.

A checklist of skills which have been taught to the particular student is very useful in making periodic evaluation and review more systematic. Informal teacher-made tests covering those skills listed on the check sheet serve the dual purpose of evaluation and review. Graphs of the pupil's progress, files of worksheets completed, and any records which the pupil keeps on his own progress will also aid in assuring that all skills taught are reviewed.

Summary

Planning remedial reading instruction must be based upon the overall objectives of the remedial reading program and on the individual needs of each student. The general organization of the program and the scheduling of students should be planned cooperatively with the classroom teachers.

Instruction for each student should be based upon a thorough analysis of the needs and abilities of that student. If needs are written in behavioral terms, it will help to place the emphasis where it belongs— on the objectives which the child should reach—rather than on the things the teacher should do.

Instruction should begin on a positive basis with emphasis on strengths and encouragement. Group instruction may be given when all students in a group need help in the same area. When only part of the group needs this instruction, the teacher can work with these students while other children work independently. If a group has widely divergent needs, the instruction may need to be completely individualized, a task which requires the teacher to spend most of the time planning with individual students and checking their progress rather than giving direct instruction.

The teacher should make daily records of students' progress and their reaction to the instruction which they receive; this evaluation should be the basis for future instruction.

Recommended Related Reading

Ekwall, Eldon E. "Important Operational Procedures for the Teacher," in *Diagnosis and Remediation of the Disabled Reader*. Boston, Mass.: Allyn and Bacon, 1976, pp. 32–43.

Seventeen valuable suggestions for making instruction effective.

Harker, W. John. "Lesson Planning for Remedial Reading," *The Reading Teacher* 29 (March 1976): 568–71.

A general outline for providing for the needs of each student.

Harris, Larry A., and Carl B. Smith. "Organizing for Instruction," in *Reading Instruction: Diagnostic Teaching in the Classroom.* New York, N.Y.: Holt, Rinehart, and Winston, 1976, pp. 367–95.

A variety of ideas for individualization of reading instruction.

Kochevar, Deloise E. "Seven Steps to Classroom Organization for Remediation," *Individualized Remedial Reading Techniques for the Classroom Teacher.* West Nyack, N.Y.: Parker Publishing Co., Inc., 1975, pp. 22–25, and 200–202.

Suggestions for overall planning of reading instruction.

Moyle, Donald. "Sequence and Structure in Reading Development," in *New Horizons in Reading,* Newark, Del.: International Reading Association, 1976, p. 220.

Emphasizes relating reading to the entire curriculum and the involvement of children in planning their own work.

Siegel, Ernest. "Task Analysis and Effective Teaching," *Journal of Learning Disabilities* 5 (November 1972): 5–18.

Planning instruction based on a task analysis of each student's needs and breaking instruction down into sequential steps.

Wallen, Carl J. "Grouping for Instruction," chapter 19 in *Competency in Teaching Reading.* Chicago, Ill.: Science Research Associates, 1972, pp. 472–82.

Good practical ideas on grouping to meet the individual needs of every student in the classroom.

Welborn, Lydia, and Pauline Hickey. "Team Reading," *Grade Teacher* (November 1970): 96–98.

Describes a method by which all children are paired off in teams of two and help each other in developing reading skills.

Wilhoyte, Cheryl H. "Contracting: A Bridge Between the Classroom and Resource Room." *The Reading Teacher* 30 (January 1977): 376–78.

Suggestions for planning, with the child, a reading program to be carried on in both his regular classroom and the remedial class.

Zintz, Miles V. "Scheduling Time for Corrective Reading Instruction," in *Corrective Reading.* Dubuque, Iowa: William C. Brown Co., 1966, pp. 90–114.

Contains practical suggestions for ways for the classroom teacher to schedule corrective instruction.

8

Oral Reading

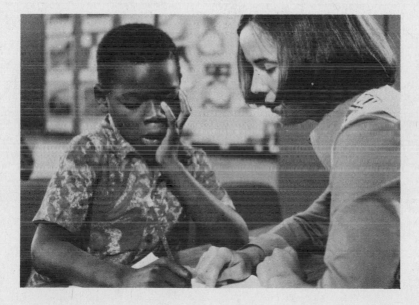

Oral reading has a very important place in the remedial reading program. If handled properly by the teacher, it adds enjoyment and creates a pleasant atmosphere, gives the teacher an opportunity to show an interest in what the child does, and makes it possible for her to keep track of the student's progress. Oral reading encourages the child to use the word analysis skills he has been learning. It also enables the teacher to give him the help he needs when he needs it, thus it is the foundation on which silent reading skills are built. It provides an opportunity for motivating activities such as dramatization, role playing, choral reading, and discussion of shared ideas. It also provides an opportunity to develop group spirit and cooperation, eliminating many discipline problems. It is, in fact, the avenue through which many reading skills can be evaluated and taught most readily.

Developing an Ability to Evaluate Oral Reading

Many reading problems can be discovered only through evaluation of the child's oral reading. The use of an oral reading test for determining the child's reading level and identifying his problems was discussed in regard to the original diagnosis in Chapter Six. However, careful observation and evaluation should continue throughout instruction whenever the teacher has an opportunity to listen to the student read aloud.

Evaluation of oral reading is not an easy task, yet practice in careful observation and recording of data is necessary. This practice can be obtained most easily through the use of an oral reading checklist, such as the one in Instructional Guide 8.1, while reading orally. The teacher practicing evaluation should have a copy of the checklist for each child whose oral reading is to be observed, and should make notes next to the items noted.

INSTRUCTIONAL GUIDE 8.1
Oral Reading Observation Checklist

Emotional Problems	*Word Analysis*	*Habits*
Attitude	Beginning sounds	Pointing, head movements, etc.
Sign of tension	Ending sounds	
Aggressive actions	Consonant sounds	Unusual voice
Withdrawal tendencies	Vowel errors	Unusual posture
	Parts of words omitted	
Fluency	Reversals	*Speech*
Pauses or hesitations	Difficulty in blending	Stuttering
Omissions of words	Prefix and suffix endings	Articulation problems
Insertions of words	Syllabication	Enunciation
Substitutions of words	Uses of context	
Poor phrasing		
Poor interpretation		

Some teachers prefer, after several observations of the child's reading, to record their observations on an evaluative scale, such as the one in Instructional Guide 8.2, which rates each characteristic on a scale of one to seven.

INSTRUCTIONAL GUIDE 8.2

Oral Reading Evaluation Scale

Meaningful Oral Reading

1	2	3	4	5	6	7

word by word—meaningless .... meaningful—expressive

Use of Context Clues

1	2	3	4	5	6	7

does not use .... excellent use

Reversals

1	2	3	4	5	6	7

reverses often .... no reversals

Pronunciation of Words

1	2	3	4	5	6	7

mumbles, indistinct ....clear and distinct

Regressions

1	2	3	4	5	6	7

repeats frequently................. .... no repetitions

Skipping Words

1	2	3	4	5	6	7

many skips.. no words skipped

Insertions

1	2	3	4	5	6	7

many extra words... no words inserted

INSTRUCTIONAL GUIDE 8.2 *(continued)*

Fluency

1	2	3	4	5	6	7

very halting .... some hesitations .... fluent, natural

---

As with all other evaluation, evaluation of a child's oral reading is of value only insofar as it changes the instruction which the child receives. Instructional Guide 8.3 lists many of the kinds of oral reading errors which may be observed and offers suggestions for remediation of them. It should be noted that some observations are listed in more than one group and that several possible causes are listed for each group. When these oral reading defects are observed, it will be necessary to evaluate further to determine which probable cause, or causes, applies in this particular case and then plan the instruction accordingly.

INSTRUCTIONAL GUIDE 8.3

Oral Reading Fluency, Interpretation, and Comprehension

Observations	Possible Causes	Recommendations
Very poor fluency in general. Great variation in speed. Lack of voice content and rhythm.	Material too difficult. Poor word attack. Poor eye-voice span.	Tape record and play back his oral reading for the student. Use easier material. Check word analysis skills. Emphasize meaning.
Many pauses and hesitations. Stumbling. Little expression in voice. Failure to anticipate and express meaning.	Eye-voice span too narrow. Focus only on word being said.	Check by covering with card in the middle of a sentence. Prepare oral reading in advance—no sight reading. Have child practice trying to look up without causing a pause in reading—use easy material. Practice phrasing with child. Have child practice with tachistoscope for quick recognition.

Observations	Possible Causes	Recommendations
		Use material student can understand and interpret. Demonstrate monotonous vs. meaningful reading.
Slow, plodding reading. Word by word or sound by sound reading. Pause after each word. Monotonous voice. Choppy reading.	Sight vocabulary poor. Loses place easily. Poor eye control. Possible learning disability—uses much time for simple tasks.	Build phonetic attack. Use marker above line. Use easy material. Build vocabulary. Practice phrase reading with child. Practice with tachistoscope for quick recognition of common words. Check eye movement.
Omission of words. Reading too rapidly. Reading with little expression. Poor enunciation when reading.	Eye-voice span broad. Looking too far ahead of reading.	Check by covering words with card. Teach to pause at punctuation. Make tapes for student.
Oral reading too rapid.	Rapid silent reading. Lack of interest in developing oral reading skills. Tension. Poor concentration.	Tape record reading and play it back. Have child listen to material read by good oral reader and then practice reading the same material. Read simultaneously with the child. Have child practice interpreting ideas to an audience.
Poor enunciation.	Hurrying through material. Poor speech habits. Feelings of insecurity. Imitation of poor speech models.	Same as those given above but use easy materials. List and practice words on which individual student has poor enunciation.

Observations	*Possible Causes*	*Recommendations*
Poor phrasing. Words not grouped in thought units.	Using material that is too difficult when learning to read.	Have child read low vocabulary material for meaning.
Word by word reading. Ignoring punctuation. Reading in monotone—does not express meaning.	Poor comprehension. Poor sight vocabulary. Lack of instruction in importance of punctuation to meaning.	Use easy material containing much conversation. Have child practice before oral reading with special attention to phrasing. Punctuate material to show meaning. Mark phrases for reading. Read with him with tachistoscope one phrase at a time. Tape record and let student listen to recorded drama—imitate it. **Group work with plays and poetry.** Read sentences with good phrasing and have the student repeat them. Read to others for specific purposes. Have child practice and then read reports and other stories to others. Use choral reading. Practice to create different moods and meanings by reading same material different ways. Choose important words—read them for emphasis. Read to the student stories with much conversation and different moods; student listens.

Observations	Possible Causes	Recommendations
		Teacher read narration, child read what people say.
Habitual repetition.	Attempt to sound fluent. Habit developed early. Possible learning disability. Material that is too difficult. Insecurity.	Have student slow down and read carefully. Tape record student's reading and help him set objective. Check visual perception. Practice with easy material. Practice oral reading on easy material. Cover with card as he reads so he can't backtrack.
Omissions. Insertions.	Effective context reader. Rapid silent reading. Careless reading. Inattention. Attempt to sound fluent. Poor eye movement. Over-reliance on context.	Same as those listed above. Have child prepare material and read it to an audience.
Skipping lines.	Poor eye movement.	Use marker above line.
Refusal to attempt to read a word.	Poor vocabulary. Poor word attack. Insecurity. Fear of criticism.	Build word attack skills. Use easy material to build confidence. Praise every success—use no criticism.
Failure to recognize common words. Substitution of "the" for "a," "and" for "for," etc.	Poor sight word recognition. Early confusion when learning to read. Good rapid reading.	Check with Dolch list. Practice with flash cards or tachistoscope. Use word box. Tape and have child listen for own error.
Word substitutions, harder words.	Poor phonetic skills. Failure to apply phonics. Carelessness. Attempt to sound fluent.	Check basic word analysis skills. Apply all skills in reading when taught. Slow down. Relax.

Observations	Possible Causes	Recommendations
Slurring of sounds. Mumbling. Poor enunciation.	Lack of confidence. Poor phonics skills. Cultural background. Fear of making error. Influence of friends.	Give feeling of security, no criticism. Check word analysis skills. Frequently record child's reading and play back.
Consistent substitution of speech sounds.	Poor auditory discrimination. Physical speech defect. Family speech patterns. Immaturity. Lack of effort. Mother's baby talk. Dialect difference.	Check auditory discrimination and listening comprehension. Refer to speech therapist. Do not work on any problem caused by physical defect or dialect. Have child watch mouth to imitate sounds. Recruit aid of family.
Frequent reversals.	Directional confusion. Lack of left to right training. Poor word attack skills. Back tracking.	Check for perceptual problems (see chapter 12). Left to right orientation practice. For complete word and letter reversals, practice one until thoroughly learned, then its reverse. Kinesthetic practice. Tachistoscope practice. Follow reading with card. Word wheels changing first letter. Controlled reader. Games that call attention to first letter. Use Frostig Program.
Omission or mispronunciation of suffixes and word endings.	Poor in phonetic analysis. Accustomed to using only beginning sound and context for word analysis. Carelessness. Vision Problem.	Practice reading words in isolation. Practice on nonsense words. Check vision. Practice.

(For other word recognition problems identified through oral reading, see Instructional guides 10.1 to 10.)

Detecting problems in word analysis. Determination of the student's ability to use word analysis for identifying words in context is an important part of the evaluation of oral reading. Word analysis skills usually are evaluated through the use of specific word analysis tests, through having the student sound out isolated words, and through spelling. However, some children can repeat phonetic rules and can use them on isolated words, even though they have not learned to use these skills in reading.

It is the student's ability to use a combination of word analysis skills as an aid to reading which makes him an effective reader. Therefore, when listening to the student read orally, the teacher should gather as much information as possible about the student's ability to use phonics in reading.

Chapter Ten is devoted to the teaching of word analysis. Detailed information on skills to be observed, possible causes, and recommendations are included in the Instructional Guides in this chapter.

Observing indications of learning disabilities. Some indications of learning disabilities may be evident in the child's oral reading. For example, the oral reading of a child with learning disabilities often lacks a steady flow, since the child labors through the words slowly and in a choppy fashion. Money (1962, p. 35) has said that it is not uncommon for children with dyslexia to exhibit a general confusion about words with similar configurations, such as "quiet" for "quit." Reversals are also common among these children. Although learning disabilities cannot be identified positively through oral reading, the alert diagnostician may see indications of orientation or visual perception problems which suggest the need for more detailed analysis. Information on various types of learning disabilities is included in chapter 12.

Identifying Speech Problems

Speech problems and reading problems often go together. Because a student's speech may give clues as to the causes of reading problems, the evaluator should be on the alert for any sign of speech problems while the student is reading orally.

Speech problems may interfere with the teaching of reading in two ways. First, the child who mispronounces certain sounds may have difficulty with phonics because he thinks of the sound he says rather than the sound he hears. Second, the student who stutters has a special problem and should never be required to read orally unless he wishes to do so.

In the diagnosis of oral reading, the teacher must be careful not to identify as oral reading errors those variations in pronunciation which are due to speech defects or dialect differences.

Interpretive Oral Reading

There are two kinds of oral reading instruction, each of which has quite different objectives and is handled quite differently. One is instructional oral reading; the other, interpretive oral reading.

Reading aloud to inform others or to explain ideas to them is called interpretive oral reading. Nearly everyone occasionally needs to read aloud to other people. Adults may be required to read an item of business in a meeting; husband and wife may wish to share a letter, a news item, or a story; parents read to their children. In all these cases, the reader is interpreting the material to his listener in such a way that the listener will get the meaning.

Every child should have an opportunity to practice interpretive oral reading. When he finds a paragraph, a joke, a story, or a poem that he would like to share with the other students, he should have an opportunity to do so. But before he does so, he should have an opportunity to read the material through for practice, either silently or aloud, as many times as he feels necessary before reading it to others.

The selection that the student reads to a group for practice in oral interpretation should be material that the other students have not read before, and they should not have a copy of it when he is reading. All his listeners should be listening attentively (practicing their listening skills) while he is reading. Since his listeners are relying on him to give them the meaning, the student has reason to read as correctly and as meaningfully as possible.

One way of getting practice in interpretive oral reading is to cut an interesting story into parts and let each student in a group practice his part individually. Then all the students come together and each reads his part to the group. Each student must try to read well to put over his part of the story, and all others are good listeners because they want to hear the rest of the story. Most stories vary within themselves so the easier parts can be given to the poorer readers and the harder parts to the better readers. If necessary, some parts can be rewritten to eliminate difficult vocabulary.

Another good way of promoting interest in interpretive oral reading is through the reader's theatre. The main differences between reader's theatre and regular drama are that in reader's theatre any material that involves characters and conversation can be used. (It does not require that the material be written in play form.) Action, staging, and costuming are suggested rather than complete, and the script is read, rather than memorized. Students taking part in reader's theatre should have a chance to practice their parts until they can do an adequate interpretation. They should have an opportunity to produce their dramatization before fellow students who have not previously read the material.

Instructional Oral Reading

The objective of instructional oral reading is the improvement of reading skills which influence silent reading. It is through this oral reading that the teacher detects reading problems and helps the student correct them; consequently, oral reading in the remedial reading class is nearly all instructional.

Oral reading can be very useful as a means of building comprehension, of keeping track of the student's progress in the skills taught, of determining areas which need emphasis, and of teaching the application of word analysis skills.

The way oral reading is conducted in the classroom is often the deciding influence in determining whether a child will like or dislike reading. The old method of "round robin" reading, going around the circle with each student taking his turn reading aloud, has received a great deal of just criticism for causing children to dislike oral reading. As generally used in the classroom, this practice has several serious drawbacks. First, the time of the better reader is wasted as he waits for the poorer reader to struggle laboriously through the page. (This criticism is just as true though if he is required to sit and do nothing while he waits for the slower students to read the material silently.) Second, some students who read more rapidly will not stay with the slow oral reader; they will not be looking at the words being read. Third, students learn poor oral reading habits by spending most of their listening time with others who are also poor in oral reading. A study of the effects of the impress method, which will be described later in this chapter, shows that listening to children who are poor readers may have a detrimental effect upon a child's reading habits. Fourth, the poorer readers suffer embarrassment by having to stumble through the material in the presence of their classmates. Fifth, being forced to follow along with another slow reader has been blamed for the development of poor eye movement and habits of regression. There are many better ways of promoting instructional oral reading.

Individual oral reading.   If students are allowed to read at their own rate, and the teacher has them come to her desk one at a time to read a page or two for her from the part of the story they have enjoyed most or the part that answers a question posed in advance, the faster readers will read three to four times the volume of material they would have read in the reading circle. Each student will do at least as much oral reading in this way as he would do in the reading circle. Just as in a circle, only one person will be reading at a time.

Sharing interesting material.   Children are social beings and enjoy things most when they are shared. Games and most other group activities of children are enjoyable largely because they are shared rather than because of the activity itself. It is logical then that reading, although it is essentially an individual activity, is more fun when it can be shared. Therefore, except in unusual cases, group instruction of two or three students is preferable to individual instruction. In completely individualized reading programs, the children lose some of their enthusiasm for reading unless the teacher can find ways for them to share their enjoyment.

Reading can be shared in many ways. For example, children can tell each other about the things they liked in the stories they have read or several children can read the same story and discuss it. They can share their enjoyment of reading and, at the same time, gain practice in interpretive oral reading by reading portions of stories, including their own experience stories, to the group.

Using material intended for oral reading.   Jokes or any humorous material are appropriate for children to read to each other because humor cannot be enjoyed fully unless shared. Laughter is a social activity; people seldom laugh when they are alone. They get much more enjoyment from humorous material when they can enjoy it with others.

The teacher should laugh with the students and let them know that laughter in the classroom is acceptable behavior. The teacher's obvious interest and enjoyment of the material also helps maintain the children's interest in reading.

Poetry, also, is meant to be read aloud. To be enjoyed fully, it either must be read orally or the reader must vocalize mentally while reading it. Narrative poems, humorous poems, and those with unusual sounds can be enjoyed together by a group of students.

Some stories also depend upon sound for interest. These may be stories in which there is much imitation of sounds or others in which certain words or sounds are repeated, such as the story of the Hucklebuck Family in which Pony Pony Hucklebuck liked to watch her father watch the watches in the watch factory. Such stories are much more appropriate when they are read aloud. Discussions of mental images portrayed and attempts to imitate sounds can also add interest to this type of reading.

Using dramatization.   Children enjoy dramatizing a story as they read it. Each child in the group may choose the character whose part he wants to take, and the teacher can then read the narrative parts while the children read the parts of the story in quotation marks. The children not only enjoy this type of activity, but they also get practice in the interpretation of mood, emotion, and character which makes reading more meaningful. Dramatization also helps the children to understand and use quotation marks and other punctuation for interpreting meaning.

Plays provide excellent material for oral reading. In fact, surveys have indicated that the majority of students prefer the oral reading of plays to the oral reading of stories. Taking part in a play which is practiced and then read to a class can be good motivation for a remedial reading student.

Each of these methods of oral reading in a group presupposes that all members of the group are reading at approximately the same level and that the material to be used is at their recreational reading level so they can read it easily or that the individual pupil has had an opportunity to practice reading his part in advance. A student should not be embarrassed by having to stumble through a selection while students who he knows could read fluently wait; nor should the other students be subjected to listening to poor reading, thereby encouraging them to be poor listeners.

Choral reading.   Choral reading can be an enjoyable activity and can add considerable variety to oral reading. Students can practice and then have individuals or groups take various parts; as an alternative, all the students can sight read in unison, following the lead of the teacher who reads loud enough for all to hear. Some students who dislike reading poetry individually learn to enjoy it through choral reading, although the technique should not be restricted to poetry.

A good way of getting started with choral reading is to pass out copies of a poem to all the students, then the teacher reads a few lines aloud. The children then read the lines in the same mood, tempo, and phrasing. Continue through the poem in this way, then all read the entire poem together. For this to be fun, the poem needs to be one that contains a lot of humor or possibilities for dramatic expression, change of pace, or action.

Expressing mood and meaning.   In all of these oral reading activities, the children are getting practice expressing mood and meaning. However, some children can go through any of these activities in a monotone, never realizing that they should be expressing ideas as they would when they are talking. One way of practicing putting meaning into oral reading is through reading the same material with different meanings. For example, have each person in the group read the same sentence with a different mood. Read the sentence, "John, don't do that!" angrily, suspiciously, hopefully, laughingly, fearfully, joyfully. Have them read each of the following words conveying three different moods, and let the others in the group guess what mood the reader is expressing: Stop! Run! No! Strike! Go! Well! In the use of the impress method, although expression is not emphasized, the student learns to express mood and meaning in the same way the teacher expresses them.

The impress method.   One of the most important developments in recent years is the system called by its originator "neurological impress." It is also called "oral impress." Neurological impress is comparable in the development of fluent oral reading to kinesthetic tracing in the development of sight vocabulary and may eventually have nearly as great an impact on the teaching of the remedial reader and the child with learning disabilities.

In using the impress method, the teacher works with one student who holds the book while the teacher sits behind and to the right of him, close enough so that she is speaking almost into the student's ear. (A book holder or slanted desk is helpful for keeping the book in proper reading position.) The teacher reads aloud, and the student reads in unison with her—or as close to in unison as is possible. At first, he may be as much as a word behind the teacher, but, with practice, he will be able to stay either with the teacher or, on unfamiliar words, a fraction of a second behind her. The student is told to try to stay with the teacher, using the same phrasing, emphasis, etc. If he does not know a word, he tries to pronounce it with the teacher if this is possible; if he cannot pronounce it, he does not hesitate but goes on with the teacher without hesitation.

As they read, the teacher points to each word with the index finger of her right hand, moving it smoothly along the line of print. This will require practice for some teachers, especially if they are accustomed to having their eyes several words ahead when reading orally. It is very important that the finger stay exactly with the voice, as the student will be looking where the finger is pointing, and he should be looking directly at each word as he hears and says it.

The teacher should read slowly and clearly, with good rhythm and emphasis, as the oral reading of the student will be patterned after that of the teacher.

Because high concentration is required of the student when using oral impress, this practice should be limited to ten minutes per day. In most cases, improvement will be seen within a short time in sight vocabulary, speed of recognition, phrasing, and general oral reading fluency.

If the student wishes to practice moving his hand with that of the teacher so that he can take over pointing to the words for part of each session, he should be encouraged to do so. Some students find that they like to use their own fingers and state that they feel that this increases their learning; other students do not agree. There is no experimental evidence to show that either method is appreciably better than the other as long as the finger is moved at the right speed.

The neurological impress method is essentially a method for individual instruction. However, there is one way in which it can be handled in a group—if the necessary equipment is available. A "language lab" is needed for such instruction, with a microphone for the teacher and earphones for each student. The reason for the earphones is that for the method to be effective, each student must hear the teacher's voice in a louder and clearer fashion than either his own voice or those of his classmates. It is the teacher's way of reading, not the way the other students read, that is to be impressed upon his mind.

The material to be read should be copied onto transparencies and placed on the overhead projector so that the students can read from the screen as the teacher points to the words on the transparency and speaks into the microphone. This can be handled in two other ways, although neither is quite as effective as the use of the overhead projector. On the one hand, the teacher can read into the microphone as the stories are projected with the controlled reader; however, the slight pauses at the end of each line prevent natural, conversational oral reading. As an alternative, each child can have a copy of the book from which the teacher is reading and follow in it, but, when this is done, it is very difficult for the teacher to know whether every student is staying exactly with her reading.

Oral reading with tape recording.   The use of tape recorded material is much less effective than the individual oral impress method. It is the personal contact and the intimacy of the teacher's voice that make the impress system work. However, some benefits can be derived from reading with the tape recorder if the student reads the material aloud while listening to it being read on the tape.

Fearn (1972) has demonstrated that the use of tape recordings with the regular classroom procedure in the basic readers will improve the reading vocabulary, reading comprehension, and total reading behavior of both the average and below average readers in the classroom.

Alternate reading with the teacher.   Often the reading of the remedial student is so slow and labored that he gets discouraged and feels that he never manages to read enough of a story for his efforts to be worthwhile. If the teacher is giving individual instruction to a student, she can solve this problem by alternating reading with the student frequently. The teacher might read every other page or even every other paragraph. Such a practice moves the story along and makes it more interesting for both teacher and student. When doing individual instruction this can be combined with the oral impress method.

The teacher occasionally should read to her students in order to promote an interest in reading, to show them how interesting reading can be, and to set an example in reading style. Alternate reading, however, is of even greater benefit because the student not only is getting practice in reading but also is learning through seeing the words as they are read. When the teacher alternates reading with the student, the student should be expected to follow in his book and watch each word as it is read. Alternate reading promotes the student's interest in material that he himself is reading.

Total-class individual oral reading.   A system of oral reading which works equally well in both the regular classroom and the remedial reading class is total-class individual oral reading. In some classrooms, this practice has taken the place of most of the individual oral reading to the teacher and of most of the silent reading, except that which is done for the purpose of practicing speed and flexibility in reading.

In total-class individual oral reading, every child in the class reads orally, at the same time, in his own materials, and at his own rate. As the pupils read, the teacher walks around among them, listening to them read. She is able to tell very quickly if any child is not reading, is trying to read material that is too difficult for him, or having any other problems. A teacher can monitor the reading of every child in the room much more quickly and efficiently this way than she could by having each child come to her desk and read a page or two from his book and then return to his seat as is necessary in most personalized reading programs.

As the teacher moves among the students, she can stop and listen to one individual child for a time if she detects a possible problem, give individual help if needed, or make a note of help or instruction that should be given later to an individual or group.

The volume of noise produced by having an entire class reading at the same time is disturbing to some teachers until they become accustomed to it. However, it seldom bothers any of the children after the first day. Even highly distractible children often find that a great many voices coming from all sides are less distracting than the voice of one child asking a question in a quiet classroom.

This total-class oral reading is an excellent method to use when all the students in the remedial reading group are doing recreational reading.

Uninterrupted sustained silent reading.   In addition to oral reading, every student will need to do some silent reading, and the teacher needs to encourage both oral and silent reading outside the remedial reading classroom. One system which the teacher can promote for use throughout the entire school is known as Uninterrupted Sustained Silent Reading, or USSR.

In the school which adopts the USSR program, a period of fifteen or twenty minutes every morning is set aside for uninterrupted reading. During this time, every person in the school stops all other activities and reads silently. By everyone is meant not only the pupils but also the teachers, the principal, the secretary, and even the janitor. Schools using the system have found that it has promoted much more reading and much more interest in reading.

If a school is unwilling to try uninterrupted sustained silent reading for all pupils, ideas from it can be adopted within the remedial reading program.

Keeping a balance between oral and silent reading.   Oral and silent reading are both essential parts of the remedial reading program and neither should be emphasized to the exclusion of the other; by keeping a balance, progress in both areas is possible. When first beginning to learn to read, the child is learning to change the written symbols into oral language. During these first stages of decoding, it is easier for the child to learn the relationship of printed symbols to spoken words if he does most of his reading orally. The amount of silent reading should increase gradually. By the time children in the regular classroom are reading more rapidly silently than they can say the words orally, at least three-fourths of their reading time should be used for silent reading so that they can develop higher silent reading speeds.

For most remedial readers though, speed is not an issue. The remedial reading teacher usually needs to be more concerned about the child's ability to recognize words and comprehend meaning than about his reading speed. Until the student is able to read well, at or above the rate at which he speaks, a large part of his reading can continue to be oral. The only reasons for including silent reading in the remedial reading program previous to this point are so that the student will learn to obtain meaning from the silent reading he must do in the regular classroom and so that he can read silently while the teacher is working with other students.

Summary

Oral reading is a very important part of the remedial reading program, both as a means of determining the need for instruction and as a method of teaching reading skills. An oral reading test is the best instrument with which to begin the original diagnosis of a student's reading problems. Close observation during this test can reveal a great deal about the student's reading problems; for example, his attitudes toward reading and his oral interpretation of the material reveal much about his vocabulary and comprehension. As the student reaches the material in which the vocabulary is difficult for him, much can be discovered about his ability to use phonetic principles as an aid to reading. Speech problems and habits that slow down reading may be revealed by the student's oral reading, and indications of possible learning disabilities may also be noted.

The remedial reading teacher should practice careful observation and evaluation of oral reading. This observation is important not only in making the original diagnosis of the student's problems but is necessary in determining changing needs and planning ways of meeting these needs throughout the entire instructional program.

Some of the ways in which oral reading can be promoted in the remedial reading classroom are individual oral reading; alternate reading with the teacher; sharing interesting material; and taking part in reading poetry, humorous material, plays, and choral reading. The neurological impress system and total-class oral reading should be used with at least some of the students in every remedial reading program.

Recommended Related Reading

Crowl, Thomas K., and Walter H. MacGinitie. "The Influence of Students' Speech Characteristics on Teachers' Evaluations of Oral Answers," in *Theoretical Models and Processes of Reading* 2nd ed., eds. Harry Singer and Robert B. Ruddell. Newark, Del.: International Reading Association, 1976, p. 440.

An experiment which showed that teachers judge answers to be inferior if spoken in a dialect other than standard English.

Fearn, Leif. "The Oral Model as a Strategy in Developmental Reading Instruction," in *The Quest for Competency in Teaching Reading,* ed. Howard A. Klein. Newark, Del.: International Reading Association, 1972, pp. 158.

Report of an experiment using taped recordings of basal readers in the regular classroom reading program.

Gilliland, Hap, and Harriet Mauritson. "Humor in the Classroom." *The Reading Teacher.* 24 (May 1971): 736-56.

Stresses the importance of the acceptance of humor as a part of teaching.

Larson, Martha L. "Reader's Theatre: New Vitality for Oral Reading," *The Reading Teacher* 29 (January 1976): 359-60.

A good description of the use of reader's theatre.

Nurss, Joanne R. "Oral Reading Errors and Reading Comprehension." *The Reading Teacher* 22 (March 1969): 523-27.

Not all oral reading errors are bad. Some may be indications of good comprehension. Self corrections require comprehension.

Oliver, Marvin E. "Improving Reading Skill Through Practice," and "An Experiment in High Intensity Practice," in *Making Readers of Everyone.* Dubuque, Iowa: Kendall/Hunt Publishing Co., 1976, pp. 51-57 and 59-80.

Experiments demonstrating the importance of uninterrupted reading practice in making gains in reading.

Packman, Linda. "Selected Oral Reading Errors and Levels of Reading Comprehension," in *The Quest for Competency in Teaching Reading,* ed. Howard A. Klein. Newark, Del.: International Reading Association, 1972, pp. 203-8.

Report of research to determine which types of oral reading errors correlated more closely with reading comprehension.

Rowell, E. H. "Do Elementary Students Read Better Orally or Silently?" *The Reading Teacher* 29 (January 1976): 367-69.

A study to determine the relationship between oral and silent reading and where the emphasis should be placed.

Seymour, Dorothy Z. "Expression as a Result," *Instructor* (March 1971).

Suggestions on developing good oral reading habits by emphasizing comprehension.

Welborn, Lydia and Pauline Hickey. "Team Reading," *Teacher* (November 1970).

Describes a good system of pairing off for reading so pairs of students help each other with oral reading, discussion of meaning, seat work.

9

Motivating Learning

Developing in a child a desire to learn is an essential part of all teaching, for no matter how good the instruction, the student will learn only if he wants to do so. Motivation can be developed through building self-confidence, making learning pleasant, using interesting materials, promoting a desire for specific skills, and insuring variety in the program.

The teacher should remember that each child will respond differently. It requires ingenuity on the part of the teacher to find the motivational technique which will work with a particular, individual child—especially the child in the remedial reading program.

Building Self-Confidence

The vast majority of remedial reading students are insecure, discouraged, and lacking in confidence in their own ability to learn to read well. Self-confidence for these children can only be built through a series of successes, for the child whose school life has been one of nothing but frustration and failure has not built that confidence. It is the job of the teacher to show him that he can succeed and then to recognize that success by giving him honest praise and appreciation without criticism.

Quandt (1972) cites research which indicates that unless remedial reading includes improvement in self-concept, reading instruction alone may be futile. His findings include the following:

1. A student who feels that those important to him do not consider him successful may use avoidance behaviors such as disinterest in or hatred of reading, lack of effort, or refusal to read.

2. If he believes, because of past experience, that he will not succeed, he may reinforce this by not succeeding.

3. Success generally leads to greater effort; failure leads to less effort which causes progressively poorer performance as the student advances in school.

Improving the Child's Self-Concept

Because reading is essential to all other subjects, inability to read influences every facet of school work. A child who is poor in arithmetic or some other subject can shrug it off with, "Oh, I'm not very good at math. I prefer to study science." But it is not so easy to be unconcerned about reading. Because reading is so essential to all subjects, the child who cannot read begins to think of himself as "too dumb to do anything." He is often ridiculed or "looked down upon" by his classmates, and before long, he loses confidence in himself as a person.

Before the child can have a good opinion of himself, the teacher must have confidence in him as her student. The teacher must have faith that the student can succeed and faith in her own ability to teach him to read. Only then will the student have reason to believe that he can be successful. The teacher not only needs to show the pupil that she has confidence in his ability to learn but she also must show by her actions that she respects the pupil as an individual—that the personal worth of the student is not dependent upon his achievement.

The student who is having difficulty not only needs acceptance and approval but also understanding and appreciation. He needs to be recognized when he does well and to receive frequent praise. The praise, however, must be sincere, for the child will detect insincere flattery. In class or elsewhere, the teacher should be an enthusiastic booster for her student. To do this, she must watch for the good points in the student and his work and comment on them, while ignoring any failures she may notice. The teacher also must see to it that the child is successful every single day. Successes must be given sufficient emphasis so that the child thinks of himself as being successful and knows that the teacher, too, has recognized his success.

A word or two at the end of each session about what the child has done well that day helps to give him enthusiasm for the next lesson. A vague statement, such as, "You did a good job today," is of little value. To show the child that the statement is sincere, the teacher should be more specific: "Well, five more words in your word box, all learned and filed away. Isn't that great? And your reading for that play was much smoother today!" If there are several children in the group who are all working independently, this reinforcement may have to come at the end of the time when the teacher works with an individual child rather than at the end of the class period. Regardless of the time it occurs though, praise must be a daily practice.

Helping the Child to Read at the Right Level

As was discussed in Chapter Six, materials that are too difficult not only cause the child to dislike reading but also cause emotional upsets which make progress very difficult. Most of the materials used in remedial reading instruction, therefore, should be at a level at which the student can enjoy his reading. This means he must be able to read it without difficulty, for most people enjoy doing what they can do well. Even the very good reader will often get discouraged and quit reading a book—even if the content is interesting to him—if the vocabulary level and sentence structure are such that he has to struggle to comprehend the content. Evaluation of the student's reading should be continuous, so as to keep him at the proper reading level as he progresses. Short selections bound separately also are an aid to motivation, for remedial readers are discouraged by thick books and fine print.

Using Self-Evaluation to Help the Child

Self-evaluation is one way of insuring that the child recognizes his own progress. To aid in this, the student can make his own charts and graphs on which he records his progress. A chart on which the child records his own progress, no matter how crudely drawn it may be, is more meaningful to him than one drawn to perfection by the teacher.

Many kinds of charts can be used. For younger children, there are race track charts with horses or cars to be moved around the track, map charts with the children's markers moving across the country, pet charts with animals to be added. For older students, bar or line graphs may be more appropriate, or a system of recording success on a bowling score sheet or golf card might be invented. Almost any activity can be graphed—new words learned, phonetic principles mastered, pages read, and comprehension or speed increased. Since the goal of trying to beat one's own score is a real incentive to most individuals, it is largely this motive that makes such individual sports as golf popular. This same motivation can give the child who cannot compete with others a sense of real accomplishment. Each child can be keeping a record of his progress in three or four areas at any one time. As the emphasis in teaching shifts to new skills, new graphs can be developed for him to use in evaluating these new areas.

Letting the student keep his own progress records is just one of the means by which the teacher can help the student to feel responsible for his own learning. With the student of any age, the teacher can discuss problems and let him set many of his own goals. She can ask for his ideas and then use them. She should remember that the more mature the student, the more he may be able to help in planning his own program.

Convincing the student who has never been asked his opinion before to evaluate his needs is difficult at first, but if the problems are faced honestly and the student realizes he no longer has to bluff his way through and pretend he is a good reader, he usually is ready to take on responsibility for his own learning. Students who are aware of their own goals usually make better progress than those who are not.

Developing Confidence in the Child through Helping Others

Students boost their self-concepts by helping set their own goals, but they also can help themselves by teaching each other. Nothing gives a student more confidence in his ability to do a task than to know he has taught someone else to do it too. In addition, the child who has had difficulty with a certain concept but finally has come to understand it is often better able to understand and to help clarify the problems that another child is having with that concept than anyone else.

Every teacher realizes that when she teaches a skill for the first time, she learns even more than the pupils do. McWhorter (1971) found that when students tutored other students, the tutors raised their own reading levels by an average of 2.4 years in four months, while those being tutored gained 1.1 years in the same period.

As Frager and Stern (1970) have said, a sixth grader reading at first- or second-grade level may be indignant if asked to use primer type material for practice in reading. However, if he is asked to help a first or second grade child who is having trouble, reading this same material takes on status and responsibility. He builds his self-concept and self-confidence as he builds his reading skills.

The tutor does not need to be older than the child he tutors. One remedial sixth grader who has some skills that another remedial sixth grader does not have can tutor that student. If properly planned, this can be of great benefit to both.

Using Language Experience to Help the Child

One method of improving the self-concept of the student and of letting him feel that his ideas are worthwhile is through letting him create his own reading materials. These can be stories of his own experiences or creative stories.

The development of language experience stories should be based on a topic of interest to the student. It can begin with conversation and discussion between the teacher and the student. The student should be encouraged to talk about his interests. When enthusiasm about a topic is apparent, the teacher can suggest that the student tell about the experience or make up a story about the subject. Often it is necessary to further stimulate the child by using pictures, showing filmstrips, reading books, or providing interesting experiences in which the child can participate. Field trips, science experiments, parties, art projects, and even games often provide the motivation for a language experience story. Once a topic is chosen, the student tells the story, the teacher writes it, using the student's exact words. The teacher then types the story or prints it in manuscript form so that the student can read it the following day. If the student enjoys drawing, the story can be typed at the bottom of a page, thus leaving room at the top for him to illustrate his ideas.

Stories should be kept quite short for the beginning reader or the student who is very unsure of his reading ability, although the selections can be lengthened as he grows in confidence. The more important words can be analyzed and discussed to aid in word recognition, but the student must realize that he is not expected to recognize every word.

These stories are used for practice in oral reading, for work on sight vocabulary, and for practice in word analysis. Students may also read each other's stories. The stories may be bound into individual scrapbooks or into class anthologies; they also may be used on bulletin boards made by the class members; or they may be combined into class newspapers. After a student has read a story several times, he may wish to take it home to read to his family.

When the student feels confident enough in his writing ability so that *he* feels he wants to do so, he can begin to take the responsibility of writing the stories himself. If he feels more comfortable recording his stories, this is possible too. One teacher created a recording booth from a refrigerator box and put a cassette tape recorder inside. Whenever a child had a story to record, he would go into the recording booth, turn on the recorder, and tape his story. A volunteer teacher's aide then typed these stories and had them ready for the next day's reading.

Too often, it has been assumed that language experience methods are appropriate only for the beginning reader, but they can be used equally well with older children. The writer has found language experience to be successful in his reading clinic with students of all socioeconomic levels and with all ages from beginning readers to adults. It has been especially valuable for disadvantaged adults.

Developing Interest

The student who makes progress in reading is the one who reads in his spare time—who chooses reading over other activities. But before he will do this, he must have a reason for wanting to read.

Making Reading Fun

Perhaps instead of saying "Make reading fun," we should say, "Have fun"—to both teacher and student. If a teacher has fun teaching a class, the children nearly always have fun, too. The classroom should have a relaxed and enjoyable atmosphere. It should be free from tension and pressure. Humor should have a definite place in every classroom— remedial or regular. Mauritson (1971) has said:

In many classrooms, learning is serious work, which can never be taken lightly by either the pupil or the teacher. Yet in other classes, very similar in outward appearance, a feeling of the joy of learning pervades the atmosphere, as humor pops in and out of the environment, pictures, and language experience work. It is enjoyed together whenever it is found in stories read aloud, or in the child's personal reading. Children learn to see the humor in the little errors and problems that could otherwise cause frustration.

The teacher can be alert to capitalize on any humorous situations that occur in the classroom. If the teacher is willing to laugh at herself and appreciate the humor the children see in the situation, she will develop a relationship with her students in which they can laugh at themselves and are not afraid to laugh and enjoy the funny incidents that occur.

Most of the humor that takes place in the classroom is spontaneous. It is difficult to plan a funny situation. However, there are many humorous things which can be read, and the student himself can create humorous pieces of writing by telling funny things he has heard, seen, or said. Humorous descriptive words can be listed to help with the writing. The child also can mix up favorite rhymes or add funny endings to his writing and make up his own nonsense rhymes.

Any collection of remedial reading materials should contain a number of humorous pieces. A child who will not tackle a novel or even a short story may not hesitate to read from books of jokes or riddles. Even the most reluctant reader will usually attempt to read the captions which accompany humorous cartoons.

Humorous stories probably have as much, if not more, universal appeal than any other one kind of writing. Books such as *Homer Price* by Robert McCloskey, *Mr. Popper's Penguins* by Richard T. Atwater, *Mary Poppins* by Pamila Travers, *Henry Huggins* by Beverly Cleary, *Tom Sawyer* by Mark Twain, *Pippi Longstocking* by Astrid Lindgren, and the books by Dr. Seuss are always among the most popular in children's libraries.

Humorous stories often offer special appeal to culturally disadvantaged students who are able to draw little from typical middle-class fiction. Especially appropriate for such a child are humorous stories about his own ethnic group. For example, of the more than seventy books in the Indian Culture Series,[1] the two most popular with Indian children are two humorous ones, *Grandfather and the Popping Machine* and *No One like a Brother.*

---

[1] Published by Montana Council for Indian Education, 1810 3rd Avenue North, Billings, Montana 59101.

Some of every student's reading should be done purely for the purpose of enjoyment. This pleasure reading should be free from interruptions and from skill development activities. The teacher should let the student know that he is to read for the fun of reading and that he will not be asked detailed questions when he has finished about what he has read.

Activity should be a part of the reading class whenever possible. The child can read instructions for making something and carry out the activity. He can be part of "treasure hunts" in which the children read a series of notes carefully and follow the instructions in order to find the treasure.

Action and humor can be added to drill by playing games such as "Twister," in which words are written on the floor and two children try to put a hand or foot on each word as it is read without removing their other hand or foot—or falling down.

Enthusiasm from the teacher is more important than any humorous materials. The teacher who says, "I'll teach him if it kills me!" usually feels "dead" at the end of the day—and so do the students.

Fitting the Material to the Student

The material to be read must be appropriate to the maturity and interests of the student in any remedial reading class. In addition, the format and interest level should be appropriate to the age level of the student, while the vocabulary level must be low enough for the student to read the material without difficulty. The usual interests of students at different age levels are discussed in Chapter Thirteen.

Not only must the teacher know something of the usual interests of students of different ages, but she also must know every individual in her program and his likes and dislikes, for each student should have a part in choosing his own reading materials.

Remedial reading instruction usually begins with a discussion of general interests. Additional information about the student's enthusiasms may be gathered throughout instruction by starting discussions on topics such as TV programs and movies that the student likes, his play and recreation, vocational interests, and his spare time reading—if he reads in his spare time. Stories or incidents the the child tells during language experience sessions often give additional clues to interests that he might like to pursue further.

The conference with the parents also should give the teacher information about the child's interests. A conference with the classroom teacher is important too, for she may know of subject areas in which the child is interested and of other things which might interest or motivate him. If the classroom teacher is one who promotes reading by getting the students so excited about a science or social studies unit that they will hunt for more information about this subject, then the remedial reading teacher should keep close tab on what is going on in the classroom and find reading material that will supplement classroom projects.

Even if a child is not enthused about what is happening in the classroom or is struggling to complete his assignments, he may appreciate help in reading material on the subject he is studying or help in finding material which is simple enough so he can read it.

If, however, the student wants to avoid reading anything related to his regular classroom activities, he should not be pushed to do related reading, as this may cause his dislike of his other classes to carry over into the remedial reading class.

Interests in reading can be developed by placing objects around the room which are not a part of the reading program but can lead to reading. Such objects include globes, maps, science equipment, cages with small animals, pictures, records, tapes, filmstrips, and book review clippings. Reading materials related to these objects should be handy. If a child comes in and spontaneously begins reading about these objects, he should be given time for this reading in place of some of the other reading that originally was planned for him.

Promoting Interest through Creative Drama

Dramatizing a story can add interest and a reason for practice in remembering what has been read. Let each student choose a part. Then have the students read the story silently, trying to remember as much as possible about the action and their own part in it. When all have read the story, they attempt to dramatize it without referring to the book. Reading as preparation for dramatization promotes a variety of reading skills: remembering sequence, main idea, details, dialogue, understanding of character, and sensitivity to mood. It provides a reason for working for high comprehension.

Teachers may find that upper elementary students who have not previously participated in spontaneous dramatization will at first be inhibited. However, they should not be discouraged if it does not go smoothly the first time. Further opportunities will often produce a great deal of enthusiasm.

Another variation of this activity is having a student read a story up to a certain point, then act out the ending as he thinks it should be. Children also enjoy acting out comprehension questions about a story they have read.

Creative drama can also be used as a means of improving vocabulary and clarifying the meanings of words. Children can act out verbs to show different connotations of meanings: walked, dashed, sauntered, strode, glided, shuffled. They can be given cards with words they have recently learned. Each child acts out one as the others try to guess what he is: a dejected girl, a greedy elf, a voracious lion.

Scheduling Remedial Reading When There Are No Conflicts

Choosing a time for remedial reading instruction which will not conflict with other activities which the student enjoys is particularly important. The student cannot be expected to want to participate in remedial reading instruction or learn to enjoy it if it takes him away from physical education, art, or any other school activity in which he can feel a measure of success or if it takes him away from the after-school ball game which is his main interest in life.

Promoting a Desire to Learn

Instruction in reading includes more than reading stories. There are specific skills to be taught. But a strong desire to understand the plot of a story does not motivate a young child (or all older ones) to learn which sound of *e* to use when sounding out a new word.

It is essential that the student see a need for what he is attempting to learn. He should understand what skill is being taught, its application, and why it is important to him. An older child or adult who is reading at a low level is often motivated to work hard on a skill if he knows it will help him to read better. If the teacher explains how this particular skill will help him to sound out words or to comprehend what he reads, this understanding may be all the motivation that is needed. As Joanna Sullivan (1969, p. 349) says:

> If those of us who develop a remedial reading center show children that books make them feel excited, sad, courageous, show them places they have never been, help them to build model planes, gain a driver's permit, pass a Civil Service exam or the College Boards, and, most important, help them find themselves, then we can begin to develop skills. Students will have a reason for learning.

Another important way of motivating practice is through the use of games and puzzles. After a phonetic rule has been taught, for example, practice on the use of that rule may be accomplished as easily through a game as through any other means. Games can be invented which will reinforce almost any reading skill. Their use is discussed more thoroughly in chapter 13.

Use of oral reading skills can be promoted by letting a student select a portion that he likes from a story and practice it in preparation for reading it to other children. The material may be a short selection to be read to his own group or a complete short story to be read to a younger brother or to the younger children in a different class.

Reading for good comprehension can be motivated in a similar fashion by letting the child read a story and then tell it to the other children. In telling a story or reading it aloud, the tape recorder can be a good means of motivation. When the child thinks he is ready to present his story to the class, he records it and then listens to himself to see if any improvements are needed.

Using Variety

A variety of types of materials and subject matter should be used in every program. Even the student who has a high degree of interest in a particular area may tire of reading only one kind of material. Consequently, a variety of very short stories should be used to help locate other areas of interest for each student. An individual student may develop a greater interest in a new subject as he learns more about it.

Each Day's Instruction Should Be Different

The remedial program should not become so routine that the child will assume that each day will be "the same old thing." The fact that instruction is based on the child's needs (as determined through diagnosis) does not mean that the teacher must use only one type of instruction, for several methods can be found for working toward any one goal. The remedial reading teacher should know good developmental reading methods well enough to feel secure in the use of a variety of techniques. In addition, she should try to be as creative as possible in searching out new ways of teaching the same skills and should not continue to use any one technique over and over until it loses its value.

Some children, especially the slow learners, like the idea of a routine. They find security in knowing what to expect. For these children, some of the activities which they particularly enjoy should be repeated every day for as long as the children are accomplishing important objectives by using them. However, within this routine, there can be variation and activities with an element of surprise. Daily planning of part of the next day's program with the student is usually a better way of meeting his needs for security than repetition which can become monotonous.

Variation in teaching methods is easier to accomplish if there is a variety of materials available. This does not mean that expensive equipment is necessary. Projected materials can add interest and help to meet needs, but these too can become monotonous, and sometimes even discourage the teacher from adjusting the instruction to the needs of the individual student. Good materials are helpful, but a creative teacher is much more important in providing the program with variety, interest, and success.

Variety is especially important for the remedial reader with very high ability because he is usually bored by routine. Many new and different ideas and opportunities to think for himself are needed to maintain his interest. Providing variety does not necessarily mean having new and different materials. They may lead to boredom if used in the same old way. It means using those materials that are available in new and creative ways. It means adapting materials to a variety of teaching methods and pupil needs. It means promoting pupil creativity and using pupils' ideas as well as the creative ideas of the teacher.

Each Class Period
Should Be Different

Long, uninterrupted periods of instruction are impossible for most remedial readers to endure. A good rule to follow in working with remedial readers is never to stay with one type of activity for more than twenty minutes at a time. This means that there must be at least four different activities planned for each hour of instruction, since some of these activities will not take a full twenty minutes. Even when the child is still enthusiastic about a story or activity, the teacher should discontinue it at the end of its allotted time. Continuing the activity until concentration becomes difficult will lessen the child's enthusiasm for returning to the story the next day as well as the value he will derive from the time he has already spent. Each new activity should be as different as possible from the one preceding it.

**Remedial Instruction Should
Be as Different as Possible
from Regular Instruction**

The remedial reader usually has become so discouraged in regular classes that he does not think he can learn at all. If his remedial program is a repetition of the type of instruction he has already experienced, he may feel that, since he could not learn to read this way in regular classes, he will be unable to do so now—and he may very well be correct in his assumption. If the remedial instruction is different from his past experience, the student may be encouraged to try harder, and the teacher may find techniques which are more suited to him. For this reason, it usually is not advisable to use basic readers for remedial instruction— the basic reading skills *should* be reviewed, but not in the same old way.

The student should not be pressured or given material that is too difficult for him; nor should he be allowed to waste time or spend his time working on that which he already knows. The gifted underachiever in particular needs to be challenged with different ideas and with learning that is meaningful to him. As David Hawkins has said, "Many remedial programs give students the same program that is already boring to them, only more slowly." [2]

Removing Obstacles to Learning

Many things are done in the name of education that kill the interest of the student. The teacher will do well to think carefully on each of the following "Ten Commandments for Motivating Reading".

1. Do not use any word, gesture, or tone of voice that will take the fun from the printed page, the smile from the lips of the child, or the sparkle from the eye of the reader.

2. Do not take any student from his physical education class, art class, recess, or any other activity which he particularly likes or does well for remedial reading. This may take from him his only opportunity for the success which is so essential to him.

---

[2] Statement made by Dr. David Hawkins at the national Upward Bound meeting, Estes Park, Colorado, April, 1968.

3. Do not force a child to write a book report on every book he reads. He may stop reading.

4. Do not make him analyze critically every story or every poem he reads.

5. Do not bore the student with material that is too easy, too hard, or on an inappropriate subject for him.

6. Do not ask a student to read without letting him know the purpose for which he is reading.

7. Do not spend more time talking to the student than listening to him.

8. Do not label a child or use a label as an excuse for not teaching him to read.

9. Do not subject any child to nagging or threats; do not allow any other teachers or parents to do so.

10. Do not subject any child to failure.

Summary

Motivating the student to want to read is one of the most essential factors in teaching reading. Suggestions for increasing motivation are summarized in Instructional Guide 9.1.

INSTRUCTIONAL GUIDE 9.1

Motivating Reading

Observations	Possible Causes	Suggested Treatment
Self-Concept		
Coming to class reluctantly. "Hang-dog" expression. Making disparaging remarks about own ability. Hesitating to try anything new.	Lack of self-confidence. Failure at reading. Attitudes of teacher, parents, or classmates. Material that is too difficult. Comparison with better readers.	Use easy reading material. Trust, appreciate, and respect the child. Praise the child sincerely. Demonstrate success daily.

Observations	Possible Causes	Suggested Treatment
Lacking confidence. Insecurity. Oversensitivity. Slumping in seat. Overdependence on approval from others. Giving up easily.	Implications that he is unworthy as an individual because he cannot read. Discouragement.	Have child demonstrate progress with graphs, charts, and score cards. Have child set own goals and keep a record of his achievement. Have child create his own materials. Have students teach each other. Compliment everything child does well. Never mention his failures. Show interest in child as an individual. Record the child's experiences.
Easily upset emotionally. Inability to accept criticism.	Poor self-concept.	Start with easy material. Keep material at child's level. Create a relaxed atmosphere. Use behavior modification techniques. Use a structured program. Let the child help others. Emphasize the child's success.
Interest Making no real effort. Acting bored. Showing no enthusiasm for stories. Poor comprehension. Saying he does not like reading.	Lack of interest in reading. Material that is too difficult. Material that is slow-moving.	All of the above. Use a variety of subject areas and kinds of materials. Change activities often. Recheck child's reading level. Obtain materials at his recreational level. Use student-made materials. Get fast-moving materials.

177

Observations	Possible Causes	Suggested Treatment
	Not enough action to maintain child's interest.	Use adventure stories. Check story and remove unnecessary passages. Use materials written for remedial reading.
Acting bored.	Lack of variety.	Change activity often. Use humorous stories, plays, poems, cartoons, jokes, riddles, and games. Keep classes active with treasure hunts, drama, and action games.
	Child has not learned to enjoy reading.	Capitalize on humor. Read to the student the beginning of a story and then alternate reading pages. Let child read for fun, with no interruptions and no questions. Have fun reading, thus being a model for the student.
	Reading is not related to student's interests.	**Develop interest centers in the classroom.** Know the student's individual interests. Use materials appropriate for the child's age —primary grades, realistic stories, animal stories, fairy tales; intermediate grades, adventure stories, sports stories, biographies, science stories, animal stories, fantasy stories; high school, mystery stories, vocational reading, stories about dating.
No effort in skill areas.	Cannot see need for reading skills. Final objective of enjoyment in reading is too remote from present instruction.	Teach skills through games, creative dramatics, tape, recordings, and machines.

INSTRUCTIONAL GUIDE 9.1 *(continued)*

Dislike for reading.	Negative teaching. Experience with failure, boredom, labels, criticism, threats, nagging, book reports, overanalysis of fiction, pointless reading, conflicts with other activities, teachers who talk too much.	Be a cheerful teacher. Create a relaxed atmosphere. Encourage the child. All of the above.

Recommended Related Reading

The books, chapters, and articles listed below cover a variety of ideas for motivating reading. You may also wish to refer to the list of recommended related readings at the end of chapter 13 as it lists research studies on the reading interests of children of different ages and different cultural groups.

Alexander, J. Estell and Ronald Claude Filler. *Attitudes and Reading.* Newark, Del.: International Reading Association, 1976, 73 pp.

Contains many ideas on building positive attitudes toward reading. Based on research.

Barufaldi, James P. and Jennifer W. Swift. "Children Learning to Read Should Experience Science." *The Reading Teacher* 30 (January 1977): 388–93.

Using science experiences at the beginning reading level to develop readiness and communication skills.

Boraks, Nancy and Amy Roseman Allen. "A Program to Enhance Peer Tutoring." *The Reading Teacher* 30 (February 1977): 479.

Good, practical suggestions on setting up a program in which one remedial student tutors another remedial student from his own grade.

Gilliland, Hap and Harriet Mauritson. "Humor in the Classroom." *The Reading Teacher* 24 (May 1971): 753–56.

Suggests a variety of ways in which the teacher can make use of humor to improve the atmosphere of a classroom.

Criscuolo, Nicholas P. "Mag Bags, Peg Sheds, Crafty Crannies, and Reading." *The Reading Teacher* 29 (January 1976): 376–78.

Creative ways to enhance the basal reading program.

Fostering Reading Interests. New England Consortium for the Right to Read, University of Rhode Island, 1976, 14 pp.

Review of research related to interesting children in reading.

Frager, Stanley and Carolyn Stern. "Learning by Teaching." *The Reading Teacher* 23 (February, 1970): 403–5+.

Usable suggestions for setting up a tutoring program in which older elementary students tutor younger students.

Hall, Mary Anne. *Teaching Reading as a Language Experience,* 2d ed. Columbus, Ohio: Charles E. Merrill Publishing Co., 1976, 118 pp.

A book that gives thorough background and instructions for the teacher interested in using the language experience method.

Harris, Larry A. and Carl B. Smith. "Creating Interest in Reading," in *Reading Instruction: Diagnostic Teaching in the Classroom.* New York: Holt, Rinehart, and Winston, 1976, pp. 233–60.

Ways of motivating children to read.

Henderson, Mary Ann. "Reading While Becoming: Affective Approaches," *Journal of Reading* 20 (January 1977): 317–26.

A good article with many ideas for improving self-concept through reading related activities.

Holdaway, Don (New Zealand). "Self-Evaluation and Reading Development," in *New Horizons in Reading,* ed. John E. Merritt. Newark, Del.: International Reading Association, 1976, pp. 181–91.

The importance of pupil feedback in making progress in reading. Outlines skill levels in reading.

McWhorter, Kathleen and Jean Leve. "The Influence of a Tutorial Program on the Tutors." *Journal of Reading,* 14 (January 1971): 221–24.

Shows that the student who tutors gains even more than the one he teaches.

Noland, Ronald G. and Lynda H. Craft. "Methods to Motivate the Reluctant Reader." *Journal of Reading* 19 (February 1976): 387–91.

Fifteen approaches that have proved to be successful in causing students to want to read. These include charting self-concepts, stressing enjoyment of reading, student authors, realistic goal setting, and others.

Oliver, Marvin E. *Making Readers of Everyone.* Dubuque, Iowa: Kendall/Hunt Publishing Co., 1976.

Chapter 2, "Influencing Attitudes Toward Reading," covers such topics as "Teachers influence attitudes toward reading," "Learning to avoid reading," "Relax the pressure," and "Fear and anxiety generate avoidance of reading."

Chapter 3, "Increasing the Desire to Read," includes ideas on cross-ability tutoring, partner reading, and pupil-team learning.

Olson, Joanne P., and Martha H. Dillner. "Language Experience Approach," chapter 8 in *Learning to Teach Reading in the Elementary School.* New York: The Macmillan Publishing Company, Inc., 1976, pp. 149–69.

Good instructions for the teacher planning to use Language Experience.

Quandt, Ivan. *Self Concept and Reading.* Newark, Del.: International Reading Association, 1972.

Suggestions for developing self-concept.

Pienaar, Peter T. "Breakthrough in Beginning Reading: Language Experience Approach." *The Reading Teacher* 30 (February 1977): 489-96.

Description of a language experience type program in reading and writing found successful in Canada, England, Australia and South Africa.

Ross, Elinor P. and Betty D. Roe. "Creative Drama Builds Proficiency in Reading." *The Reading Teacher* 30 (January 1977): 383-87.

Using dramatizations of various kinds to promote comprehension and reading skills.

Smith, Lewis B. "They Found A Golden Ladder." *The Reading Teacher* 29 (March 1976): 541.

Describes a variety of benefits from having students tape their experience stories.

Sullivan, Joanna. "Developing a Remedial Reading Center," in *Reading and Realism,* ed. J. Allen Figurel. Newark, Del.: International Reading Association, 1969, pp. 347-52.

Contains good suggestions for getting children interested in reading.

10

Word Recognition

The purpose of all reading is to obtain meaning. However, no one can get meaning from printed material without first recognizing the printed words. Therefore, teaching children decoding skills, or the translation of printed words into the spoken words which they represent, is one of the main concerns of the remedial reading teacher. Although occasionally a child with good word recognition skills will have such poor comprehension that he will be placed in a remedial reading class, the majority of students in remedial reading programs are there because of difficulty in word recognition. To further complicate the problem, many remedial reading students are unable to build a large sight vocabulary as easily as other students; therefore, they need to rely much more heavily on word analysis skills in reading.

Evaluating Word Recognition Skills

Before beginning instruction in word analysis, the teacher must know exactly what word recognition skills the student has learned, and how well he uses these skills in independent reading. This information cannot be obtained from any one test, although some information can be obtained through group tests of spelling, some through oral tests of phonetic skills, and some through listening to the students read in such material as the Informal Reading Inventory. Few, if any, of the standardized group achievement tests ordinarily used to classify children give any usable information on the student's needs in word recognition.

In reading, word recognition is dependent upon the combined use of many different cues. This includes not only grapheme (letter) to phoneme (sound) transfer, but also syntax (the grammatical structure of the sentence) and semantics (the meanings behind the words). Whenever a reader overuses any one of these systems of identification, his reading breaks down. This breakdown more often results from the overuse of phonics than from overuse of the other cues. This is probably due to the attempts in some instructional systems to teach the phonetic cues in isolation from the other cues. All are necessary for effective word recognition in reading.

If children are taught from the very beginning of their reading to see the relationship of reading to their oral language, they can use their language sense to predict, and when the predictions are not right, to correct their miscues.

Miscue Analysis in Oral Reading

The diagnosis of a person's reading problems should nearly always begin with an oral reading test. This test is not only used for determining a student's reading level. It also provides an opportunity for analyzing nearly all his reading problems, including any specific patterns of word recognition problems.

This analysis of his word identification skills in reading is more important than the other tests of phonetic or word analysis skills which may also be used because it helps to evaluate the child's ability to identify words *when he is reading* and gives clues as to the reasons for his substitutions. It therefore also provides clues to the kind of instruction which may be needed by this individual.

Even the best oral reader will occasionally substitute another word for the word he sees, when the grammatical or context cues cause him to predict a different word. Such substitutions are termed "miscues" because the error is usually a misinterpretation of the cues, rather than a random guess.

By examining an individual's miscues in oral reading, we obtain much information on the whole process of reading as used by this student. Reading words from a list does not provide us with this information because some of the cues which the student needs are missing. Kenneth Goodman (1965) found that when words were in context, young readers could read at least two-thirds of the words which they were unable to read in isolation.

Grammatical structure is learned early as a part of oral language and is therefore a more important factor in choice of words than is usually recognized. Yetta Goodman (1976) states that "There is a tendency for young readers to produce more syntactically acceptable sentences than semantically acceptable sentences. This is especially true when the concepts of the material are complex for the reader. The reader seems to be able to manipulate grammatical structure even when semantic meaning is not easily accessible."

Recording and analyzing miscues. As the pupil reads aloud in the oral reading test, the teacher should not only record every miscue, but should record all other observations as well:

1. Does the student use word analysis to a different extent in easy and difficult material?

2. Does the student appear to use context to verify his word analysis? Does he discover errors and correct them?

3. How much effort does he make to sound out unknown words?

4. Which cues does he appear to use?

Since the examiner cannot stop the test while the child is reading to analyze the cause of a miscue, most of the analysis will have to be done after the child has finished reading, and it will be necessary for an exact record to be made while the child is reading. It is particularly important that when a word is miscalled the child's pronunciation of it be written phonetically over the word on the examiner's copy of the test.

After the child has finished reading, the examiner should go back over the test, listing and analyzing all miscues to see if a pattern can be detected:

1. Is a mispronunciation of a nonphonetic word a correct use of phonetic principles?

2. Is a mispronunciation a correct pronunciation in the child's dialect or in the language patterns of the community?

3. Does the word substitution fit the grammatical structure of the sentence? Does it result in an acceptable grammatical structure?

4. If the grammatical structure is changed, has it been changed into a structure that is more common or more familiar in the cultural background of the child?

5. Does the miscue change the meaning? If the omission or substitution does not change the meaning, then it is not an error in the traditional sense, but indicates the child's unique method of processing information.

6. If it does change the meaning, does it still make sense?

It is only through analysis of the probable causes of the miscues that the teacher can determine what instruction is needed to help this individual.

Use of a miscue analysis chart. A chart such as Instructional Guide 10.1 can be used as an aid in analyzing the unexpected responses found in a child's oral reading. The chart is used as follows: After completing the oral reading test, turn back to the first word that the student misread. Write this word in the first column. In the next column, entitled "substitution," write phonetically the word the student said. Follow that row across the chart and check all the appropriate columns. Example: In reading the sentence "Before John went to the store, his mother gave him a pill," the student read "Befoe John gone to stoe his mom give him a bill." The pronunciations of *before* and *store* are obviously dialect differences and need not be recorded in the oral reading inventory. If they were recorded and were listed in the chart, only the "Dialect

INSTRUCTIONAL GUIDE 10.1

Analysis of Miscues in Oral Reading

	Substitutions										Consonants				Vowels			Word Structure							
Correct Word	Substitution	Not a word	Substitute word or phrase	Grammatically correct	Grammatically incorrect	Semantically correct	Semantically incorrect	Meaning unchanged	Meaning changed	More common expression	Dialect difference	Initial consonant	Medial or final consonant	Consonant blend	Digraph	Short vowel	Long vowel	Team, R-controlled, aw, al	Contractions, poss., plurals	Prefixes	Endings	Letter clusters	Compound words	Reversals	Insertions

Repetitions: _____

Omissions: _____

Revised from *Test of Individual Needs in Reading.* Reprinted by permission of Montana Reading Publications.

187

Difference" column should be checked. *Went* will be listed in column 1 and *gone* in column 2. Following that row across the chart, the following columns will be checked: "Substitute word or phrase," "Semantically Correct," "Meaning Unchanged," and "Dialect Difference." The same columns will be checked for *mother-mom* and *gave-give*. For *gave-give* the letter *a* could be listed above the diagonal line and *i* below the line under long vowel. The word *the* will be listed in the upper left part of the chart under "omissions." After *pill* and *bill* the following columns will be checked: "Substitute word or phrase," "Grammatically correct," "Semantically correct," and "Meaning changes." Under "reversals," the letter *p* will be listed above the diagonal and *b* below it.

Although it does not show in the chart, the teacher should note that the miscue "bill" for "pill" may be the result of the child's mind set, that is, his prediction of meaning from the cues in the sentence.

The amount of reading material found in the oral reading test may be insufficient to do an adequate job of miscue analysis. If this is true, the pupil should be asked to read orally from additional material at his instructional level until enough miscues have been evidenced for the miscue analysis to be completed.

Dialect differences.   Unexpected responses in oral reading which are changes in sentence structure or in pronunciation which are due to dialectical differences should not be considered as misidentification, either for determining reading level or for planning needed instruction. It is important that the teacher working with children whose dialect differs from standard English know that dialect well enough to know which apparent miscues are changes to fit the dialect, and which will affect the meaning for the child reading in this dialect.

Determining Ability to Predict a Word in Context

Skilled readers do not look at words letter by letter. They use a combination of context and either whole word recognition or partial analysis of the word. It is seldom that the skilled reader completely sounds out even a word which he has not seen in print before. Rapid silent reading, and smooth, easy oral reading are possible only when the reader can predict in advance most of the words and can use his predictions along with a minimum of word analysis to identify unknown words. He uses both syntax and semantics to make these predictions. Since the reader is already familiar with the oral structure of the language, he knows that only a limited number of words will "fit" in a particular spot in a sentence. The meaning of what is being said will further narrow the possibilities and make his predictions more accurate. Other word recognition techniques are then used only to select from the words he has already predicted. Most of the miscues of good readers are words which fit the context, both grammatically and semantically, and also have some resemblance to the appearance of the word, such as the same beginning sound. This type of miscues should be recognized as signs of good reading skills, rather than of poor ones.

When a person is reading in an area with which he is familiar he can read much more difficult material than in an area in which he has no previous knowledge or interest. This is because he not only knows some of the specialized vocabulary, but is also able to predict what will be said. Thus he is able to identify words in this specialized field that are otherwise unfamiliar to him.

Since the cloze test is a good means of testing the student's ability to use a combination of meaning and structure to predict the word, a brief cloze test could well be included in every reading diagnosis. For this purpose, any word which fits into the sentence should be considered correct. To check the student's other word recognition skills, beginning letters and other word parts can be inserted into some of the blanks in the cloze test. This will help to determine whether the student can use these other word identification clues in conjunction with the concept to identify the word. If the student is unable to fill in the blanks with logical words, part of his instruction should be practice in predicting words through context. He should also be given a cloze-type test orally to determine whether he needs oral practice in these skills before practicing them through reading.

Individual Diagnostic Tests

Although much of the needed information on a pupil's word recognition skills can be obtained through miscue analysis of his oral reading, it is usually best to verify this information by checking his ability to identify words in isolation. Some of the standardized oral reading inventories include additional tests for testing knowledge of phonetic skills. Two of the best of these are:

Diagnostic Reading Scales by Spache. An oral reading inventory followed by analysis of phonetic skills. Evaluation is somewhat subjective.

Test of Individual Needs in Reading. An oral reading inventory followed by an individual phonics test. Graph of skills and miscue analysis chart help to pinpoint specific instruction needed.

In both of these tests the oral reading inventory and the phonics test are in the same booklet. However, if you are making your own Informal Reading Inventory, you could use with it the phonics part of one of these tests, or you may prefer one of the following individual word analysis tests:

> *Durkin-Meshover Phonics Knowledge Survey.* Individual tests with sixteen subtests, useful in any grade.

> *Durrell Analysis of Reading Difficulty.* Includes phonics along with a variety of reading skills. Scores are based on speed as much as on skill.

> *Gillingham-Childs Phonics Proficiency Scales.* Individual test evaluating letter-sound correspondences, and reading and spelling of both nonsense and real words.

> *Roswell-Chall Auditory Blending Test.* For grades 1-4. The child pronounces phonemes separately, then blends them together into words.

> *Roswell-Chall Diagnostic Test of Word Analysis Skills.* Tests a variety of skills in grades 2-6.

> *Sipay Word Analysis Tests (SWAT).* Sixteen individual word analysis tests.

> *Test of Phonic Skills.* Includes nineteen individual subtests of ability to relate symbol to sound, and a taped auditory discrimination test.

These tests will indicate which types of skills have been mastered, and which will need more work. For example, the test may indicate that Billy Jones knows and can use beginning consonant sounds, but that he needs help in using vowel sounds. However, the teacher must use her own originality and observation to determine just exactly what vowel sounds and vowel rules Billy knows and to what extent he can use them.

Group Word Analysis Tests

It is sometimes advantageous to supplement the individual testing with a group test. Some valuable information can be obtained from these tests. Many teachers prefer to give a group test to all the students, then determine from it what individual testing is needed. If an oral reading inventory has been used, and has been accompanied by a thorough miscue analysis, then the group word analysis test may be all the additional testing that is needed. However, the group test cannot give all the information that is needed. Either a miscue analysis or individual word analysis test is needed.

Group word analysis tests are of two types: spelling tests and standardized reading achievement tests. A spelling test designed for the purpose of measuring word analysis skills provides an indication of the student's ability to apply phonetic skills. The way in which a pupil spells words tells much about his ability to use phonics. The spelling test is usually shorter than other group tests and does not require that each student have a copy of the test. However, it may take longer to analyze the results to determine which skills the child has than to score other tests. Four other cautions should be kept in mind:

1. Since there is no way of knowing whether the student used phonetic spelling or already knew how to spell the word, nonsense words may be better for testing older children. The teacher must be sure she pronounces them according to the phonics rules, and counts as correct any spelling which follows the rules.

2. There is more than one way of spelling many words phonetically. If, for example, the student always uses a final *e* to indicate the long vowel, there is no way of knowing whether or not he knows other rules.

3. A student might not use in reading a rule he can use in spelling.

4. If the dialect spoken by the teacher is not the same as the dialect spoken by the student, the test may be invalid.

These problems are common to some of the other tests also. If they are kept in mind, the spelling test may be a very useful tool, especially to check on or give practice in using specific skills which have just been taught.

The teacher may want to make her own spelling test to fit a particular need, or may in the original diagnosis, prefer to use a printed test such as the McKee *Inventory of Phonetic Skill.* The *Phonovisual Diagnostic Test* also diagnoses word analysis skills mainly through spelling. A number of group reading achievement tests also are, or include, tests of word analysis skills. Some of those available are listed below:

Botel Reading Inventory. Evaluates phonics skills and whole word recognition.

California Phonics Survey. A group phonics test with eight subtests, designed for grades 7 through college.

Diagnostic Reading Test, Word Attack Skills. Group and Individual test of phonetic and structural analysis for grades 4-13.

Doren Diagnostic Reading Test of Word Recognition Skills. Group test for grades 2-8. Covers ten phonetic skills.

McCullough Word Analysis Test. A good group test for grades 4-6. Seven subtests.

Checking for Specific Skills

Regardless of the tests that have been used, some of the evaluation of word analysis skills will have to be done individually by the teacher to get further information on the specific instruction needed. Suppose, for example, the test has indicated that Billy Jones can use consonants adequately for word recognition but has made errors in the use of vowel sounds. As a result, the teacher first will verify this fact by checking to see if he wrote all the consonant sounds correctly in spelling. If he did so, no further testing of consonant sounds is needed, unless he makes errors in recognition of consonant sounds during oral reading.

The teacher will then begin a careful analysis of Billy's knowledge of the generalizations regarding vowel sounds. To do this, she will have Billy read several words containing each sound of each vowel. She will need to include words which apply each of the vowel rules which she thinks it is important for Billy to know.

Although new words to be learned are presented in context, words for testing are presented in isolation so that the teacher will know that the student can recognize the word through phonetic analysis alone. Some of the words should be nonsense words so that the student will have to use phonetic analysis rather than sight word recognition. All words must be pronounced according to the rules of phonetic analysis.

The teacher may want to ask the student why he used a certain sound; however, it is not necessary that he be able to express his reason in words if he can apply the phonetic skill correctly.

Evaluating progress daily. Diagnosis of the child's problems before beginning instruction is helpful; however, much of the evaluation can be accomplished during the early part of the instructional program if necessary. Regardless of when the diagnosis is done, it results in a *tentative* plan of action which will be altered as more information is gained through daily observation of the child's reading and of his progress in the skills in which he is being instructed. It is only through daily observation that instruction can be adjusted to the child's changing needs, and continuous progress can be assured.

Teaching Word Analysis to Remedial Students

Emphasizing meaning and the use of context.   As letter sounds, and other word identification skills are taught, practice in using them should always include use of these skills in reading meaningful material, so that the student learns to use a combination of the skill being taught and context in identifying new words.

Teaching students to use only as much word analysis as is necessary.   Completely sounding out each unknown word is inefficient and does not promote meaningful reading. For example, if the reader sees the word "unrecoupable," breaking the word into syllables and then sounding out each syllable, letter by letter, will require much time and still may not help him in understanding the passage. However, if he first looks for known parts of the word, he may recognize the root word, the prefixes, and the suffix. Such knowledge not only will give him the pronunciation quickly but also will give him a good idea of the meaning of the word.

There are eight main methods of word recognition, some of which can be used more quickly than others. They are listed below in the order of the length of time which it takes to use each one to identify any particular word.

1. Sight word recognition

2. Context

3. Beginning sounds

4. Prefixes, suffixes, and root words

5. Familiar letter clusters

6. Syllabication

7. Complete phonetic analysis

8. Use of the dictionary

The student should learn to use all of these skills when it is necessary but should use them in this order and go only as far down the list as necessary in sounding out any particular word. He should be taught only those phonetic generalizations which are frequently useful in analyzing new words. Teaching many rules that are seldom used will only confuse the remedial reader and may prevent his use of the important ones.

Teaching letter clusters. Research by Rubeck (1975), Glass (1973), Hardy, Sonnett, and Smythe (1973) and others shows that children seldom utilize either vowel rules or single letter sounds other than the beginning sounds of words in identifying new words. They use, instead, the sounds of familiar letter clusters. Vowel sounds should therefore be taught mainly as parts of letter clusters instead of as single letter sounds with rules to identify the correct sound. Most good readers will automatically give the correct vowel sound to endings *ide* and *id* without ever thinking of the final *e* rule. Groups of letters such as *ight* are not confusing if taught as letter clusters. But if they are sounded out letter by letter with rules for silent letters and so on, they can only lead to confusion for the remedial reader.

Using the discovery method. A few of the most common and most useful vowel rules can be taught so that the child can fall back on them when he meets a word in which the vowel is not part of a familiar letter cluster. The rules should be taught through the discovery method. Letting a child discover a vowel rule by analyzing several words which illustrate that rule is much more effective than telling him the rule and expecting him to memorize it. If he discovers the rule through experimentation, he will remember it longer, understand it better, and be able to apply it more effectively.

Emphasizing consonant sounds. Consonant sounds are much more predictable than vowels and are much more useful in word identification since almost all words can be identified through consonant sounds and context alone. However, vowel sounds should be taught along with the consonants because they are necessary in the analysis of isolated words and letter substitutions. In addition, it is easier to pronounce a consonant-vowel combination than an isolated consonant sound.

Teaching the sounds of the letters through key words. Teaching the child that *b* represents the beginning sound of the key word "ball" eliminates the necessity of attempting to isolate the sound by saying, in the traditional way, that *b* says "buh" which it does not. The key word should begin with the letter and should be an easily illustrated noun. If it can be illustrated by a picture which resembles the letter, the illustration will help to reinforce the image and make learning the letter easier for the child. Key words are especially important in teaching the short vowel sounds and those consonant sounds which are not contained in the names of the letters, such as the hard sounds of *c* and *g*.

Teaching the child to expect exceptions when using phonics. Phonetic analysis gives only an approximation of the sound of the word—near enough for recognition but still not complete. If the sounds the child tries do not make a sensible word, the teacher should encourage him to try other sounds of the letters.

Practicing phonetic skills on words from the student's reading. This can be done most effectively by the use of the word box described in the next section.

Teaching Whole-Word Recognition to Remedial Students

Some children who cannot build a sight vocabulary easily must learn to read almost entirely through the use of phonics. However, even these children must learn to recognize some common nonphonetic words as whole words. The more words the student can recognize at sight, the more rapid and effortless his reading can become. Therefore, instruction for every child should include an effort to increase his sight vocabulary.

A sight vocabulary can be improved most by reading much material at the student's recreational reading level. However, the use of a word box, kinesthetic instruction, tachistoscopic techniques, and group oral response all will aid in improving whole-word recognition.

Using a Word Box

One of the most useful tools for teaching whole-word recognition is the word box. Each child should have a three by five inch file box, a set of alphabetical index cards, and some lined cards for his word box. If the child is reading at a low primary level or if he shows any evidence of poor visual memory, tagboard cards eight to ten inches in length are preferable to index cards, as they can be used for kinesthetic practice. Cheese boxes make good file boxes for these longer cards.

At each remedial reading session, if the child does not recognize a word as he reads, the teacher writes that word on a piece of paper. If the student is reading independently, he can put a light pencil check mark beside any word he cannot identify, and after he has finished reading—when the teacher goes over the word with him—they can analyze the word phonetically and discuss ways of remembering it. The student then writes the word and, under it, an original sentence using the word. This should not be done with more than eight words in any one day (six, if the child is reading at first-grade level). If more than eight words are missed, the eight most important should be chosen. These may be words which are on the basic word lists or words particularly important to the child's interests.

Before the next day's reading session, the teacher types the word on one of the cards for the word box and the child's sentence on the back. (Good manuscript writing can be used in place of typing if necessary.) The cards are then placed in the front of the child's word box.

At the next remedial reading session, the child takes the cards from the front of the word box and reads each of the words and sentences. If the word is one which can be illustrated, he may want to draw a small picture above the sentence to help him remember it.

Because the picture and sentence are on the back rather than the front of the card, the child can check himself at any time that he wants extra practice. He simply reads each word and then turns the card over so the sentence and the picture will tell him whether or not he has read the word correctly.

Since it helps the child to be more independent, the teacher should be sure that the sentence which the child writes using his word indicates the meaning of the word. The child may also wish to divide the word into syllables and spell it phonetically in writing it.

As the student goes through the cards, he places in one pile those which he can recognize without turning them over to check the sentence. Those which he does not recognize immediately, he places in another pile. He places a check mark in the corner of the card above the sentence containing each word that he knows and a small circle on the card of each word he did not know. He then goes through the pile of the unknown words again to see if he can work them over into the known pile.

More words will be added to the word box each day, but only enough to make up eight unknown words at any one time. If, for example, there are eight words in the box and the student misses three but gets five right, then no more than five new words can be added to the box on that day. He now will have thirteen words in his word box, but only eight are unknown. If he gets all but two of these eight right tomorrow, he can add six new words. It is important not to exceed more than six or eight unknown words, for more than this number will decrease rather than increase the number of words the student actually learns.

The series of check marks and circles on each card provides a record for the child of exactly which words he needs to practice. When a word has three check marks in a row, thereby indicating that it has been recognized for three days in succession, the student files it in his alphabetical index. If, on the other hand, a word is missed three days in a row, this is a sign that for this word the child needs to be taught by a different approach. This word probably should be taught kinesthetically.

In addition to providing necessary practice for the student, the word box also serves several other purposes.

1. It provides the student with a record of the number of words he has learned, thereby adding to his motivation.

2. It provides a record of the child's reading vocabulary which the teacher can use in future planning.

3. It provides a reference in which the child can check the spelling of words when doing creative writing.

4. The child can use the cards in creating and playing various word games.

5. It provides words for sentence-building and word-matching activities.

6. It provides the teacher and student with words to use as examples in the study of phonics and other word analysis skills.

Using Kinesthetic Instruction

Some children with poor visual memory find it almost impossible to remember sight words simply by seeing the word and being told what it is, no matter how many times the word is repeated. These students must rely for the most part on sounding out each word phonetically. However, some of the more common words as well as some of the less phonetic words will need to be taught kinesthetically to these students.

Even the child who has no trouble with most words may find certain words which continue to confuse him. Kinesthetic instruction usually will be helpful in eliminating these confusions.

The usual word recognition techniques rely on two senses, sight and hearing. Kinesthetic instruction aids the building of a clear mental image of the word by using two additional senses—the kinesthetic, or the movement of muscles, and the tactile, or the sense of touch. In the most common method of teaching kinesthetically, the word to be learned is written in large manuscript letters on smooth paper with a wax crayon. The student places his index and second fingers on the word and traces over it from left to right, following the lines in the same order as if he were writing the word. He first says the word aloud before tracing, then traces over it, and, finally, repeats it aloud again. He repeats this process as many times as he himself feels is necessary in order to gain a clear picture of the word.

Next, he covers the word while he writes it on a clean sheet of paper. He then checks his word against the original to be sure he has written it correctly. If it is correct, he writes it once more and then files it away so that he can check his recognition of it the following day. If he has written it incorrectly, he should start again with the kinesthetic tracing.

This kinesthetic practice should be repeated each day until the student can recognize the word; he then should continue to check the word each day until he can recognize it unaided for at least three days in succession.

This kinesthetic instruction can be varied in many ways to add variety and to become more effective. For example, a thin layer of salt can be spread over the bottom of a large baking pan which has a black bottom, and the child can write his word in this salt with his fingers, or the word can be cut from old beaded motion picture screens and glued on cardboard. The word also can be written in glue and then have salt poured over it while the glue is still wet; when the excess **salt is shaken off, the word will be raised and have a rough texture** which aids in the use of the sense of touch for building the mental image of the word.

If the child does not recognize all of the letters of the alphabet, and is using kinesthetic tracing for learning the letters, large letters cut from plywood or heavy cardboard can be used, for they can be handled as well as traced. Games can be played in which the child handles the wooden letter with his eyes closed and tries to identify it. The old-fashioned alphabet blocks also can be useful for kinesthetic instruction.

For most kinesthetic instruction, words should be in manuscript (printed) form and should be traced carefully by the student, as it is the printed form of the word which he needs to recognize when reading. If, however, the kinesthetic instruction is for the purpose of eliminating reversals, the word may be in cursive writing and should be traced rapidly in order to develop a sense of movement from left to right.

Kinesthetic instruction is essential for words which the child can learn in no other way. However, because it is time-consuming, it should be used only to the extent that it is needed. Wasted time will be eliminated to a great extent if each word with which the child has difficulty is placed in the child's word box, studied and analyzed phonetically, said in context, and reviewed each day for three days. If, after this analysis and exposure to the word, the child still has not been able to recognize it, the word should be taught kinesthetically.

Using Flash Cards and Tachistoscopic Techniques

By flashing the words from the word box on a screen or with flash cards so that the student sees them for only a fraction of a second, the teacher can tell whether or not the student is able to recognize each word without stopping to analyze it phonetically. Quick-flash techniques help some students to learn to visualize the word as a whole. They are also very good for motivating some children toward the building of quick recognition of words.

Any type of tachistoscope can be used for teaching quick recognition of words. The most commonly used, however, is a projector equipped to flash a word or picture on the screen for a short, measured length of time. The speed usually can be adjusted to fit the needs of the students. Small hand tachistoscopes are also available for individual use. More information on tachistoscopes is included in chapter 13.

Using Group Response Techniques

Every student should be an active learner at all times. And all instruction should be individualized so that each student is working on the specific skills which he needs. Individualized instruction, however, does not always need to be individual. Sometimes more than one student needs the same instruction at the same time. In this case, it is most efficient to give instruction to a group.

Most group instruction, however, is inefficient because every student is not an active learner. Most students are either listening to the teacher or awaiting their turns while others respond to the teacher. There are, however, oral group response techniques which give much more practice on skills than does individual response within the group. By using these techniques, each pupil is given almost as much practice in a large group as in a small one or in individual instruction. There are several ways of using group oral response for practice.

Using one-word group oral responses. One-word responses are used for teaching new material and, later, for review of material already learned. In practicing new words through one-word responses, the teacher holds up a flash card, and every pupil in the group says the word. After the students have learned enough phonics to sound a word out completely, the teacher can hold up phonetic words and say, "Sound out the word together, one sound at a time, as I point—good. Once more, now; say the whole word once. Very good—once more." The teacher must watch the entire group closely to make sure every child is responding every time.

The teacher may want to break into the group oral response occasionally to call for an individual response from a child if: she thinks the child is responding incorrectly; she wishes to give positive reinforcement to an individual; or she wants to provide a change of pace.

To increase speed of recognition, the teacher may use a stopwatch and say, "Let's see if you can read this list in fifteen seconds—good. Now let's see if you can do it in thirteen."

Responding to a partner.   Half the children can be responding to comprehension questions at one time instead of only one if the other pupils take the place of the teacher as listeners. For example, if the children are to answer a question such as, "How would you have ended this story?" They are paired, and before asking the question, the teacher says "Answer to your partner." While the students are answering, the teacher should be moving through the class listening to as many individuals as possible.

Using repeated group oral response.   Using repeated responses has two advantages over using single responses. First, it gives each child more practice, for he says the word more times while he looks at it. Second, it allows the teacher to monitor every pupil without any pupil sitting idle.

To use the repeated response, the teacher says, "Read this word over and over clearly, as many times as you can while I point to it. When I take my hand away, stop. Each of you read rapidly over and over. You don't need to stay together. Now, keep your eyes on the card! Ready—Start!"

The teacher holds the card in one hand and points with the other. The card may be moved up, down, or to one side slowly, so that the teacher can be sure that all eyes are following it and that every child is seeing the word while he says it. With practice, the teacher will be able to monitor every child in the class within a few seconds.

If any child puts his hand near his mouth, the teacher's view may be obstructed, so the teacher should remind the whole class to sit up and to keep their hands away from their faces

Repeated group oral response also can be used for experience charts or charts listing new words. For this purpose, the instructions will be: "Read these sentences out loud. Go at your own speed. You do not need to stay together. When you finish, start over and read them again."

The teacher should walk through the class, monitoring each child and giving help where it is needed. The children should not be allowed to speed up to the point that they are distorting words or losing expression. This same method may be used for reading material projected with the overhead projector or for reading a short selection from a book if every student has his own copy of the book.

Using cards for group response. Another type of group response can be used for answering questions. Each child has three cards on his desk, with the numbers *1, 2,* and *3* printed on them. The teacher asks all questions in such a way that they can be answered with one of these numbers or so that possible answers are given numbers. As the teacher asks the question, each child holds up the card that indicates his answer. This technique can be varied to fit the individual situation. For example, in discussing vowel sounds, each child might have two cards, one of which says *long* and the other *short.*

Choral Reading. For variety, the pupils may read in unison. Choral reading in unison and group oral reading each have advantages. Although when reading individually most pupils read more rapidly, and therefore get more practice, in choral reading, children who do not know all the words will be aided by the others.

In any of the group oral response systems, some pupils may, at first, try to move their mouths without reading aloud. With practice, the teacher can detect this easily. Pupils should be told they should all read loud enough so the teacher can hear them. The noise may bother a teacher who is accustomed to a quiet classroom at first, but it seldom bothers the children.

Correcting Deficiencies in Word Recognition

Throughout the students' reading, the teacher should observe critically to identify flaws in word recognition techniques. Whenever a student has difficulty in identifying a strange word, the teacher should note the means he uses to analyze it for any clues to the cause of his problems. Thus, she can determine the specific remediation which will help the student to develop the necessary skills.

In the Instructional Guides which begin below, a large number of commonly observed difficulties in word recognition are listed. Along with each problem are listed some of the common causes of the difficulty and some of the treatments which have been found effective in treating the specific problem. Through observation of the student, the teacher should be able to determine whether one or more of the common causes listed is the probable cause of this child's difficulty. She then should be able to read through the suggested treatments and either pick one which she feels will be effective with this student or, using these suggestions as a starting point for thinking, develop a remedial technique adapted to the individual student's needs.

INSTRUCTIONAL GUIDE 10.2

Motivational Problems in Word Analysis

Observations	Possible Causes	Recommendations
Lack of effort. Lack of interest in learning phonics.	Monotonous instruction. Failure to see need for word analysis skills. High visual but low auditory perception. Dislike for reading.	Demonstrate value of word analysis skills. Teach with games, riddles, puzzles, word wheels, films, film strips, charts, and recordings. Motivate reading with high interest, easy reading materials.

INSTRUCTIONAL GUIDE 10.3

Readiness Problems in Word Analysis

Observations	Possible Causes	Recommendations
Auditory Discrimination		
Inability to recognize words which begin in the same way. Inability to recognize rhyming words. Inability to tell if two words sound alike.	Poor auditory discrimination. Auditory perception problem.	Practice recognition of beginning and ending sounds. Use auditory perception practice from readiness workbooks. Check the student with *Wepman Test of Auditory Discrimination.* **See Instructional Guide 12.4.**
Visual discrimination		
Inability to tell if two printed words are alike. Confusion of similar letters.	Lacks visual readiness skills. Poor visual perception. Poor visual memory. Lack of motivation.	Practice with tachistoscope. Use visual discrimination practice from readiness workbooks.

Observations	*Possible Causes*	*Recommendations*
		Play games requiring letter discrimination. Practice on two or three concrete letters at a time and overlearn them. Engage in kinesthetic tracing. Practice writing confused letters on chalkboard while naming them aloud. See Instructional Guide 10.2.

INSTRUCTIONAL GUIDE 10.4

Problems in Use of Context for Word Identification

Observations	*Possible Causes*	*Recommendations*
Meaningless reading		
Inability to guess a probable word when he comes to an unknown word in reading. Inability to think of words to fit the blanks in a cloze test.	Overemphasis on word recognition to the exclusion of meaning. Does not relate reading to speech and meaning.	Read very easy material for meaning. Discuss meaning of everything read. Pupil read aloud then teacher read aloud then discuss. Read with emphasis on expression of meaning.
	Cultural difference, shy. Will not state a guess until sure.	Use group oral response techniques. Use easy material, work for self-confidence. Give feeling of security. Use written instead of oral response. Have him pretend to be character in story and answer as they would answer. Use culturally related material.

Observations	*Possible Causes*	*Recommendationbs*
Mental Content		
Substitutes for unknown word, a word that does not fit the meaning of the sentence or paragraph. Cannot think of a word to fit space.	Any of above. Material outside his background of experience. Reading material too difficult.	Find material relevant to background. Build background of information. Use easier material. Use IRI standards to check appropriateness of material for student.
Language problems		
In reading, substitutes word which does not fit the grammatical structure of the sentence.	Any of above. Bilingual background. More familiar with structure of another language.	All of above. Much oral language exchange. Much listening to good reading.
Unable to use context and beginning sound to identify unknown word.	Any of above. Does not know consonant sounds. Confused by trying to do in combination, skills in which he is not secure.	Any of above. Check thoroughly knowledge of each consonant; teach. Practice each skill separately, then combine.

INSTRUCTIONAL GUIDE 10.5

Sight Word Recognition Problems

Observations	*Possible Causes*	*Recommendations*
Small Vocabulary		
Very small sight vocabulary.	Poor visual memory. Inattention. Lack of motivation.	Use oral impress method (see Chapter Eight). Practice Dolch Word List with word box or kinesthetically. Have student do much reading of very easy material. Play games like "Word Bingo."

Observations	Possible Causes	Recommendations
		Practice with flash cards. Act out words. See activities for Instructional Guide 10.1.
Easy Words		
Errors on small words.	All of the above. Started reading too early without readiness and became confused on beginning words. Poor visual memory for details. Good silent reader; thinks ahead of oral reading.	All of the above. If the child knows the harder words but makes errors only on the small words, ask the small words after reading. If the child can recognize the small words in isolation and his comprehension is good, do not remediate. Emphasize silent reading and flexibility. Tape record and let child listen to his own reading.
Memory for Words		
Inability to remember word he has been told repeatedly.	Poor visual memory. Poor visual discrimination. Lack of motivation.	All of the above under "Small Vocabulary." Test visual memory. Use auditory instruction. Teach kinesthetically. Give visual discrimination exercises from readiness workbooks. Use word box. Do not work on more than six unknown words each day, including those taught but not remembered from the previous day. Play word recognition games.
Word-by-Word Reading		
Word-by-word reading. Sounding out each word laboriously.	Overemphasis on phonics. Lack of attention to meaning.	Ask comprehension questions before reading; have child read to answer questions.

Observations	*Possible Causes*	*Recommendations*
	Poor sight vocabulary.	Use easier material.
	Material that is too difficult.	Use recreational reading of easy material.
	Concentration on word recognition to the exclusion of meaning.	Divide sentences into phrases and read as word groups.
	Poor comprehension.	Dramatize stories or read plays.
	Lack of interest.	
	No understanding of phrasing and punctuation.	Practice making quotes sound like the person speaking.
	Inability to see relationship between print and meaning.	Use language experience materials.
		Use easy silent reading.
		Read sentence orally and then flash final word with tachistoscope.
		Tape record and let child analyze own reading.
		Develop sight vocabulary (see "Small Vocabulary" on preceding page).
		Motivate the child (see Instructional Guide 10.2).
Slow Reading		
Extremely slow reading.	All of causes listed for "Memory for Words" on page 205.	All of activities listed under "Word-by-Word Reading."
	Lack of sight vocabulary; must analyze every word.	Use tachistoscopic training with words and then with phrases.
	Poor visual memory for words.	Test visual memory.
	Reading everything for detail.	Use accelerator.
		Practice skim reading for one fact.
	Has been taught to read everything carefully instead of adjusting to purpose.	Practice reading for a specific purpose.
	Narrow visual span.	Read a paragraph over and over for speed.
		Use much easy fun reading.
		Check student with the Dolch 220 Word List; practice words missed with flash cards and tachistoscope.

INSTRUCTIONAL GUIDE 10.5 *(continued)*

Observations	*Possible Causes*	*Recommendations*
Nonphonetic Words		
Inability to recognize nonphonetic words like *one, the.*	Poor visual memory. Overemphasis on phonics.	Practice these words kinesthetically. Point out phonetic parts and use context. Use word box. Practice with tachistoscope. Check visual memory (see chapter 12).

INSTRUCTIONAL GUIDE 10.6

Problems in the Use of Consonant Sounds

Observations	*Possible Causes*	*Recommendations*
Knowledge of Letter Sounds		
Inability to remember letter sounds.	Trying to learn too many sounds before first sounds are fixed firmly in the mind. Meaningless memorization. Failure to apply to enough known words.	Teach key words. Superimpose letters on key word pictures. Overlearn one letter before starting instruction on another. Teach letter sounds through comparison with known words. Use "Consonant Rummy" and other letter sound games. Have students make up silly words using the letters being taught.
Beginning Sound		
Inability to think of words which fit into context and beginning sound.	Poor auditory perception. Poor auditory discrimination. Inability to relate oral to written language. Poor comprehension. Failure to learn to use context to predict what next word will be.	All of "Knowledge of Letter Sounds" above. All of "Auditory Discrimination" in Instructional Guide 10.3. Practice auditory discrimination from readiness workbooks. Use the cloze procedure.

Observations	*Possible Causes*	*Recommendations*
	Not knowing letter sounds.	Use the language experience approach. Teach sounds not learned through the discovery method. Teach listening comprehension. Read to student and test his comprehension. Give readiness tests. Give *Wepman Test of Auditory Perception.*

Ending Sound

Omitting endings. Placing wrong consonant at end of a word. Using wrong inflectional ending on a word.	Overdependence on beginning sounds. Failure to see endings. Lack of awareness of effect of endings on meaning. Failure to use context as an aid.	Complete sounding of words in isolation. Practice adding different endings—*ly, -ed, -ing, -er.* Practice pronouncing and using words in sentences. Choose from words with different endings the one to fit a blank.

Spelling Words

Saying letter names instead of sounds when attempting to sound out words.	Has been told spelling word will help identification. Has been taught by alphabet-spelling method. Parents tell him to spell words when he asks them to pronounce them for him.	Teach key words for letter sounds. Practice blending consonant and vowel sounds.

Digraphs

Beginning *ch* word with *c* sound. Trying to sound each letter of digraph.	Has not learned digraphs. Has had too much emphasis placed on sounding single letters.	Teach digraphs. Give much practice of sounding out words containing digraphs. Play word games containing digraphs.

Observations	Possible Causes	Recommendations
Multiple-Sound Consonants		
Inability to sound out words in which c sounds like s. Inability to recognize words in which g sounds like j.	Knows only one sound of c or g. Does not remember to try another sound. Does not know "hard" and "soft" rule.	Teach both sounds of c and g. Practice on list of familiar words, most of which have a "soft" sound. Practice oral group response with flash cards with ca, ce, ci, co, cu, cy, cla, ga, ge, gla, gy. If problem persists, teach rule.
Silent Letters		
Inability to recognize words beginning with silent k or g. Inability to sound out words containing silent gh.	Does not know or cannot apply rule for kn, gn, pn. Is too dependent on phonetic analysis. Does not know or cannot use rule.	Teach these words as sight words. Give student a dictionary and let him hunt out and list all the words he knows beginning with kn or gn. Teach ight and ought as phonograms.

INSTRUCTIONAL GUIDE 10.7

Problems in the Use of Vowel Sounds

Observations	Possible Causes	Recommendations
Vowels Not Used		
Failure to use any vowel sounds in sounding out words. Lack of knowledge of short vowel sounds.	Has not been taught short vowels. Has had improper instruction in vowels. Has not learned key words for vowels.	Teach vowels through discovery method of comparing words. Teach a key word for each short vowel. Practice spelling words and nonsense syllables phonetically.

Observations	*Possible Causes*	*Recommendations*
		Use flash card pictures representing short words. Play "Phonics Rummy" and other vowel letter games. Encourage much reading from linguistic readers. Use programmed readers.

Errors in Use of Specific Vowels

Making errors on one particular vowel sound. Lack of knowledge of one particular vowel sound.	All of the above. Lacks knowledge of the vowel and its key word. Has not been taught memory clues for vowels.	All of the above. Teach the key word for the vowel on which the child makes mistakes. Practice spelling words containing the vowel which the child does not know.

Determination of Long and Short Vowel Sounds

Using wrong sound of vowel. Not following vowel rule. Inflexibility in use of phonics; if vowel sound does not follow rule, the child cannot identify the word. Failure to understand the real word or to have the word make sense in a sentence.	Knows only one sound of a vowel. Does not know which sound to try first. Lacks practice for flexible use of vowels in words. Does not know vowel rules. Has memorized rules but cannot apply them. Has learned rules that are too cumbersome. Believes that rules do not work. Is confused regarding vowel sounds. Fails to check word through context. Does not see the need for the rule when it is taught. Taught rules only through memorization.	Check knowledge of vowel sounds. Teach child to try long vowels if short vowels do not work. Emphasize use of context to check accuracy of phonetic analysis. Practice use of rules for a variety of words. Practice writing words phonetically. Hold a contest on writing rules in the most condensed form. Teach sight recognition of common non-phonetic word parts. Develop rules not known through study of words. Review each rule, one at a time, and apply it to reading and spelling many different words.

Observations	*Possible Causes*	*Recommendations*
	Places too much emphasis on vowel rules.	Use catchy expressions to remember rules. Practice using context and consonant sounds only. **Teach vowels with consonants following as letter clusters.** Teach the importance of using rules as a clue and then trying various sounds. Play games by putting the wrong word in a sentence to see if others in the group can think of the right word (e.g., "I milked the car last night.") Make a game of seeing how many different sounding words students can get from the same printed word.

No Long Vowel Sounds

Always trying to use short vowel sounds. Inability to identify words containing long vowels.	Has not learned long vowel sounds. Does not use context to help identify words. Is not flexible in use of vowel sounds. Does not know vowel rules.	Check knowledge of vowel sounds; teach them if necessary. Practice sounding out each word with both short and long sounds and then trying out both words in the sentence. Check knowledge of vowel rules. Have child tell what rule applies to each of a list of words.

No Short Vowel Sounds

Always uses long vowel sounds in sounding out a word.	Does not know short sounds.	All of recommendations for "No Long Vowel Sounds."

Observations	Possible Causes	Recommendations
	Has trouble recalling short sounds. Cannot use vowel rules.	Check knowledge of short vowels. Teach key words for short vowels. Teach child to try short sound first. Develop vowel generalizations.

Remembering Rules

Inability to think of a rule to fit a vowel sound in a word even though rules have been taught.	Memorizes rules without enough application. Does not understand the reason for a rule. Rules are too long or complicated for him.	Reteach through discovery method. Play games in which the child states which rule applies to each word. Let students rewrite rules in the form of telegrams. Have child hunt through a paragraph to find all of the words to which a specific rule applies. Play "Vowel Rummy" and "Authors" games in which the child finds sets of words with similar vowel sounds.

Use in Context

Inability to use words in context, although he is able to do so on isolated words.	Has been taught rules in isolation, without context as an aid. Has not been taught what to do when a rule does not apply to a word. Emphasizes memorization rather than meaningful application. Has been taught rules through memorization rather than discovery.	All of the recommendations for "Determination of Long and Short Vowel Sounds" and "Remembering Rules." Practice rules on many words in context; the rules should apply to most, but not all, of the words.

INSTRUCTIONAL GUIDE 10.8

Problems in Blending Letter Sounds

Observations	Possible Causes	Recommendations

Inability to Blend Sounds into Words

Inability to blend sounds into word, although he can say letter sounds separately.
Inability to recognize words that he can say.
Sounding out words with added sounds so that they cannot be recognized (e.g., "Buh-aa-Duh" for *bad*).

Improper teaching of consonants with *uh* sound added.
Does not understand use of letter sounds.
Does not know letters as beginning sounds of key words.
Attempts to isolate consonant sounds.
Attempts to say consonant sound before looking at the vowel.
Thinks of letter names rather than of sounds.

Teach sound blending by beginning practice with two letters, a vowel and a consonant (like *m*) which can be pronounced alone.

Say sounds and have child repeat the word

Teach consonants as beginning sounds of key words rather than as isolated sounds.

Have student practice one consonant with different vowels: *ba, bu, be,* etc.

Have student look at the consonant *p*, hold his mouth in position for the *p* sound, and then look at the vowel *e* and say the two together; repeat this exercise with other vowels and then other consonants.

Have pupil see how fast he can give letter sounds (not names) of letters that can be sounded alone: *a, e, f, h, i, j, l, m, n, o, r, s, u, v, z;* do not permit the child to follow the letter with an "uh" sound.

Think sounds together mentally rather than sounding them audibly.

Observations	*Possible Causes*	*Recommendations*
Reliance on context		
Inability to analyze word in isolation. although he can do some in context.	Over-reliance on context.	Use all of the above. Practice blending sounds to form words and reading a list of phonetic words.

Reliance on context is not a problem if the student is really able to identify words when he encounters them in context. The purpose of practice out of context is to insure his being better able to identify words in context. But be sure he is actually using letter sounds and sound blending along with the context for word recognition.

Confused by Context		
Inability to read words in context that he can read in isolation. Inability to sound out a word in a paragraph that he can sound out in isolation.	Has figure-ground perception problem. Has been taught phonics as an isolated subject rather than as part of reading. Over-emphasizes rules without applying them in context.	See Instructional Guide 12.5 "Figure-Ground Constancy" Present all new words in context. Practice phonetic rules on words only in context. Practice skills in difficult material with many unknown words for a small portion of reading; stop to analyze each new word. Use liner above line of print. Read through card with a slot large enough to expose only one word or short phrase at a time.
Consonant Blends		
Leaving out part of a consonant blend.	Has possible vision problem. Lacks patience with blending consonant sounds. Does not know some consonant sounds.	Check vision. Check knowledge of single consonant sounds. Practice saying vowel sound, then consonant-vowel sounds blended, and then consonant-consonant-vowel sounds blended: *a, la, bla; e, es, est.*

Observations	*Possible Causes*	*Recommendations*
		Use all recommendations from "Inability to Blend Sounds into Words." If consonant sounded is often the second letter of the consonant blend, refer to the "Reversals" section of Instructional Guide 12.5.

Reversals

Reversing letters such as *b* for *d.* Changing order of letter sounds.	Lacks training in directional attack. Has possible learning disability.	Reversals are discussed in detail in the section on perception in chapter Twelve.

Over-Analysis

Over-analyzing. Analyzing known words. Sounding out words letter by letter. Breaking long words into too many small parts. Making equal number of errors regardless of difficulty of material. Making more mistakes on small words than on longer words.	Has been taught phonics as an isolated skill separate from reading. Over-emphasizes phonics. Skills, when taught, were not applied to reading. Lacks use of context. Has poor sight vocabulary Has poor visual memory. Vocalizes sounds of all words. Has not learned common letter clusters. Lacks knowledge of prefixes and suffixes.	Use cloze technique with beginning sounds and context. Teach prefixes, endings, and common letter clusters. Read easy material with an accelerator. Use flash cards. Use a tachistoscope. Check visual memory—if it is poor, do not pressure the student for a change in reading pattern.

215

Substitutions

Observations	Possible Causes	Recommendations

Substitution of Sounds

The words given in the "Observations" column below are examples. To make effective use of them, find in the child similar problems to the ones observed in the guide. For instance, if a child in your class says *so* for *show*, this is a problem similar to the first example, *trow* for *throw*.

Says:

Observations	Possible Causes	Recommendations
trow for *throw*	Has immature speech. Difference in dialect.	Practice auditory discrimination. Learn of family background and accept the child's language as correct if it is according to the dialect.
	Does not know digraphs.	Practice digraphs.
wabbit for *rabbit*	Has immature speech.	Practice auditory discrimination.
witch for *which*	Has enunciation problem.	Hold paper before lips and practice *w* and *wh* sounds.
	Looks at first letter only.	Study digraphs.
dog for *bog*.	Reverses letter.	Practice letter kinesthetically. **See Guide 12.5.**
timmer for *timber*.	Lacks attention to middle of words.	Practice consonant substitution with middle letters.
Fin for *fish*. *forcing* for *forces*.	Lacks attention to ending sounds.	Practice making rhymes and writing rhyming words. Use word wheels that change the ending sounds of words.
grow for *glow*.	Does not know consonant blends.	Practice blending *s, l,* and *r* with various letters.
ran for *rain*.	Uses wrong vowel sound.	Teach child to apply rule for two vowels together.

216

Observations	*Possible Causes*	*Recommendations*
pet for *Pete.*	Uses wrong vowel sound.	Teach child to use final *e* rule.
gvve for *give*	Follows rules too closely. Lacks flexibility in using phonics.	Practice using context to check a word after sounding.
curtain for *certain*	Uses wrong sound of *c*.	Practice checking context. Teach rules for *c* and *g*.
Substituting words with similar beginnings	See listing above. Relies only on beginning sounds. Is unable to use vowel sounds. Guesses because it is easier than word analysis. Lacks attention to meaning and context. Observes first letter or two and guesses at the remainder. Is unable to sound out words completely.	Use recommendations listed above. Practice more on word analysis skills. Practice changing endings. Use word wheels which change ending sounds. Emphasize context to check correctness of word. Use oral expressive reading. Practice sound blending. Practice complete analysis of isolated words. Pronounce words by syllables.

Substitutions of Words with Similar Sounds

Substituting word similar in sound but not in meaning. Substituting word that does not fit context. Inability to identify word if phonetic rules do not apply. Inability to tell from context if word is wrong.	Relies too much on phonics. Has any of the possible problems listed above. Fails to use context or to read for meaning. Is reading material that is too difficult so that he must ignore meaning and concentrate on word analysis. Over-emphasizes phonics. Fails to anticipate a possible word.	Use all of the recommendations listed above. Practice sounding out words in context. Use easier materials and concentrate on meaning. Use materials related to the child's interests. Develop games for using context. Use *SRA-Reading for Understanding* kit and similar materials. Combine pictures with verbal context.

Observations	Possible Causes	Recommendations
	Fails to check to see if a word makes sense. Is so concerned with word analysis that he cannot get meaning.	Read a story aloud and then pause to allow the child to supply the next word. Teach him to finish a sentence and then come back to an unknown word. Use exercises that employ beginning sound and context to supply word (e.g., Houghton-Mifflin readiness materials). Use the cloze technique but give a choice of two words for each blank, give all the consonants, give beginning and ending letters, give beginning letter and length of word, or give beginning letter only. Substitute silly words in a paragraph and let students replace them with the correct word. Make reading easy material fun. Practice choosing word through first letter and context. Give comprehension questions and then have the student read to find the answers.

Substitution of Words with Similar Meaning

Substituting words that are similar in meaning but not in sound. Guessing at new words and making no attempt to sound them out phonetically.	Relies too much on context and ignores sounds. Has poor knowledge of letter sounds. Places too much emphasis on speed or sounding fluent.	Have the student reread a story after finishing it; if error persists in rereading, help him analyze the words phonetically. Teach those phonetic skills needed for this word.

Observations	Possible Causes	Recommendations
Recognizing "hard" but not common words. Guessing inaccurately.	Uses sight vocabulary alone: has learned meaning of word through context. Has poor vision. Has poor perception. Has possible learning disability. Has learned phonics separately rather than as a part of reading. Reads rapidly and fluently silently and with good comprehension.	Practice discrimination of phonetically similar words. Test vision. Practice the printed word and spoken substitute in a variety of sentences using their various meanings. Use only positive reinforcement. Practice sound blending. Check comprehension; if it is good, ignore the error and encourage the student. See the recommendations for Instructional Guide 10.5, "No Short Vowel Sounds."

Phrase Substitution

Substituting several words or part of a sentence.	Guesses. Relies too much on pictures or context. Lacks word recognition skills.	Use all of the recommendations listed under "Substitution of Words with Similar Meanings." Practice reading isolated words. Read sentences aloud to answer questions. Check phonetic analysis skills.

INSTRUCTIONAL GUIDE 10.10

Problems with Omissions, Repetitions, and Regressions

Observations	Possible Causes	Recommendations
Omitting Sounds		
Omitting one or more sound from a word.	Has vision problem. Hurries phonetic analysis too much. Does not know some sounds.	Check vision with telebinocular, watching for poor visual acuity, poor fusion, suppression of vision in one eye.

Observations	*Possible Causes*	*Recommendations*
	Lacks reading for meaning.	Remove pressures. Check knowledge of letter sounds. Practice using context to determine if word used is correct.

Omitting Words

Observations	*Possible Causes*	*Recommendations*
Omitting difficult words. Omitting unknown word and going on. Unwillingness to attempt an unknown word. Skipping small words. Reading rapidly and skipping words.	Hurries. Skims over known parts; has poor word recognition skills. Lacks word attack skills. Is unable to apply the word attack skills he knows in reading. Has vision problem. Is shy. Is insecure. Is criticized by classmates. Fears being wrong. Fears criticism. Is indifferent. Reads fast silently with good comprehension but is slowed down by oral reading.	Motivate good oral reading. Have child read to others. Have child tape record reading and listen to self. Use oral impress methods. Use group oral response techniques. Use easy reading materials with child. Check word skills. Have child practice applying word attack while reading. Have child make own material, using words missed. Test vision. Repeat successful experiences in word recognition. Praise child when he does well. Use behavior modification techniques. Remove pressures. Eliminate all criticism. Check silent reading comprehension and, if good, do not overemphasize oral reading.

Repetition

Observations	*Possible Causes*	*Recommendations*
Repeating words or phrases in oral reading.	Has any of problems under "Omitting Words."	Use all recommendations under "Omitting Words."

Observations	*Possible Causes*	*Recommendations*
	Has developed habit in early reading or from too much difficult material. Has been compared with more fluent readers. Is embarrassed while reading orally. Has poor sight vocabulary; stalls while analyzing the next word.	Use oral impress method (see Chapter Eight). Reread easy paragraphs. Use choral reading of easy material. Use much easy reading. Keep a relaxed atmosphere. Be informal. Build security. Practice basic vocabulary with tachistoscope.

Insertions

Inserting extra words while reading orally.	Has any of the problems listed under "Omitting Words" and "Repetition." Relies too much on context. Guesses.	Use all of the recommendations listed under "Omitting Words" and "Repetitions." Have child reread carefully.

Large Regressions

Rereading whole sentences or phrases when reading silently	Has poor concentration. Lets mind wander. Has short attention span. Lacks interest. Has poor comprehension. Is reading material that is too difficult. Has formed a habit. Is unsure of ability to get meaning.	Use controlled reader. Use accelerator. Use card above line of print. Push for speed. Have child relax, slow down, and read carefully the first time. Have child read easier material. Have him read for pleasure with assurance that there will be no questions. Use oral impress method.

Small Regressions

Excessive small eye movement regressions in silent reading.	Has poor sight vocabulary. Has slow word attack.	Have child read for speed in easy material. Practice basic sight words

Observations	Possible Causes	Recommendations
	Has narrow vision span. Has poor vision. Has formed a habit. Is reading material that is too difficult.	with tachistoscope and flash cards. Practice identifying short unknown words or syllables on tachistoscope phonetically. Check visual acuity.

INSTRUCTIONAL GUIDE 10.11

Problems in Structural Analysis of Words

Observations	Possible Causes	Recommendations
Letter Clusters		
Inability to sound out words containing *ought, tion, sion, ight,* etc.	Has not learned to look for letter clusters. Depends too much on single-letter phonics. Does not know common combinations.	Teach common letter clusters and phonograms. Practice with flash cards and tachistoscope.
Compound Words		
Inability to see separate words in compound words.	Lacks understanding of compound words.	Practice finding root word in compound and multi-syllable words. Play games guessing the meaning of long words.
	Has figure-ground perceptual problem.	Check with *ITPA, Frostig Test,* or *Bender-Gestalt.* Use Frostig materials.
Suffixes		
Omitting endings. Placing wrong inflectional ending on word.	See Instructional Guide 10.6, "Ending Sounds."	
Syllabication		
Trying to sound out compound or multi-syllable words one letter at a	Lacks knowledge of affixes and root words. Places too much empha-	Learn meanings of common word parts through discovery.

Observations	Possible Causes	Recommendations
time. Inability to sound out long words. Dividing words into syllables before looking for affixes.	sis on decoding through letter sounds alone. Lacks concern for meaning. Lacks knowledge of common letter groups or of their use. Fails to use context for word identification. Does not know rules for dividing into syllables.	Practice structural analysis of words. Play "Word Domino" and other games using word parts. Present long words in context and then look for clues in meaning. Teach student that he should: (1) look for affixes and roots, (2) syllabicate, (3) analyze syllables, (4) use dictionary. Teach rules for dividing into syllables. Help him develop interest in word origins.

Syllabication: Exceptions

Observations	Possible Causes	Recommendations
Dividing blends or digraphs when syllabicating words.	Does not recognize blends. Does not know that blends are not to be divided. Follows rules routinely without thought.	Teach the child to consider digraphs and blends as single consonants. Practice on words with three letters between vowels. Use context with syllabication for word recognition.

Accent

Observations	Possible Causes	Recommendations
Accenting wrong syllable when sounding out multisyllable word.	Does not use context adequately to aid word analysis. Fails to try various accents.	Have student listen to the word as he pronounces it in the sentence in which he finds it. Have student try various accents and listen for familiar sounds. If he has done these and still cannot recognize the word, tell him which syllable to accent and the rule for this or have him use the dictionary.

Teaching the Teacher to Teach Word Analysis

Before the teacher can be effective in evaluating the needs of the student and in teaching to meet those needs, she herself must have a good understanding of word analysis. Information on phonetic rules and other word analysis skills is not included in this book as it is assumed that teachers planning to teach remedial reading already have a good knowledge of word analysis. However, a great many teachers do not have an adequate background in the phonetic and linguistic principles of word recognition. Dolores Durkin's *Phonics Test for Teachers* [1] will give the teacher a good idea of her need for additional background. If she feels that her knowledge of word analysis skills is inadequate, the teacher can build an adequate knowledge of phonetic generalization by studying *Programmed Word Attack for Teachers.* [2]

It is also recommended that the teacher keep up with the latest developments, especially in linguistics and its relation to reading, through such journals as *The Reading Teacher* published by the International Reading Association.

Summary

Reading consists of decoding, or the changing of written symbols to spoken words, and comprehension, or the getting of meaning from those words. In order to get meaning, which is the ultimate purpose of all reading, the student must first be able to decode.

When the student enters the remedial reading program, he should be tested to determine his ability to use word analysis skills. This testing will give an indication of the general area in which instruction must begin. As instruction proceeds, the teacher must check in detail the child's ability to use each skill. If the child is found to be deficient in any skill, he must be given special instruction in that skill, followed by a variety of practice in using the skill. The teacher must then re-evaluate carefully to be sure that the student can use the skill effectively for recognition of words in his independent reading.

Since rapid effective reading requires instant recognition of most words, new words must be identified and sight vocabulary built through the use of the four word analysis skills:

---

[1] Dolores Durkin, *Phonics Test for Teachers* (New York: New York Teachers College Bureau of Publications, 1964).

[2] Robert M. Wilson and MaryAnne Hall, *Programmed Word Attack for Teachers,* 2d ed. (Columbus, Ohio: Charles E. Merrill Publishing Co., 1974).

1. Use of context

2. Phonetic analysis

3. Structural analysis

4. Use of the dictionary

There are seven general principles that should be kept in mind when planning instruction in word analysis for remedial reading. Briefly stated, they are:

1. Emphasize consonant sounds as the key sounds in the decoding process.

2. Teach the sounds of letters through key words rather than in isolation.

3. Use the discovery method of teaching.

4. Teach the child to expect exceptions when using phonics.

5. Teach the use of context to verify every phonetically analyzed word.

6. Teach students to use only as much word analysis as they find necessary.

7. Practice phonetic skills on words from the student's reading.

To become a fluent reader who can concentrate on meaning, the student also must build as large a sight vocabulary as possible. He can be helped to increase this sight vocabulary through:

1. Use of a word box.

2. Use of flash cards and tachistoscopic techniques

3. Kinesthetic instruction

4. Practice sessions using group response techniques

A large portion of this chapter has been devoted to Instructional Guides which list commonly observed problems in word recognition, along with possible causes and recommendations for remediation. When a child demonstrates problems in word recognition, these Instructional Guides will help the teacher to determine possible causes, and a variety of possible ways of helping the child.

Recommended Related Reading

Downing, John. "The Bullock Commission's Judgment of i. t. a." *The Reading Teacher* 29 (January 1976): 379–82.

Reviews the most thorough and extensive research on use of the initial teaching alphabet.

Cagney, Margaret A. "Children's Ability to Understand Standard English and Black Dialect." *The Reading Teacher* 30 (March 1977): 607–10.

A study that indicates that reading language experience stories to children in their own dialect did not improve their comprehension of those stories over reading them in standard English.

Dahl, Patricia R., and S. Jay Samuels. "Teaching Children to Read Using Hypothesis/Test Strategies." *The Reading Teacher* 30 (March 1977): 603.

Good information on helping children predict the word through context clues.

Ekwall, Eldon. "Diagnosis and Remediation of Educational Factors: Word Analysis Skills," in *Diagnosis and Remediation of the Disabled Reader.* Boston, Mass.: Allyn & Bacon, 1976, pp. 86–124.

Thorough coverage of evaluation and teaching of word analysis.

Glass, Gerald G., and Elizabeth H. Burton. "How Do They Decode? Verbalizations and Observed Behaviors of Successful Decoders." *Education* 94 (September/October 1973): 58–64.

Research on children's use of word identification skills.

Goodman, Kenneth. "A Linguistic Study of Cues and Miscues in Reading." *Elementary English* (October 1965): 641–43.

The study upon which Miscue Analysis is based.

————. "Miscue Analysis: Theory and Reality in Reading," in *New Horizons in Reading,* ed. John E. Merritt. Newark, Del.: International Reading Association, 1976, pp. 15–26.

Explains the basic concepts of analysis of reading errors on the basis of meaning and semantics as well as grapheme-phoneme relationships.

Goodman, Yetta M. "Miscues, Errors, and Reading Comprehension," in *New Horizons in Reading,* ed. John E. Merritt. Newark, Del.: International Reading Association, 1976, pp. 86–93.

Discusses the relationship of meaning to miscues in word identification.

———— and Carolyn M. Burke. *Reading Miscue Inventory Manual: Procedure for Diagnosis and Evaluation.* New York, N.Y.: The Macmillan Co., 1972, 133 pp.

Complete instructions for carrying out miscue analysis.

Hardy, Madeline, R. G. Sennett, and P. C. Smythe. "Word Attack: How do they 'Figure Them Out'?" *Elementary English* 50 (January 1973): 99–102.

Study of children's use of word analysis skills.

Lucas, Marilyn S., and Harry Singer. "Dialect in Relation to Oral Reading Achievement: Recoding, Encoding, or Merely a Code?" *Journal of Reading Behavior* 7 (Summer 1975, National Reading Conference): 137–48.

A study of the relationship between reading, Mexican-American dialect, and the amount of Spanish spoken in the home. It indicates that dialect interferes with reading only when sentence structure changes.

Miller, Wilma H. "Correcting Difficulties in Context Usage." *Reading Correction Kit.* The Center for Applied Research in Education, Inc., p. 93.

Suggestions on ways of improving the ability to use context clues for word recognition.

_____. "Inventories in the Word Recognition Techniques." *Reading Diagnosis Kit.* The Center for Applied Research in Education, Inc., p. 163.

A variety of tests for use in evaluating word analysis skills. Includes information on constructing additional tests.

Ramsey, Wallace and Dorothy Harrod. "Diagnostic Measures of Phonic Analysis Skills," in *Reading and Realism,* ed. J. Allen Figurel. Newark, Del.: International Reading Association, 1969, pp. 642–44.

Compares different means of testing word analysis.

Rubeck, Patricia A. *Pupil Self-Analysis of Word Attack Cues.* Bowling Green, Ohio: Bowling Green State University, College of Education, February 1975, 72 pages.

Ways in which students can aid in analyzing their own problems.

Schneyer, J. Wesley. "Reading Achievement of First Grade Children Taught by a Linguistic Approach and a Basal Reader Approach—Extended into Third Grade." *The Reading Teacher* 22 (January 1969): 315–19.

Research study which shows some of the strengths of each method.

Singer, Harry, S. Jay Samuels, and Jean Spiroff. "The Effect of Pictures and Contextual Conditions on Learning Responses to Printed Words," in *Theoretical Models and Processes of Reading,* 2d ed., eds. Harry Singer and Robert B. Ruddell. Newark, Del.: International Reading Association, 1976, p. 291.

Experiment to determine condition under which a student can learn words more quickly.

11

Comprehension

Since the sole purpose for reading is to get meaning, the instruction in all the other reading skills is pointless if a student does not develop good comprehension of what he reads. This will be true throughout his life no matter whether he reads for pleasure or information. The good reader must be able not only to recognize printed words but also to get ideas from those words and to relate those ideas to experience, organize them, weigh them, and use them. Although comprehension is the most important part of reading, it is usually the most poorly taught. This is because it is most difficult to analyze, to diagnose, and to prescribe specific teaching strategy. Most comprehension is caught rather than taught.

The teacher usually asks comprehension questions, and if the child gets the wrong answers, tells him the right ones with no instruction on how he could find the right answer for himself. This is like giving the students a group of mathematics problems, and if they get the wrong answers, giving them the answers with no explanation of why they are wrong, then exhorting them to do better next time. It is as important in reading as in math that we teach the child *how* to find the right answer. Yet in reading it is much more complicated. Teaching isolated comprehension skills as separate entities may not lead to comprehension of passages. Nor will understanding each sentence in a passage necessarily lead to comprehension of the entire passage. Comprehension requires seeing the relationship between sentences, between paragraphs, between stated and implied ideas, and between the content of the material and the reader's experiential background.

We cannot identify through tests the way a child obtains comprehension nor the information we must give him for him to be able to internalize the content of a paragraph, relate it to his previous understandings, and end with an approximate understanding of the author's meaning. We can, however, ask questions which relate to a variety of types of comprehension, then help the child who can not answer a question to analyze the material until he has an understanding of what was necessary for him to get the right answer. We can show him how to combine his experience with his knowledge of what the passage says and come up with meaning. It is this kind of analysis, done frequently and repeatedly, that enables the child to generalize within himself ways of thinking that will help him comprehend other materials that he reads.

Although comprehension skills can not be completely isolated or diagnosed separately, we can do some diagnosis of general levels of comprehension, and general areas needing emphasis.

Evaluating Comprehension

Information on a student's comprehension skills can be obtained from three sources: standardized reading tests—both group and individual, teacher-made tests, and informal observation and discussion. Each of these sources can and will contribute some information that is not easily obtainable from the others; consequently, no single form of evaluation should be used alone.

Using Standardized Tests for Evaluation

Standardized tests have an important place in the evaluation of comprehension. While teacher observation and questioning give more information on specific areas of strength or weakness, standardized tests usually are a better way of getting the first overall picture of the student's comprehension. The teacher can follow such testing up with the kind of questioning and discussion that cannot be included in the standardized test. Therefore, a complete diagnosis should include both.

Selecting the test to be used. The reading teacher must select the standardized test to be used with a particular student not only on the basis of the validity and reliability of the tests available but also on the basis of the reading level of the student and the information needed to plan a remedial program. The level of the test to be used will depend upon the reading level of the student.

If an achievement test is to be a basis for tentative selection of students for a remedial reading program, the results cannot be used for diagnostic purposes for those students whose reading levels fall below the lower limits of the test. All tests written for particular grade levels give a distorted picture of achievement for students whose scores fall at the highest or the lowest levels of these tests. The student may be in the eighth grade but reading at third grade level. However, if he takes a test written for junior high-school students, a few correct guesses will place him at least at a sixth-grade level. To get any truly valid information on this student, the teacher should use a third-grade level test. She will know what test to use if diagnosis begins as it should—with an oral reading test. She can then select the particular achievement test to be used with a student on the basis of his reading level as determined from the oral reading test.

If the oral reading test used is an Informal Reading Inventory, then a group standardized silent reading test should follow. If, on the other hand, the oral reading test is a part of one of the standardized individual reading tests which include information on comprehension, the reading specialist can make the decision after this test has been evaluated as to whether an additional standardized test is needed and, if so, which test is most appropriate.

The individual oral reading test will usually give more valid information than the group test on all areas except silent reading comprehension and, perhaps, speed and study skills. The silent reading achievement test usually has longer passages and more questions which thus make it a more valid measurement of comprehension.

Although a few tests break down the comprehension score into component parts, most tests rate comprehension as one item. Scores on these tests usually are stated in terms of grade levels or percentile rankings. Scores on most tests can be converted to either of these terms. Grade-level scores are much more useful to the remedial reading teacher. For example, if a high-school student takes a test written for the fourth-grade level because that is his reading level, percentile norms will be meaningless. Only the grade-level scores will be of use to his remedial reading teacher.

The test to be used must be chosen on the basis of what skills the examiner wishes to test and what types of norms are available. The standardized test being used in a school often does not reflect the reading skills being emphasized in that school. The teacher should examine a number of tests and select one which will provide information on the student's ability to use the skills which are particularly important in the reading program of the school, and which she will wish to emphasize for students who are not proficient in those skills.

Instructional Guide 11.1 lists some of the skills identified by five of the most commonly used individual reading tests and two group silent reading tests (see pp. 234-235). Under each test, those sections are listed which are designed to evaluate the skills enumerated on the left-hand side of the table. Additional tests which may be useful in testing each of these areas are listed in the right-hand column. The tests listed are not the only tests available to evaluate these skills, nor are they necessarily the best available, but the table will show the reading teacher the type of test analysis she should use to aid her in choosing the test to be used.

Administering and evaluating the test.   Standardized reading tests are intended to be used by the classroom teacher. They do not require any special training to administer. The following precautions should be kept in mind, however. The student's rating on the test is determined by comparison with norms which have been established by administering the test according to specific instructions; therefore, the results will be valid only if those instructions are adhered to strictly. Time limits must be observed exactly, and instructions must be given by reading the instructions as they are written so that the student has *precisely* the information he requires. Scoring also must be done exactly as outlined in the manual. Any deviations from these will invalidate the test scores.

There are, however, points on which the examiner may wish to change testing procedure in ways which will not invalidate the results. Timing is an example of such an instance. Some tests allow the student as much time as he needs for comprehension exercises, while others limit the time so that the result is as much a measure of speed as it is of comprehension. Because the scores on these tests do not indicate whether a low score is caused by poor comprehension or low speed, the teacher may wish to place a check on this variable by going over the child's answers to determine how many of those marked wrong are actually incorrect answers and how many are questions that were not answered. If nearly all the questions which were answered are correct, this is a good indication that the student's comprehension may be much better than the scores would indicate. In this case, the student's real problem is slow rate of reading or of answering questions.

If most or all of the questions are answered but many answers are incorrect, this is an indication that the student may be rushing through the material too rapidly to attain good comprehension. Or he may merely be guessing at answers without making any real effort to read carefully. Still another possibility is that the material may be above his reading level so that he cannot read it. Finally, one should consider the possibility that he may have poor comprehension of all that he reads. It should be obvious that individual observation and discussion will be required to determine the exact cause of poor comprehension.

Another method of checking comprehension on a test with short time limits is to stop the students at the end of the allotted time, hand them each a colored pencil, and tell them to continue, marking the rest of their answers with the colored pencil. This procedure will result in two comprehension scores for each child, one which is derived from the norms and based upon a combination of speed and comprehension, and another which is a measure of what the student can do if his time is not limited. This latter score cannot be related to the norms, however, as all students on whom the norms were established were reading within the time limits, and most could have done better with unlimited time.

Even when machine scoring is available, all tests used in remedial reading should also be hand scored so that the examiner can observe such factors as the grouping of correct answers, paragraphs on certain subjects which the student reads with higher comprehension than others,

Skills Identified by Some Standardized Reading Tests

	Botel Reading Inventory	Diagnostic Reading Scales (Spache)	Durrell Analysis of Reading Difficulties	Gates-McKillon Reading Diagnostic Tests
Individual or Group	Individual or Group	Individual	Individual	Individual
Grade Levels	1-6	1-7	1-6	1-6
Instructional Reading Level	Word recognition test	Oral reading passages		
Word Analysis Skills	Consonants Rhyming words Vowels Nonsense words	Consonants Vowels Syllables Blending letter sounds	Letters. Hearing sounds in words Sounds of letters Phonetic spelling of words	Letters Nonsense words Vowels Blending Syllabication
Word Meaning	Word opposites			Oral vocabulary
Paragraph Comprehension			Silent reading Oral reading	Oral reading
Study Skills				
Speed				
Listening Comprehension		Reading Passages (listening)	Listening Comprehension	
Visual Perception			Visual memory for words	
Auditory Perception			Hearing sounds in words Learning to hear sounds in words	Auditory discrimination

Test of Individual Needs in Reading (Gilliland)	Stanford Diagnostic Reading Test	STS Diagnostic Reading Test	Other Tests Which Evaluate This Skill
Individual	Group	Group	
1-7	2-4 4-8	2-4 4-6	
Basic Reading level (oral reading)			Gilmore Oral Reading Test Diagnostic Reading Tests Reading Diagnosis Kit
Context Consonants Reversals Vowels Affixes Syllables	Syllabication Beginning and ending sounds Blending Sound discrimination		McKee Inventory of Phonetic Skill California Phonics Survey Woodcock Reading Mastery Test
	Vocabulary	Word meaning	Nelson-Denny (H.S. and Adult) Metropolitan Reading Test Woodcock Reading Mastery Test
Comprehension	Reading Comprehension: 1. Literal 2. Inferential	Recall Reading for meaning, direction, description	Gates Basic Reading Tests California Reading Test Woodcock Reading Mastery Test Nelson-Denny (H.S. and Adult)
		Sources Index Contents Locating Information	SRA Reading Record Iowa Basic Skills Survey of Study Habits and Attitudes
Silent reading speed	Rate of reading	Rate of reading for meaning	Reader's Digest Skill Builders Nelson-Denny Reading Test Standard Reading Inventory Durrell Listening Reading Classroom Reading Inventory
			Gilliland Learning Potential Examination
	Auditory discrimination		Wepman Auditory Discrimination

or a particular kind of question which is missed consistently by a particular student.

It is essential that the teacher who is to use the results of the test know the test itself as well as the skills being assessed and understand exactly what the scores mean. For example, in one test a "vocabulary" score may depend entirely on word analysis skills; in another, it may depend on understanding of word meaning. "Comprehension" may test direct recall of details or may include inference and evaluation. A student's ability to match words with their synonyms may be called "word recognition," "vocabulary," or "comprehension of words." If a student makes a low score in "comprehension," the score gives the teacher no indication of what skills need to be taught unless the teacher has examined the test carefully and knows what skills were tested in this particular case.

The teacher should also realize that although the test is said to measure "comprehension," it may not be a test of comprehension skills at all for a given child. Rather, it may be a test of the child's emotional reaction to the passage, the test, or the teacher—or it may be a test of word recognition. If a student cannot recognize the words in the testing material, his comprehension of it will be poor no matter how well he understands the material which he can read. On the other hand, a low score on silent reading comprehension along with a higher score on oral reading may indicate either poor comprehension, a lack of concentration when reading silently, or a need for verbalization in order to comprehend.

The examiner's attitude while giving the test can greatly affect the results of the test. If she is pleasant and relaxed, the results will be much more valid than if her attitude builds tension in the students. Nonetheless, some students will develop nervous tension in the testing situation regardless of the teacher's actions. The examiner should be alert for such signs of tension as twitchings, scratching, or biting the lips. If they are present, she should note the fact on the test and take it into consideration when evaluating the results.

Limitations of achievement tests.   A standardized reading test is a small sampling of a student's comprehension of certain kinds of reading matter which may be biased for or against this particular student because of his interest in or dislike for a certain subject area or because of the particular kinds of questions asked on the test.

Standardized tests may give some measure of understanding of vocabulary, of speed at getting answers, of ability to follow directions or choose main ideas. They do not ordinarily contribute any information on the student's interest in reading, his ability to adjust rate and comprehension to his purposes, his motivation to achieve, his attitudes, his ability to organize or use the ideas contained in the reading matter, or his appreciation or enjoyment of reading.

Using the Cloze Procedure

Development of a cloze test was discussed earlier in Chapter 6 (see page 117). But the cloze test also provides an excellent means of evaluating an individual's comprehension. The cloze test measures the student's comprehension of a particular piece of material. Therefore, it can be used to determine whether a student can read material of a certain level of difficulty adequately, whether he can understand material of a certain type, or whether he can comprehend material on a particular subject, such as one area of science. The cloze technique can be used not only for testing but also for teaching various comprehension and communication skills. The cloze technique forces the student who has been concentrating on word calling to focus on the meaning of the word in order to predict what it will be.

In practical terms, when testing the understanding of fictional material, the teacher may delete every fifth word. However, for factual—especially scientific or technical—material, the deletions should occur at every tenth word. For instructional purposes, selected deletion is usually preferable. For example, the technique can be adapted to the teaching of a better understanding of pronouns by deleting all the pronouns. Deletion of nouns can help in teaching children to remember certain facts in science and social studies if the material is reviewed orally when it is completed.

When the cloze technique is used for testing, only the exact words of the author should be accepted as correct. However, for instructional purposes, any synonym should be accepted. If he is being tested for vocabulary development and ability to choose expressive words, the student can be asked to choose two words to fit each blank.

When improvement of comprehension is the objective, discussion of the processes the student uses in selecting words is important, for this can help him learn to determine whether a word is sensible and whether it "sounds right" when read aloud.

Completion tests in which the student completes each sentence with one or more words have a similar function to the cloze test and can be used both for testing and for instruction. Some excellent materials, such as the SRA *Reading for Understanding* kit and the *Using the Context* workbooks, use completion tests as the method of teaching comprehension skills. The teacher can construct materials of this type to teach both factual recall and inferential reasoning.

Informal Procedures

Much of the diagnosis of a child's reading comprehension must be accomplished through informal devices and teacher-made tests.

One of the best ways of checking general comprehension is through paraphrasing, that is, having the student repeat in his own words what he has read. If necessary, the paraphrasing can be followed by questions of the "who," "what," "where," "when," "why," and "how" type. Paraphrasing can also be used as a means of improving comprehension. Again, after the child has told his own version of a story, the teacher can lead him to more critical thinking through carefully selected questions.

Informal tests of specific comprehension skills, such as the ability to recall events in sequence or to relate details to the correct major ideas, can be created by the teacher. Higher cognitive skills such as application and analysis of ideas can also be tested informally, as they are rarely included in standardized tests.

Although some individual diagnosis may be done before remedial instruction begins, most of it will be a part of on-going instruction and will be in the form of diagnostic teaching, serving both as instruction and determination of needs for further instruction.

Causes of Comprehension Problems

Throughout both diagnosis and instruction, the teacher should be watching for possible causes of problems in comprehension. The purpose is, of course, to try to eliminate these causes through instruction. Instructional Guide 11.2 lists some of the common causes of failure to comprehend adequately. Along with each of these causes are listed ways of identifying these causes, as well as suggestions for remediation.

INSTRUCTIONAL GUIDE 11.2

Common Causes of Comprehension Problems

Observations	Possible Causes	Recommendations
Lack of Motivation to Comprehend		
Failure to seek meaning actively. No evidence of curiosity. No enthusiasm. Lack of alertness when	Is not concerned about good comprehension.	Read exciting story beginnings to students, have them predict outcomes, and then read rest of story.

Observations	*Possible Causes*	*Recommendations*
reading. Satisfaction with word calling—no demand for comprehension. Lack of attention. Failure to recognize inconsistencies in his own answers. Failure to ask logical questions.		Share the student's interests. Help students visualize characters, scenes, feelings, sounds. Learn about regular classroom activities in which student is very interested or needs help. Help him find and read information on subject that interests him. Listen to student. Have student draw cartoons and illustrations, to show meanings. Read different materials to students: popular song lyrics, riddles, cartoon titles. Evaluate progress together with student frequently. Graph comprehension scores. Do not reread same material. Promote free reading with no questions. Make reading fun. Read instructions to carry out activity.

Failure to Relate Written and Oral Meanings

Poor comprehension. Inability to discuss material read. Lack of effort to comprehend. All of above.	Does not relate printed material to oral speech.	Use language experience approach. Use dramatization. Have student follow in book while listening to meaningful reading on tape. Have student relate to experience, firsthand and vicarious.

Observations	*Possible Causes*	*Recommendations*
Overemphasis on Word Recognition		
Poor comprehension. Lack of interest. No attempt to get meaning. All of above.	Early instruction concentrated on word recognition without attention to comprehension. Must concentrate on word analysis to recognize words.	Have student do much reading of easy material. Set a definite purpose and ask questions of student before he starts to read. Have student read to find answers. Use tachistoscopic practice for sight recognition of basic vocabulary. Encourage student to read jokes and other short, interesting material. Have student read only high interest material. Emphasize fun in reading.
Too Difficult Level of Reading		
Poor comprehension. Lack of effort to understand. Satisfaction with word recognition without comprehension. No enjoyment from reading. All of above. Embarrassment or refusal to read aloud.	Is being made to read material that is too difficult.	Check reading level carefully. Be sure material is at recreational reading level. Whenever student starts new story, listen to him read aloud to make sure he is not missing more than one or two words per 100 words.
Visualization of Action		
Poor comprehension. Inability to answer questions regarding appearances, feelings, personalities.	Does not visualize action, characters, settings, emotions.	Stop to discuss appearances, similarity to places students know, people they have seen, feelings they have had. Have students act out scenes. Have students imitate characters. Use facial expressions in reading to students.

Observations	*Possible Causes*	*Recommendations*
Verbalization		
Poor answers on "why" questions. Inability to choose main ideas. Response to questions with words of author. Failure to be disturbed by partial understanding.	Overemphasizes verbalization and memorization of details.	Set purpose before reading. Outline material for student showing relationship of ideas. Ask some direct recall questions but follow answering of each with a related inference or "why" question.
Physical Setting		
Poor comprehension. Inattention. Restlessness.	Noisy surroundings. Poor lighting. Uncomfortable seats— too high, too low, wrong shape. Many distractions.	Attempt to improve physical facilities.
Distractibility		
Reading without meaning when anything else is going on. Short attention span.	May have learning disability. Lacks interest. Material is too difficult.	See Instructional Guides 12.1 and 12.2. Shorten reading time. Read in a small cubical. Use total class oral reading. Use all of above.

Reading According to Purpose

No one reads without purpose, whether that purpose is to enjoy a story, learn to make something, pass an examination, or merely to occupy time.

The good reader has many speeds and many ways of reading which he adapts to the purpose for which he is reading. An important object of instruction in reading should be the development of this flexibility. Therefore, the student must *always* know the purpose for which he is reading. If his only purpose for reading is "because the teacher said to," he cannot build proper reading skills. He may assume from past experience that the teacher means for him to read for all the details because she may ask anything, while, in reality, a reader would seldom, if ever, read for all the details. For example, in reading a problem in

241

mathematics, he will identify all the information and remember most of it, yet, even here, there may be extraneous material which he will wish to ignore.

When a person decides, on his own, to read something, he has already set his purpose, although he may change that purpose as he reads. When the teacher tells the child to read, she should always indicate the purpose for which he is to read or, better still, discuss the reading with him and let him set his own purpose.

After reading, the teacher may check the student's comprehension by asking questions, but those questions *all* must relate to the set purpose. If the purpose was "to get the main idea," the teacher should not ask, "What was John's cousin's name?" If the student learns that questions not related to his purpose will be asked, he also will learn to read all material slowly and methodically, trying to remember every detail and not to read according to his purpose. This not only hinders the development of speed but also prevents the student from concentrating on those details that he should be remembering and so decreases his useful comprehension. If the only purpose for reading is the teacher's command, "Read this," the only fair question to ask is, "Did you read it?" (This question really means, "Did your eyes go down the page?")

Questions used to set purposes for reading should represent purposes which would apply naturally to the material. Poorly chosen questions used to direct reading can be detrimental to building good reading skills if they direct the student toward insignificant happenings or facts instead of directing him toward the most important elements. They may teach him to try to remember all the insignificant facts rather than help him to learn to choose those which are relevant and important.

When questions are asked after reading, the student should go back and reread to determine the answers to questions he has missed. It is only in this way that he can find out why he failed to get the correct information the first time and improve his comprehension.

If students learn to adapt their reading to the specific purpose for which they are reading, they not only will greatly increase their comprehension of that which is important, but they also will cease to waste time on that which is unimportant, thus defeating one of the reasons some students dislike reading. As Francis Bacon has said, "Some books are to be tasted, others swallowed, some few to be chewed and digested."

The object of setting purposes for reading is to aid the student in learning to select and remember that information which is important to his purpose, and to adjust reading speed and comprehension to his purpose. This is not to imply that each purpose entails a different set of skills. There is a great deal of overlap. Most of the research on reading comprehension indicates that improving reading for one of these purposes improves reading for the others also. However, there is some difference in the amount of skill required for gaining different types of comprehension. The National Assessment of Educational Progress classified comprehension questions in four categories: understanding word meanings, gleaning facts, comprehending main ideas, and drawing inferences. The students tested understood word meanings best, comprehended main ideas second, gleaned significant facts third, and drew inferences least well.[1] It is well to keep this order of difficulty in mind when teaching comprehension skills.

In helping children set purposes for reading, it is advisable to be even more specific. Keeping in mind some of the purposes which are discussed in the following sections will help in organizing instruction.

Reading for Enjoyment

Reading for fun should be part of every child's program every week. When reading for enjoyment, the student should be allowed to read in his own way, skimming to get the plot, or carefully reading to determine the way in which something is done or the author's way of expressing an idea. No questions should be asked, except to give the student an opportunity to tell what he enjoyed.

Literal Comprehension

Recall of directly stated facts should be motivated by one of the following purposes:

Reading for the main idea. An interesting way of teaching, this is having students write their own newspaper headlines for the material they have read.

Recognizing subordinate ideas and their relation to the main idea. This is essential to the organization and use of information. Outlining is helpful, but should not be overdone or it can kill interest.

Skimming to locate specific information. Skimming quickly to locate the answer to a specific question greatly speeds up study and should be practiced by all students who read at fourth-grade level or above. Until they have adequate practice in skimming, students will plod through the material until they stumble onto the answer. Pupils should never

---

[1] *NAEP Newsletter*, vol. 9, no. 4 (August 1976):9.

be asked to attempt to skim read without a definite, stated purpose. They must know what information they are to locate.

Recalling relevant details. The student should not attempt to recall all details, only those relevant to another purpose.

Reading for sequence. This is an important skill in following directions, working problems, and retelling a story, and should be practiced in relation to one of these.

Following directions. Skill in following directions should be taught by having students carry out an activity; it should not be done merely by repeating the directions. In carrying out the activity, students should rely on their reading of the directions. Teachers often defeat their purpose in teaching children to read directions by giving them directions for an activity, then, after they have read the directions, telling them orally how to do the activity.

Story Comprehension. In summarizing research on story comprehension, Guthrie (1977) states that teachers of reading unwittingly create obstacles for their students' achievement of good comprehension by expecting types of comprehension based on specific patterns, when the stories they are reading do not contain the patterns the students are expected to discern.

The usual structure of a story contains a setting, a theme, a plot, and a resolution. The setting consists of the characters, the location, and the time of the story. The theme consists of the main goal of the main character. An understanding of the story is based on the hierarchy of the sentences within the story. The higher the position of the sentence in the hierarchy, the better it is remembered by the reader. Stories without a theme or a plot are incoherent and difficult to recall. Texts or tales which contain violations of the rules of grammar are perceived as incomprehensible and hard to remember.

Some generalizations can be made regarding development of story understanding, according to age groups. Readers from the first grade through adulthood easily remember settings and resolutions. Children as young as six years of age recall story beginnings and conclusions. Children in general tend to be less able to recall episodes within a plot than are older readers. Children also tend to be less able to comprehend reactions and causes, since making such inferences requires more complex cognitive operations. Children expect stories to have structure.

It is the teacher's responsibility to assist the children in formulating appropriate questions by presenting appropriate questions because haphazard questioning is very confusing to the reader. Main idea questions are usually inappropriate for stories since there is usually more than one major idea to the story. The teacher should be sure that the comprehension questions asked are valid. Do not assume that "detail" questions contained in the teacher's manual ask only for the recognition of details. Investigate! Sometimes those questions actually require the students to make inferences. Maybe there is not *one* "main" idea to the story; maybe there are five.

Interpretation

Interpretation is the supplying of meanings not directly stated in the text and is much more difficult than simple recall of directly stated facts. Therefore, many of the questions asked in teaching comprehension should be directed toward the development of the skills of interpretation. Each student's background must be considered in this instruction, for the interpretation given a piece of reading material is largely dependent upon the background of the reader. Interpretation skills can be taught most easily by focusing on the following areas:

Translation of nonliteral language. This includes figures of speech, metaphors, similes, personification, and poetic expressions.

Recognizing cause and effect. As students read a story, they should continually be asked questions which force them to make a conjecture, or reasoned guess, as to what will happen next and what will be the outcome of an action. As students develop the habit of anticipating outcomes, they not only improve their ability to make inferences, but also learn to choose and remember those details that are significant, to organize their thinking, and to read to verify a statement.

Inference. Questions should be asked which check the child's ability to note ideas which are implied but not stated directly and to think beyond a statement to its implications in other situations.

Evaluative reading. Unless the student learns to read critically, to recognize inferences and emotive language, and then to evaluate what he reads, he has no defense against media advertising and propaganda of all types.

An example of excellent instruction in this area is a study of newspapers which was made by a class under Mrs. Ann Regan, a reading specialist at Lincoln Junior High School in Billings, Montana. At the time of her study, the city was in the midst of a controversy over beginning flouridation of the city's water supply. Feelings were strong on both sides of the question, and newspapers contained reports, editorials, and letters which ranged from straight reporting to strong propaganda and high emotion.

Each day, the students in the class cut out any items pertaining to the controversy and analyzed them, discussing evidence of each writer's purpose, emotive language, etc. The students combined these newspaper items into a booklet in which they evaluated each item and classified it according to its purpose and technique. The booklet was used by later classes for developing evaluative reading techniques.

Critical reading should be taught at all levels of reading ability. One way of doing this is to include much reading of factual material and, in setting the objective for the reading, include questions which relate to the author's objectives and biases.

Reading newspaper advertisements is a good way to develop discussion of propaganda techniques.

Creative Reading

Speaking at an International Reading Association breakfast, Hazel Horn Carol quoted a fourth grade child who said, "I like books that mean more than they mean." Children should be given the opportunity to read material that leads them beyond the printed content to imaginative and creative thinking.

Instructional Guide 11.3 summarizes methods which may be used to teach the specific skills listed under "Reading According to Purpose" (see pages 246–251). The "Possible Causes" column included in most of the other Instructional Guides has been omitted from this guide since inadequate or inefficient instruction in the particular skill is the main cause of problems in these areas.

INSTRUCTIONAL GUIDE 11.3

Developing Ability to Read for Specific Purposes

Purpose	Recommended Instruction
Flexibility.	Always set purpose before reading. Ask only questions related to the purpose.
Enjoyment.	Use easy reading with high interest content.

Purpose	*Recommended Instruction*
	Set purpose which appeals to child as being important.
	Read to find humorous or exciting part, to settle an argument, to select material or prepare to read to others in class, younger brother or sisters, or for dramatization.
Gaining main idea.	Begin by selecting the main idea of short paragraphs; lengthen passages gradually.
	Have child preview chapter before reading it.
	Choose from statements in reading one that relates to entire selection.
	Have student make up appropriate titles for articles or headings for paragraphs.
	Have student read very rapidly to get main idea only.
	Remove headings and have pupils match them with the selections.
	Have pupils skim to find only one fact.
Locating information.	Ask for one specific piece of information.
Skim reading.	Have pupils skim to find dates and names (when did an event take place?); then proceed to facts (what are the leading industries of Utah?); eventually, ask for reasons and abstract ideas or for answers to more than one question and for main idea.
	Have two students of equal ability race to find information; discontinue race if one wins consistently.
	Have student practice running eyes over material, looking for specific information only in textbooks and newspapers.
	Have student skim for other purposes: to get general idea of content,

Purpose	*Recommended Instruction*
	to determine if article deals with a certain subject, to select a story to read, to prove a point from a story already read.
Recalling relevant details.	Always have students read for particular details, not for details in general. Do not expect student to retain everything.
	Help student to develop ability to separate relevant from irrelevant details through oral reading and discussion.
	Have student read a page and then retell it in as much detail as possible.
	Have student read and then dramatize a story.
	Have student draw pictures showing events of story.
	Help student draw maps or make graphs interpreting material read.
	Read arithmetic problem containing unneeded information and have students tell which information is needed.
	Have student read to find "who," "what," "where," "when," "why," and "how."
	Have student read for a purpose and answer questions; check his answers immediately and have him reread to find answers to questions missed.
	Tell main idea and have students read to find supporting evidence.
	Add irrelevant sentences and let pupils find these sentences.
Reading for sequence.	Read to: construct timelines, draw comic strips, put pictures in order, follow directions. Read complete information before starting activity.

248

Purpose	*Recommended Instruction*
	Put in order sentences or paragraphs that tell steps in sequential story or activity.
	Follow an event through a series of daily newspapers. Represent with numbered pictures and timeline.
	Write activities of the day.
	Retell a story in order.
	Put up an action picture and have students list events that led to this picture as well as those which might follow.
	Scramble instructions for making something; then let pupils put information in right order and carry out activity.
Following directions.	Read directions for playing game and then play the game.
	Have students read directions and then build model cars, do science experiments, or make buckskin.
	Have students read from *Popular Mechanics* and *Boy Scout* or *Girl Scout Handbook*, and carry out activities.
	Have students make puppets, cook, sew, and make Christmas decorations, from written instructions.
	Have students read and solve math problems.
	Leave one part out of directions and let pupils decide what it is.
	Let pupils write directions for getting to a location or for playing a game developed in class.
	Practice following oral directions containing several steps.

Purpose	Recommended Instruction
Using ngures of speech. Misinterpreting or stopping and puzzling over symbolic language.	Draw cartoons showing literal and actual meanings of expressions, such as "a wolf in sheep's clothing" and "he has a chip on his shoulder." Choose from child's reading.
	Have student make up riddles using analogies: "Its teeth bite into the wood"—saw.
	Show student that metaphors, similes, and personification have comparison as their basis. (Do not use technical terms.)
Predicting outcomes. Showing surprise at events student should have anticipated.	Base discussions on why something happened and what may happen next.
	Use guessing the outcome as purpose for reading.
	Show own curiosity and anticipation.
	Find phrases that predict action.
Interpretation.	Set purposes: to draw conclusions, to decide what the students themselves would do to visualize an incident.
	Help student determine author's purpose: Was it to entertain, to inform, to persuade?
	Have student tell how a person in a story felt—happy, worried, pleased, etc.
	Have student identify mood in a story.
	Have student find phrases that convey a certain feeling.
	Have student locate words that produce emotion.
	Help students interpret in such a way that they gain insight into their own lives through reading.

Purpose	*Recommended Instruction*
Inference.	Ask questions which require the student to discover and use ideas or facts that are implied by the author but are not actually stated.
	Teach student to distinguish emotive and informative language.
	List and discuss propaganda devices. Read advertisements and political speeches and have students identify devices used.
	Teach student to identify humor, irony, sarcasm, exaggeration.
	Discuss connotations of words.
	Help student recognize implications.
	Have student read a slanted editorial and rewrite it slanting it in the opposite way.
	Have student write two stories about a school football game (or a fight) from two opposite viewpoints.
	Help student look for emotional reactions, motives, character traits in a story.
Evaluative reading.	Start with simple question of whether a selection is fiction or fact and then ask if it is fact or opinion.
	Move to verification of information by comparing more than one source, by checking author's background, credibility, probable motives, and propaganda techniques.
Creative reading.	Answer questions such as: How would you have solved this problem? What might have resulted if John had done such-and-such?
	Have children take a story placed in Africa and tell how the plot could be transferred to their own neighborhood.

Understanding Words, Sentences, and Longer Passages

The psycholinguistic study of reading has recently contributed much useful information for analyzing students' reading problems. Studies indicate that reading comprehension depends largely on recognition of relevant syntactic structures. Recognizing syntactic structure helps the reader to relate the content of each phrase to the whole sentence, and the content of the sentence to the whole passage. Syntactic clues used by readers are: the word order and knowledge of relations it reflects; pattern markers such as word inflections and signal words which indicate the grammatical structure of the sentence; and punctuation, which sets off phrases, clauses, and complete sentences. All of these are recurrent and predictable.

A student's ability to comprehend more abstract or complex relations expressed at higher levels may depend on his stage of cognitive and linguistic development. A student may need help in making the transition from the concrete, linear narration of basal readers to the more abstract complex relations in the content areas.

Teaching Word Meaning

Unless the reader knows the meanings of the words, he cannot comprehend the meaning of the passage. It should not be assumed that just because the student can pronounce the word when he sees it, he understands its meaning. Even if he says he knows what it means, his ideas may be hazy or he may know only one meaning for a word that has many meanings. Since he thinks he knows individual words, he does not understand why he cannot understand the sentence clearly.

Achievement tests may give some indication of the general level of a child's meaning vocabulary. However, only discussion or the use of teacher-made tests will reveal a student's knowledge of the meaning of a certain group or type of words. For determining a student's understanding of a specific list of words from a certain group, a measure which is simple to use and is interesting to the student is associational fluency—the student's ability to name rapidly other words similar in meaning, or related in some way, to a given word.

When a child begins to read new material, it is worthwhile to check his understanding of key words—those words which are necessary for good comprehension of that material.

One advantage of intensive training in word meaning is that it makes the student word conscious and shows him ways in which he can learn the meanings of words, thus continuing to improve his vocabulary of other words in addition to those which are being studied. The teacher should encourage the demanding of understanding of all the words the student reads.

Some methods of teaching the meaning of words include:

Using direct instruction. The teacher and the students discuss the word, giving definitions, illustrating them with sentences, and finding synonyms.

Using context. The children get the meaning through the context, and the teacher checks their knowledge through discussion. This method has the advantage of helping the students to become independent in their vocabulary building. A good supplement to it is to study the words in context and then create as many new contexts as possible for the words to sharpen the meaning. All word study should be associated with the use of words in context.

Using author's definitions. The author frequently defines the word in the context. Pupils must learn to watch for and recognize these definitions.

Using prefixes, suffixes, and root words. A study of common root words and affixes, along with study of context, helps the students to determine the probable meanings of words. Lists of prefixes and suffixes to be memorized are seldom of value, especially to remedial readers. However, if students develop lists like the following through their own analysis and discussion of words found in their reading they can be very useful in vocabulary building:

ab-	means *away*	abduct, abstain, absent
ad-	means *to*	adhere, admit
auto-	means *self*	automobile, autobiography
bi-	means *two*	bicycle, biannual
dis-	means *not*	disbelief, displease
hydro	means *water*	hydroplane, hydrant
micro-	means *small*	microscope, microfilm, microbe
post-	means *after*	postscript, post dated
pre-	means *before*	preheat, preview
-al	means *belonging to*	regional, functional
-ee	means *one who is*	employee, attendee
-er	means *one who acts*	runner, pacifier
-ful	means *full of*	respectful, regretful

Vocabulary games. The teacher and students can invent a variety of games using synonyms, antonyms, and prefixes.

Word origins. If a teacher can get a group of students enthused about studying the origin of words, she can lead them to the learning of the meanings of a great many new words. This does not necessarily require high level reading skills. One second-grade teacher found it very successful with her students.

Using picture clues.   Children can determine the meanings of words from appropriate illustrations.

Classifying words.   Words can be printed on cards and classified by the children by putting them in an appropriate envelope according to what subject they are related, such as school, sports, food, etc.

Using the function of words.   Children find and underline transition words, such as "furthermore," "in the first place," and "besides," and discuss their interpretation in reading. Time words, place words, etc. can also be used in this exercise.

Relating words to subject.   Discussion of the subject to which a group of words is related may clarify the meanings.

Using adequate exposure.   Wide reading insures that the child will be exposed to many words and to certain words many times; it provides an opportunity for the student to build his reading vocabulary in the same way everyone originally builds a listening vocabulary. Some students, usually—though not always—the better readers, build a large vocabulary this way, while other students skip over all unknown words, learning few, if any, new words through reading.

Using the dictionary.   Research shows that the actual increase in vocabulary is much greater when words are taught by the teacher than when looked up in the dictionary. Children reading at fourth-grade level or above should be taught the skills required for obtaining the meaning of a word from the dictionary, since the dictionary is a source which is available when personal assistance is not. A habit of checking meanings through the dictionary can be a valuable asset to the advanced student; however, expecting that remedial readers will look up words on their own initiative is, in most cases, unrealistic.

Sentence Meaning

Recognizing words and their meanings is important, but it is the relationship of these words to each other that gives meaning to sentences. In fact, this syntax tells us which of several meanings to assign to a word. Word recognition, however, is necessary to understanding syntax. Certain words place restrictions on the meanings, and occurrence of other words in a sentence. Therefore, the placement of a word in a sentence may change the meaning of the sentence entirely. Thus, also, if a reader misunderstands one word, the sentence may take on a completely different meaning.

Spoken language consists of syntax, intonation, facial expression, and body movement. All of these help convey meaning. Because they also add variety and interest, the speaker does not need to use the variety of sentence structure usually found in printed material. The writer tries to add to the interest and convey details of thought through a variety of sentence structure, beyond that which would be appropriate in ordinary conversation. As Walter MacGinitie once said of a passage from a social studies book, "If anyone actually spoke like that in a conversation, you'd ask him to turn in his social security number for a Dewey decimal number!" [2] Since writers use sentence structures not common in oral language, we have to give students help in understanding and predicting these more complicated linguistic structures.

There are many exercises which emphasize understanding derived from word order and word clue relationships. Some exercises to use include: making meaningful substitutions for words in nonsense sentences; placing scrambled sentences in order; identifying words which are spoiling the sentence meaning; and constructing a sentence collage with words from newspapers and magazines. Transforming sentences from the active to the passive voice and changing sentences from declarative to interrogative are also helpful. Certain words are used as signal words to show the relationship of the other words in a sentence. A study of these words can be very fruitful in improving comprehension. One way of doing this is to have students list signal words according to their use. Examples of this would be:

Words signaling comparison: both, although, but, on the other hand.

Words signaling cause: because, due to, therefore, since.

Words signaling sequence: first, afterward, then.

Words signaling grouping: several, these, many, another.

Words signaling purpose: in order to, so that.

Words signaling change of thought: but, however, yet.

Words signaling continuation of same thought: moreover, and, furthermore.

Words signaling emphasis: above all, indeed.

Students can take a passage and skim through it looking for examples of a particular type of signal word, then discuss how these affect meaning.

Since one of the chief systems of signaling sentence structure is through punctuation, readers must learn to watch the punctuation and

---

[2] Walter H. MacGinitie, in speech at IRA Transmountain Regional Conference, Calgary, Alberta, Canada, November 1975.

to interpret it in oral reading through intonation, stress, and juncture. Until they see the effect it has on meaning, students may pay little attention to punctuation. To help them use punctuation as a way of getting meaning, sentences can be typed with each sentence punctuated in more than one way. Students read the sentences aloud, follow the punctuation cues, and discuss the difference in meaning. The following are some examples of this approach:

It is time? The boy said that we should go?

It is time! The boy said that we should go!

"It is time," the boy said, "That we should go?"

"It is time." The boy said that. We should go.

Horses? Two got away.

Horses too, got away.

She cried; alligator tears ran down her face.

She cried, "Alligator!" Tears ran down her face.

Who said Jack called Jane?

Who said Jack called, Jane?

Who said Jack called—Jane?

Who said, "Jack called," Jane?

"Who said 'Jack'?" called Jane.

Who said "Jack called Jane"?

"Who," said Jack, "Called Jane?"

"Who," said Jack "Called, 'Jane'?"

Who said Jack called, "Jane!"?

Who said *Jack* called Jane?

Who said Jack *called* Jane?

Who said Jack called *Jane?*

Additional practice for understanding punctuation can be given by having the student punctuate a sentence in more than one way and then read the sentences aloud according to his punctuation. Sentences, such as the following, can be used for this practice:

The cowboy said Bill was a good rider.

The Eskimo without his parka is not ready to go hunting.

John called Mary.

If you leave my friends you may not come back.

Students must learn to use both context and punctuation to help in expressive reading. To accomplish this, an isolated sentence can be read in different ways to show different meanings and then be put in its place within a paragraph to show how the previous context indicates the proper stress.

Getting Meaning from Paragraphs and Longer Passages

From a psycholinguistic treatment of sentence comprehension, instruction can proceed to intersentence comprehension. This requires an understanding of the relationship between the sentences in a paragraph. The student can be helped to choose the topic sentence of a paragraph. He can then attempt to see in what way each of the other sentences enlarges upon the information contained in the topic sentence.

Instruction should begin with well-written paragraphs which begin with the topic sentence. Later, students can find the topic sentences in paragraphs in which it comes at the end and the middle. Paragraphs used for this purpose should all be paragraphs which are well constructed around clearly stated topics.

Exercises which can be used to improve the comprehension of paragraphs include:

1. Selecting the main idea from several choices.

2. Writing titles or headlines for paragraphs.

3. Giving the students several paragraphs or short articles, and the titles and having them match the title to the paragraph.

4. Having students select the topic sentence of a paragraph, then explain how each of the other sentences relates to it.

5. Drawing symbols to represent the construction of different paragraphs. The triangle, inverted triangle, diamond, circle, and

square can represent the paragraph with the topic sentence at the end, at the beginning, in the middle, one with the main idea in the middle but not in one sentence, and the paragraph with no topic sentence.

6. Giving a student a topic sentence and letting him write a paragraph by adding supporting details.

Because paragraph comprehension is important in the study of science or social studies, textbooks from these subjects should be used for part of the practice.

To fully comprehend longer selections, the student must organize mentally the material he is reading. Instruction in organization usually begins by teaching the student to find the three main parts of an article or chapter—the introductory part which usually tells the purpose or the "where" and "when"; the body or discussion; and the conclusion or summary. The material used to begin this instruction must be well organized.

Students should then learn to select the main and subordinate ideas in a selection and to see the relationship between them. Once students have become proficient at this task, they can try to separate important facts from the less important details related to these facts. They are then ready to outline by putting the important ideas in logical order and listing subordinate details under them.

This understanding of organization can be aided even more if the student writes a summary from his outline by using the main idea for the introduction, changing the main headings into topic sentences for paragraphs, and the subtopics into supporting sentences.

Students should also be given practice in drawing conclusions and in arriving at generalizations.

Comprehension of chapters can also be increased by encouraging the students to survey the material before reading, as in the manner taught in the SQ3R method of reading and by encouraging understanding of such illustrative material as maps, globes, and charts.

Asking Questions That Promote Comprehension

One of the most important techniques in developing comprehension is the asking of thought-provoking questions. The type of questions should vary according to the ability of the reader, his purpose for reading, and the type of material he is reading.

To improve her use of questioning to teach comprehension, the teacher should occasionally tape record her class and then listen to the tape analytically, asking herself, "How many of each of the types of questions did I use? Were the kinds of questions used the best for teaching the particular skills needed by this student or by each individual in the group? Did my handling of the discussion session promote interest in reading? Did it give every child encouragement? Did I allow adequate time for thinking? Did I accept every child's thinking? Did I let the children answer the questions, or did I, in one way or another, answer them for them? Did I follow up mediocre answers with additional questions that helped the child to clarify his thinking? Were all of my comprehension questions related to the child's purpose for reading?"

Asking Different Types of Questions

All of the kinds of questions enumerated in the following sections should be used in teaching comprehension skills. The proportion of each type of question will depend upon the needs and abilities of the individual child.

Guiding questions. Before the student starts to read, he can be asked to find the answers to such questions as the following:

What equipment did Lyle take for climbing the mountain?

What are the steps in scaling a cliff?

What is rappelling?

Would you like to be a mountain climbing guide?

What is the author trying to prove throughout this article?

Can you find answers to the "who," "what," "where," "when," and "why" questions?

Can you find evidence to support . . .?

The type of questions used for guiding will depend upon the particular comprehension skills which are to be developed through the lesson. Except where the purpose is to teach a skill, such as skimming to locate one particular piece of information, the questions usually will be much broader than those used for discussion after reading. In this way, several follow-up questions can be used to cover the same information. However, all of the questions asked after reading should be related to these questions or to additional purposes suggested by the student.

Direct recall.   How many dogs did Paul have?

Simple recall questions are necessary first steps in the development of comprehension for the child who is a word caller, sounding out words without getting meaning from what he reads. Yet even at this level, some "why" questions should be used in addition to those of the direct recall type in order to be sure there is some actual understanding. Direct recall questions usually do not really require comprehension. In fact, they may teach the child that understanding is not expected, only verbalization. The story below illustrates this point. The reader should attempt to read this passage with meaningful expression, rereading if necessary to give the words the proper emphasis.

Zeg and the Slir-Juk

"I'll quev the slir-juk in the novek." Zeg ilned.
"Will the slir-juk nal the novek tup better?" his tor ilned.
"The slir-juk nals the novek tup. Without the slir-juk the novek dourf not tup."
"Then mees the slir-juk," ilned his tor.
Zeg queved the slir-juk in. The novek tuped. Zeg's tor chagged.

Was it possible to read this selection with meaningful inflections? Was expression evidence of good comprehension?
The following questions concerning the selection should be answered with complete sentences:

1. What did Zeg do with the slir-juk?

2. Would the novek tup without the slir-juk?

3. What did his tor iln?

4. What else did his tor do?

Answering these questions does not require comprehension, but only verbalization, the repetition of the words of the author. Do the following modifications evaluate comprehension more adequately?

a. Was it necessary for Zeg to quev the slir-juk in the novek?

b. Why did his tor chag?

c. What would you do next if you were Zeg?

The preceding selection also demonstrates the fact that many words can be identified through context, if the reader has even a little comprehension—in this case, if he knows that in the first line, *slir-juk* is gasoline and *novek* means car. This knowledge will reveal the meaning of most of the other words. It also shows how completely the meaning is changed by a lack of adequate vocabulary.

Vocabulary Questions.   In this sentence does the word *lead* indicate an action or an object?

Questions such as the preceding should be used to check on the reader's comprehension of the vocabulary used. This is especially important when the meaning of some of the words, such as "lead," "bow," or "sail," depends entirely upon the context in which they are found and when misinterpretation of the word could cause complete loss of comprehension of the passage.

Verification.   You just told us what you think was Betty's reason for running away. Can you find a sentence that proves your answer?

Organization.   What two types of animals were in the act?

Which ones belong to the cat family?

What were Ed's three jobs, and what work did he do at each one?

What are the steps in making watermelon pickles?

Conjecture.   What do you think Diane will do next?

If Jack refuses to go, will she stay home also?

What do you suppose had to be done before Pretty Weasel could start beading her moccasins?

Explanation.   Why did Grandpa keep driving around and around the house?

How did he finally stop the car?

What did Nickifer prove when he took the seal back to the ocean?

Application.   What does this mean to you?

How can you apply some of these ideas to the club you are starting?

Justification.   Why did you say that Bob was the most important member of the expedition?

Evaluation.   Why did the author write this article?

What kind of person was Elk Shoulder?

Would you want him for a friend?

Would you have made the same decision?

Evaluation includes any question which causes the student to think about worth, acceptability, or probability.

Appreciation.   How does the author make you feel about _____?

How was the mood set?

Did you like the point of view the author used?

Using Group Response to Questions

When a group of pupils have read a story together, they will each have more opportunity to express themselves and think about answers if group response is used rather than the usual discussion in which only one person has an opportunity to respond at a time. Depending upon the type of questions to be asked, this group response can be either oral or silent. Either one can be used with any group regardless of size.

Group response using cards.   Group silent response can be used most easily with direct recall questions, but it can also be used for some questions requiring higher comprehension skills.

The most easily used group response system for beginning readers is giving each child three cards on each of which is printed the name of one character in the story. All questions asked must be answerable with one of the names on the cards. For example, the questions might ask:

"Who had the dream about the dogs?"

"Who do you think was the bravest person?"

"Which character would you rather take with you on a camping trip?"

As the teacher asks the question, each child picks up the card with the name which answers the question and holds it up with the name facing toward the teacher. The teacher can see easily how quickly each child has determined an answer, whether all the answers are correct, and whether any students are relying on others to get their answers. On a question like the last one, the teacher may want to ask one or two children who disagree with each other why they made their particular choices.

For more variety in questions, the teacher may prefer to use cards numbered "1," "2," and "3." She then says: "The person who showed the best sportsmanship was, Dick, Bill, or Jim? Dick-one, Bill-two, Jim-three. All right, show your answers—*now!*"

If the students are seated at desks, a set of these cards can be kept in each desk at all times.

If only a few questions are to be asked, answers can be indicated by the right or left hand or by the number of fingers held up, although this method gives the students more opportunity to copy each other's answers.

Giving group oral response to partners.   In using group oral response, the teacher starts with a statement such as: "As I ask these questions, I want you to answer them to your partner. If your partner disagrees, he should tell what he thinks is a better answer. If you need help, raise your hand." The teacher moves among the students, listening and stopping the discussions occasionally to give new questions.

Questions Developed by Students

Since good readers are curious readers with questioning minds, letting students ask questions instead of just answering them can be an excellent way of checking and developing comprehension. This helps the student learn to set his own purposes for reading and, as he reads, to recognize information about which questions might be asked.

In individual instruction, the teacher can ask questions about one page and then allow the student to try to ask the same kind of questions about the following page.

In a group, the students and teacher can discuss the objectives and the kind of questions that could be used to check those objectives before the reading begins and then, after reading, they can each jot down two or three questions, all of which the group will then try to answer. In addition to answering the questions, the group, with the teacher's help, also evaluates the questions.

Students also can preview material to be read and formulate questions which probably will be answered in the material. This is an important part of study reading.

Study Skills

Reading in subject-matter areas presents special problems because of technical writing style and specialized vocabulary. The classroom teacher who teaches any subject also should teach the special vocabulary and reading techniques needed for that subject. However, the remedial reading student may not receive adequate help from the regular classroom teacher in this respect, so the reading teacher should be prepared to give the student help in study skills, if this is necessary.

Evaluating needs.   If the remedial reading student is reading at fourth-grade level or above, some diagnosis of his ability to use study skills may be advisable. Both the teaching and evaluation of study skills can best be accomplished through a problem assignment. A situation is set up in which the student needs information. He then studies the resources available and decides where he can best get the information needed; he then proceeds to find the information, to evaluate it, and to apply it in solving his problem. At each step of this procedure, the teacher will need to give instruction in those skills which the student has not yet learned.

If it is considered necessary to do some evaluation of study skills during the preliminary testing, standardized tests can be used which include study skills. Tests will not show whether or not a student can evaluate information, organize it, or apply it to specific problems. They will, however, measure certain locational skills—finding words in an alphabetical list, determining what to look for in an index, knowing what is contained in the card catalog, or understanding maps and graphs.

The *SRA Reading Record,* the *Iowa Test of Basic Skills,* and the *STS Diagnostic Reading Test* all include sections on locational skills for students reading above fourth-grade level. The *California Study Habits Survey* and the *Survey of Study Habits and Attitudes* are both for students in junior high and above and concentrate more on attitudes toward study, organization of time, and mechanics of study.

Improving locational skills.   The ability to locate needed information is an essential study skill which begins in first and second grade with finding answers to questions within a paragraph or short selection. It progresses to the locating of information on a subject in several different sources. This progression may require a review of several types of material, skimming these materials to locate information on the subject being investigated, and careful reading of those parts.

This location of information will need to be followed by: evaluation of the information to determine its relevance to the subject, its reliability, and its freedom from bias; organization of the information; summarization of the information or drawing a conclusion; and application of that information to the solution of a problem.

Like evaluation, instruction in all these skills can be conducted most profitably through a problem assignment—getting a student enthused about a subject and then helping him do research on that subject. Instructional Guide 11.4 suggests remedies for problems discovered in the use of the locational skills.

INSTRUCTIONAL GUIDE 11.4

Problems in the Use of Locational Skills

Observations	*Possible Causes*	*Recommendations*
Use of Library		
Failure to use library for information.	Does not see need for library use. Lacks confidence in ability to find information. Lacks library skills.	Help student develop understanding of how library can help study. Help student use the following library resources in solving a specific problem or informational need: card catalog, location of books, various indexes, *Who's Who, Reader's Guide,* current materials, reference books.
Use of Index		
Inability to use index to find information on a topic.	Cannot choose appropriate key words to look up information. Does not know purpose of index, meaning of page numbers or cross references.	Have student practice finding appropriate key words from such a question as: "How much *wheat* is grown in *Kansas?*" Have student practice thinking of broader words related to an idea such as *agriculture* for the above question. Find student's problem by going through the process of locating a subject.

Observations	*Possible Causes*	*Recommendations*
Difficulty finding words in index file or dictionary. Slow in using index.	Does not know alphabetical order well enough.	Have student do lots of filing material behind index cards. Have student make own dictionary, using pictures from catalogs, magazines, and old work books. Use Dolch word cards or other word cards and arrange them in alphabetical order. Use "alphabet rummy" with word cards—four letters in a row can be laid down. Have student make own phone book by listing names alphabetically and looking them up in city phone book.

Use of Table of Contents

Shuffling through book to look for information without using contents or index.	Lacks knowledge of organization of book parts.	Teach how to find title, copyright date, author, publisher, illustrator, titles of chapters, index. When starting each new book, ask easy questions such as "On what pages is there information on horses?" and harder ones, such as "What is page 43 about? On what page does that chapter begin?"

Use of Encyclopedia

Failure to use the encyclopedia when it is an appropriate reference tool.	Does not know the encyclopedia's value. Is inefficient in finding alphabetical material. Has found encyclopedia too difficult.	Have him look up information important to him in an encyclopedia appropriate to his reading level. See *Use of Index*, section in this Guide.

INSTRUCTIONAL GUIDE 11.4 *(continued)*

Observations	Possible Causes	Recommendations

Use of Dictionary

| Failure to use dictionary without prompting. Inability to use dictionary pronunciation. Inability to understand dictionary definitions or choose appropriate definition. | Does not know how to use dictionary. Thinks dictionary is too difficult to use. Does not know value of dictionary. Does not understand pronunciation key. Has poor reading comprehension. Lacks attention to meaning when reading. Does not understand dictionary terminology. | Teach alphabetical arrangement, use of guide words, use of pronunciation key, word meanings. Make a game of finding as many synonyms as possible for a given word. Try to create curiosity about words. Have student practice writing dictionary-type definitions. Rewrite dictionary definitions expanding them into normal sentence form. Restate sentence in which an unknown word was found, replacing the word with synonym or definition. |

Use of Glossary

| Failure to use glossary of book. | Same causes as those for *Use of Index.* | Same as recommendations for *Use of Index and Dictionary.* |

Study Reading

The student should be taught the study techniques which will help him to read subject material at his reading level. He should be able to locate information through the use of the library, the index of a book, graphs and illustrations, and encyclopedias. He should be helped to study more effectively through techniques, such as Robinson's SQ3R reading formula, and effective organization of study notes. He also may need help in adjusting to the vocabulary and writing style used in particular subject-matter areas. Instructional Guides 11.5 and 11.6 list common problems in study reading as well as their possible causes and suggested methods of remediation.

INSTRUCTIONAL GUIDE 11.5

Problems in Study-type Reading

Observations	*Possible Causes*	*Recommendations*

Motivation for Study

Observations	Possible Causes	Recommendations
Poor attitudes toward school, studying, subjects. Inability to see need for effort. Conflicting activities. Failure to finish assignments.	Lacks motivation in subject-matter areas. Does not believe in own ability to succeed.	Provide success and self-confidence. Promote the feeling that study can be fun. Discuss interesting parts of school; be sure to include all aspects. Develop the understanding that achievement is up to the individual, not teachers or parents. Teach student to be dissatisfied with vague ideas and unfinished work. Use timed exercises and games to develop concentration among distractions.

Study Methods

Observations	Possible Causes	Recommendations
Poor comprehension in subject-matter areas.	Does not know how to apply reading skills to study.	Teach use of key words, topic sentences, introductions, and summaries. Help student to watch for special type, sectional headings, indentations in reading selections. Help student to note difference in meanings of same words in different subjects (e.g., *fold* in cooking and in geography). Teach student to read to anticipate ideas—guessing, then supporting or refuting with facts and logic.

Observations	*Possible Causes*	*Recommendations*
		Cut up old textbooks; mount paragraphs or short sections with questions; and have students answer, supply titles, find topic sentences, and outline the displayed selection.
		Read difficult portions aloud, identifying propaganda.
Hazy ideas of historical events described. Repeating words without being able to explain them.	Cannot distinguish fact vs. opinion, main idea, abstractions, figurative language, organization, summarization, relevancy, maps, graphs, globes.	Have student interpret political cartoons.
		Use time line to relate events read about to time.
	Fails to relate social studies material to own experience or previous learning.	Read and follow events on map.
		Compare fiction, editorials, textbooks.
		Teach skills of locating information.
		Break down abstract ideas and use concrete examples.
		Have student outline.
		Have student write summary paragraphs.
		Have student choose material important to a subject from an article containing relevant and irrelevant material.
		Graph progress on several kinds of graphs.
		Have student survey for organization of content.
		Have student practice finding cause-and-effect relationships.
		Have student practice

Observations	Possible Causes	Recommendations
		hunting for information on both sides of controversial issues.
		Thoroughly discuss special vocabulary, especially abstract terms, in each item read.
		Discourage memorization of material.
		Discourage use of author's terminology.
		Encourage expression of ideas in personal language patterns.
		Paraphrase.
Poor comprehension of social studies vocabulary.	Is encountering many new words (e.g., feudalism, guild) and abstract words (e.g., justice, equality).	Encourage vocabulary study using words from social studies books.
		Have student practice use of word analysis, dictionary, glossary.
		Encourage extra reading from historical fiction or a book about one event, but not from different textbook.
Social Studies		
Poor comprehension in social studies.	Does not have clear concept of time or space.	Read travel books and historical fiction for background.
	Encounters too many	

INSTRUCTIONAL GUIDE 11.6

Problems in Reading Subject Matter Material

Observations	Possible Causes	Recommendations
	concepts in a small amount of material.	Teach propaganda devices and terms that indicate opinion.
	Cannot distinguish fact, opinion, biased writing.	Evaluate progress by asking question and having students use textbook to find answer.

Observations	*Possible Causes*	*Recommendations*
		Observe methods used by students.
		Make list of questions which require use of maps, graphs, and tables.
		Watch student's methods.
Science		
Poor comprehension in science.	Does not visualize, follow directions, note details, or analyze.	Teach the special vocabulary needed in the area being studied.
	Fails to note sequence or cause and effect.	
	Cannot interpret formulas, tables, diagrams.	Arouse interest in problem-solving and new discoveries.
	Encounters technical vocabulary.	Clarify measurement terms for student by measuring.
	Encounters different meanings for common words.	Discuss possible applications of theories.
		Help student practice reading symbols and formulas.
		Read instructions for experiment with student.
		Have students visualize each step of experiment, equipment needed, process, etc., and then carry out the experiment.
		Discuss the clarity of the student's mental images.
Mathematics		
Poor comprehension of arithmetic problems.	Does not know what to look for.	Teach such mathematics vocabulary as "triangle," "perimeter," "sum," "product."
	Has difficulty with technical vocabulary.	
	Cannot picture steps in a process.	Teach steps: (1) What am I asked to find? (2) What facts are given? (3) How are they related to other problems?
	Encounters many abbreviations.	
		Type paragraphs using symbols $<$, $=$, $>$, $\div$, etc., in place of words

Observations	Possible Causes	Recommendations
		(e.g., I think King Henry > King Edward.) Read aloud. Help student visualize problem. Ask questions to check for full understanding and memory for details. Check for understanding of new meanings of such words as "base," "interest," "root," "product," etc. Have students search newspapers and magazines for all the graphs they can find. Interpret problems.
Industrial Arts		
Poor comprehension of shop manuals.	Is confused by large, specialized vocabulary.	Read on the subject under consideration from *Popular Mechanics* or other periodicals at student's reading level. Have students read instructions. Have students close book and list steps in order. Have students study specialized vocabulary as needed.

Summary

Getting meaning is the only real purpose of reading; the purpose of instruction in word recognition and all other reading skills simply is to make that comprehension possible. Instruction for improving comprehension begins with diagnosis of the student's understanding of what he reads through group standardized reading tests, individual reading tests, cloze tests, and informal procedures. Through the well-organized use of a variety of types of questions, students can be taught the particular comprehension and study skills which they lack and which are retarding their reading. Such students also should learn to adjust their speed and comprehension to their purpose for reading. The most common comprehension problems, along with suggestions for their remediation, are summarized in Instructional Guide 11.7

INSTRUCTIONAL GUIDE 11.7

Summary of Common Problems in Reading Comprehension

Observations	Possible Causes	Recommendations
Silent Comprehension		
Poor silent reading comprehension.	Fails to relate print to speech. Is an auditory learner.	Reinforce reading by listening while teacher reads aloud and student follows silently. Follow reading with questions. (Do this with standardized test for identifying potential reading level.)
Overall Comprehension		
Poor in all areas of comprehension.	Has poor sight vocabulary. Overemphasizes word analysis. Has poor knowledge of word meaning. Materials are not adapted to interests or to experiential background. Has poor phrasing.	Set purpose by giving questions before reading. Discuss key vocabulary before reading. Motivate and build readiness before reading. Use low vocabulary material. Teach paragraph structure.
	Uses word-by-word reading. Lacks experience in expressing ideas. Does not read with appropriate purpose in mind.	Practice telling main ideas and sequence. Read instructions and carry out.

Observations	*Possible Causes*	*Recommendations*
Verbalizing		
Lack of attention to meaning. Reading words meaninglessly. Failure to attempt to get meaning.	Overemphasizes word recognition. Lacks motivation. Verbalizes because he does not expect to be able to get meaning. Material is too difficult. Encounters too many strange concepts. Teacher fails to help student relate to experience. Teacher has accepted reproduction of words as comprehension. Reads without knowing purpose.	Have student read paragraph and then paraphrase; reread, if necessary. Discuss how facts are related with student. Have student write summaries. Have student outline in question form. Ask "why" questions of student. Ask questions requiring predictions of outcomes. Discuss purposes before reading.
Experience		
Inability to picture places and activities.	All of causes listed under *Verbalizing* above. Lacks experience background. Unable to see relationship to experience.	All of recommendations listed for *Verbalizing* above. Build background through experiences, films, pictures, discussions, other reading, handling objects. Bring out similarities to child's own experiences, neighborhood, and actions.
Listening		
Poor listening comprehension.	Has poor auditory perception (see Chapter 12). Has not learned how to listen, or to organize, or to retain ideas.	Give student questions; then have him listen to taped story and answer questions. Use SRA *Listening Skill Builders.* Play listening games in which each child repeats what the previous one said and adds to it.

Observations	*Possible Causes*	*Recommendations*
		Give series of oral directions to be carried out. Teach students to think as they listen by stopping in the middle of a taped presentation and asking students to tell what the speaker will say next. Teach all the reading comprehension skills in terms of listening first.

Recognizing Humor

Inability to recognize humor when reading. Inability to tell if author is serious or not. Inability to recognize sarcasm.	Cannot relate written to oral humor. Does not appreciate any humor. Does not understand what makes humor.	Read jokes and other humorous material aloud with a group. Discuss jokes—their use of exaggeration, play on words, etc.

Oral Reading Comprehension

Comprehension is poorer in oral than silent reading. Reading without meaningful expression.	Experiences tension—emotional pressures in oral reading. Oral reading is criticized by teacher or peers. Emphasizes vocalization rather than meaning.	Encourage oral reading for fun. Create a relaxed atmosphere. Emphasize good qualities with no criticism

Recall of Details

Poor recall of details.	Is overly attentive to word analysis. Rushes through material. Is inattentive. Has poor concentration.	Use low vocabulary material. Set purpose, motivate, and then read slowly and carefully. Make a game of covering material as he goes and getting answers on first reading.

Eye Movement

Excessive regressions in eye movements.	Material is too difficult. Has poor vocabulary.	Use much reading of easy material.

Observations	Possible Causes	Recommendations
	Has poor word attack skills. Has poor concentration. Has poor comprehension. Has formed poor habit.	Use marker above line. Motivate with Controlled Reader. Check word attack skills and vocabulary.
Silent Reading Speed		
Slow silent reading.	Has poor sight vocabulary. Overemphasizes word analysis. Subvocalizes. Is overly concerned with detail. Fails to use context. Points to word or line with finger. Reads everything at same speed.	Build word recognition skills. Use tachistoscopic practice. Use much reading of easy material. Avoid oral reading. Have student place fingers on lips while reading. Have student practice reading according to purpose. Use cloze procedure. Use card above line. Use accelerator. Use timed easy exercises.

Recommended Related Reading

Anderson, Richard C., Sheila R. Goldberg, and Janet Hidde. "Meaningful Processing of Sentences," in *Theoretical Models and Processes of Reading,* 2d ed., eds. Harry Singer and Robert B. Ruddell. Newark, Del.: International Reading Association, 1976, p. 580.

Report of an experiment which indicates that forcing a person to think about what he is reading improves comprehension. Has implication for use of Cloze procedure in teaching.

Beil, Drake. "The Emperor's New Cloze." *Journal of Reading* 20 (April 1977): 601–4.

Verifies standards for use of the Cloze technique.

Carter, Betty B. "Helping Seventh Graders to Understand Figurative Expressions." *Journal of Reading* 20 (April 1977): 553–58.

Emphasizes the importance of understanding figurative language for comprehending social studies texts, and gives suggestions for instruction.

Chapman, Carita A. "Teaching Comprehension to the Disabled Reader." *Journal of Reading* 20 (October 1976): 37–42.

Suggestions on improving comprehension through a linguistic study of sentence and passage structure.

Dulin, Ken L. and M. Jane Greenewald. "Mature Readers' Affective Response to Three Specific Propaganda Devices: Loaded Words, Name-Calling, and Borrowed Prestige/Borrowed Dislike," *Reading: Convention and Inquiry,* eds. George H. McNinch and Wallace D. Miller. University of Southern Mississippi Press, 1975, pp. 267–72.

Research that shows that propaganda devices do work, and the importance of making students aware of them.

Frazier, Lynne and Edward Caldwell. "Testing Higher Cognitive Skills in Young Children." *The Reading Teacher* 30 (February 1977): 475.

Gives an example of a teacher-made reading comprehension test which includes application and analysis questions.

Golinkoff, Roberta Michnick. "A Comparison of Reading Comprehension Processes in Good and Poor Comprehenders." *Reading Research Quarterly* 11 (1976): 623–59.

Reviews the research on the effect on comprehension of decoding skills, word meaning, and organizational skills.

Goodman, Yetta M. "Miscues, Errors, and Reading Comprehension," in *New Horizons in Reading,* ed. John E. Merritt. Newark, Del.: International Reading Association, 1976, p. 86.

Shows that miscues in oral reading may be the result of good comprehension rather than the cause of poor comprehension.

Guthrie, John T. "Research Views—Story Comprehension." *The Reading Teacher* 30 (February 1977): 574–77.

Discusses some problems in teaching comprehension through story material.

Miller, Wilma H. "Correcting Difficulties in Interpretive Comprehension Skills," *Reading Correction Kit.* The Center for Applied Research, Inc., 1975, pp. 201–61.

Includes samples of a variety of worksheets for developing comprehension skills.

Neuwirth, Sharyn E. "A Look at Intersentence Grammar." *The Reading Teacher* 30 (October 1976): 28–32.

Discusses the need for analysis of psycholinguistic factors in understanding comprehension problems.

Oliver, Marvin E. "Reading Word Pictures," in *Making Readers of Everyone.* Kendall/Hunt Publishing Co., 1976, pp. 101–29.

Specific suggestions on ways of teaching comprehension skills such as inviting imaginative response to literature, questioning students about their mental pictures, and using dramatics.

12

Learning
Disabilities

Why is it that Wayne, who is intelligent, interested, and has no vision or hearing problems, is unable to build a sight vocabulary and, after four years of good basic instruction, is still reading on a first-grade level?

Why does Stewart, who can reason out arithmetic problems well, mix up the order of the numerals when he writes his answer? And why is his handwriting so jumbled as to be illegible?

Why is Jim distracted by every sound or movement—even when the class is discussing the subjects that are most interesting to him?

All these boys have specific learning disabilities and are, therefore, unable to learn to read readily when taught by the usual classroom procedures. They are not unlike the many children in remedial reading programs who are there because they have learning disabilities. Consequently, the remedial reading teacher must recognize those pboblems and know how to help a child with any specific disability.

What Are Specific Learning Disabilities?

A learning disability in reading can be defined as any disorder in one or more of the basic psychological processes, which results in a child's inability to learn to read at a level commensurate with his general mental ability. The child with a learning disability can be differentiated from other "remedial readers" in that his difficulty is not caused by poor instruction, poor background, or other outside influences, or by such physical disabilities as poor vision or hearing. Rather, it is caused by an innate lack in some mental process needed for learning to read by the usual procedures.

Characteristics of Children with Learning Disabilities

Diagnosis of learning disabilities must be made on the basis of a *general* pattern, or the presence of several of a number of possible characteristics, rather than on any specific pattern. The most common characteristics of children with learning disabilities can be grouped together under two main types:

1. *Distractibility:* Short attention span, hyperactivity, perserveration, poor motor control, and problems in visual motor coordination.

2. *Perception difficulties:* Problems in visual perception, visual memory, auditory perception; problems with conceptual relationships, self concept, body image, time-space relationships, and, perhaps, lack of established lateral dominance.

Any or all of these factors may be present in varying degrees in any individual with a learning disability.

More than fifty different terms are used by different writers and organizations to identify the child with learning disabilities. Terms such as "dyslexia," "word blind," and "specific reading disabilities" are considered most descriptive of the effect of learning disabilities on reading, although "minimal brain injury" and "the neurologically handicapped child" are preferred by many educators. Emphasis upon perceptual problems and lack of motor control have brought into common usage such terms as "perceptual-motor handicap," "hyperactivity," and "hyperkinesis." Since most preschool children demonstrate characteristics similar to the older child with learning disabilities, terms such as "developmental language delays" are also appropriate.

Regardless of what title is used, the teacher and the diagnostician should be very cautious about labeling the child. Too often, a label given to a child in his early schooling creates prejudices in his future teachers and is used as an excuse for not teaching him rather than as a way of understanding him and adapting instruction to his needs. Labels are also often misunderstood and misused by parents and the general public. Emphasis, therefore, should be placed upon describing each child's specific deficits in such a way that instruction can be adapted to his particular needs.

Causes of Learning Disabilities

Learning disabilities may be of either a genetic or acquired nature. For example, some cases may be the result of injury before, during, or after birth, from high fever, or from a lack of oxygen to the brain during or after birth.

It is not necessary that the teacher know for certain the causes of a particular child's disability, and, indeed, the teacher cannot diagnose a child as having brain damage by herself; nonetheless, it is the teacher who must decide on treatment. As a result, it is her analyses of the characteristics that is important, because it is on these that the planning for the appropriate instruction must be based.

General Diagnostic Procedures

There is no one test which will identify all children with learning disabilities; nor is there any one specific pattern of test scores which will identify them. Since there are so many types of learning disabilities, they must be identified through both observation and patterns of test scores which indicate disabilities in certain areas.

Many of the characteristics typical of children with learning disabilities will be found in the normal preschool child. It is their persistence beyond the normal time that evidences a true learning disability.

Because symptoms vary with each child, teaching methods must vary accordingly. Specific methods must be developed to meet the needs determined through diagnosis. Since immaturity, emotional problems, and other factors may result in similar symptoms, it is best to rule out all other factors before concluding that a child's problems are caused by learning disabilities.

Exact diagnosis is easiest to accomplish if the child is about eight years of age. However, most learning disabilities *can* be identified when the children are between five and one-half and six years of age, and the chances of successful remediation are good if the problem is discovered before the age of eight.

Observation

Careful observation is the most important factor in the identification of a child with learning disabilities. Every child will display some of the characteristics expected of the child with learning disabilities at times. It is the persistence of a number of these signs that leads the teacher to a hypothesis of learning disabilities.

Some of the signs of possible learning disabilities to which all teachers should be alert are:

Significantly better performance in arithmetic than reading.

Poor word recognition in comparison to other reading skills.

Hyperactivity—the inability to sit still while working.

Distractibility—the inability to concentrate on that which is interesting to him when there are other sounds or movement around him.

Difficulty in recognizing likenesses and differences in similar spoken or printed words.

Inability to draw simple shapes.

Reversals of letters and order of letters in writing or change of order of sounds in a word when reading that persists beyond the first stages of reading and writing.

Lack of coordination in writing or walking.

Repetition of the same errors when he attempts to correct them.

Very poor ability to follow oral directions.

Great variability in performance in different areas.

Lack of ability to organize work.

Slowness in finishing work.

By watching carefully for the symptoms just listed, the teacher can identify children who may have problems because of learning disabilities. However, diagnosis is always tentative and needs to be verified by continued observation. In addition, simply identifying the child as having a learning disability does not indicate exactly what his problems are or how he can be helped. The more information that is obtained regarding the particular child's disabilities, the better instruction can be geared to meet his needs. Therefore, careful observation does not end with identification of a child with learning disabilities. Instead, it becomes even more important as work with the child progresses.

Parent Interview

Parent interviews can be very helpful in identifying a child with a specific learning disability, especially if the child is just starting to school. Questions such as the following in a parent interview may uncover valuable information for the teacher of such a child:

Is he now receiving medication of any kind?

Did his parents or other members of the family have difficulty with reading or spelling?

Was he premature?

Were there any problems during or immediately after birth?

Has he had any head injuries?

Does he enjoy games requiring coordination, such as jacks, marbles, baseball, or rope jumping?

Can he return easily to a place he has been by using his sense of direction?

Has he had any serious ailments, such as convulsions or encephalitis, or been hospitalized for any reason?

Has he had any high fevers?

Achievement Tests

The child with learning disabilities in reading will usually be lower in reading than in arithmetic computation and will also be lower in word recognition than in other reading skills.

Psychological Tests

The following tests are followed by some of the indications of a learning disability which the individual experienced in mental testing might detect:

Goodenough-Harris Draw-A-Man Test: A score lower than the child's actual mental age.

Bender Gestalt: A score lower than the child's actual mental age.

Learning Potential Examination: Scores on Visual Memory, Symbolic Representation, and Symbol Identification which are lower than scores on other sections of the test, or score on Listening Comprehension which is lower than any other scores.

WISC (Weschler Intelligence Scale for Children): A Verbal IQ score below 100 and fifteen points or more below performance; scores for Arithmetic, Digit Span, Information, and/or similarities which are lower than scores in other areas.

In addition to the mental tests already listed, two tests definitely intended for children with learning disabilities are the *Slingerland Test* and the *ITPA (Illinois Test of Psycholinguistic Abilities).*

No one of the tests listed above will identify definitely a child with a learning disability. However, scores from one or more of these tests, combined with observation and other information, makes identification possible.

Determination of whether or not a child "has a learning disability" is not nearly so important as the identification of his specific learning characteristics, for it is on these that his instruction must be based.

General Instructional Procedures

Good teaching, accompanied by careful observation and a willingness to revise the teaching plan as needed, can make up for many omissions and mistakes in diagnosis. The teacher must plan instruction according to the best information available and then keep trying different approaches until something works. Instruction for children with learning disabilities should always be planned for two purposes: to strengthen the weak areas and to build on those areas in which the child can do well—as a substitute for the areas in which he is weak. The emphasis should always be on the areas of strength. Many teachers and their pupils have become discouraged when they were making little or no progress because they were spending all their effort in trying to do the impossible. As an example, we might consider a child who is low in visual memory but has good auditory perception; with this child, some time may be spent using such techniques as kinesthetic training to build some whole-word recognition of nonphonetic words, but the major emphasis should be on giving him a thorough grounding in phonics so that he can sound out the words as he comes to them.

It is obvious that there can be no single type of instruction for all children with learning disabilities, although this is occasionally attempted in some schools. An individualized program must be planned according to the needs of each child.

Instruction for children with learning disabilities must be thoroughly planned for sequential development. All instructions to the pupils must be clear, concise, and brief. At the same time, the teacher must be consistent in her handling of the child with learning disabilities. The same rules and expectations must apply each day. The teacher must be firm, but the child must be able to see that her purpose is to benefit him. Although standards must be met, these standards must be based on the child's ability to follow them. The child must feel that he has the freedom to do that which will help him learn, and he must not be criticized for that which he cannot help.

Some children may have become so discouraged and upset by their inability to learn to read that they may have completely withdrawn from learning. In such cases, beginning with an attempt at reading will be impossible. Games, using behavior modification techniques, walks, and outdoor activities with the teacher may be the necessary first step with these children. Sorting, coloring, story-telling, arts, crafts, and drama may then lead into an "experience story" approach to actual reading.

The majority of children with learning disabilities need their work programmed in such a way that there will be continual reinforcement and overlearning of all skills taught.

Classroom Arrangements for Learning Disabled Children

Only a very few children with learning disabilities are so handicapped as to need to have all their instruction in special classes. Most can be handled, appropriately, in the regular classroom. However, it is important that the classroom teacher have a good understanding of their problems and adapt their instruction to their individual learning styles. Too often, the hyperactive or distractible child is considered a discipline problem and is treated as an intentionally disruptive child. This may only aggravate his problems since he cannot understand why he is penalized when he is doing his best. Likewise, the child with visual or auditory perception problems may be expected to participate in the regular basic reading program, and finds that he is able to make little or no progress.

If the learning disabled child can receive his reading instruction from a reading teacher who does a thorough diagnosis of his strengths and weaknesses, and adapts the instruction to his individual needs, he can usually make good progress. This may be in the regular classroom, with a program planned cooperatively between the classroom teacher and the reading specialist, in a remedial reading room, or in a special education resource room.

It is very important that the resource room teacher who is to work with children with learning disabilities has had thorough training in remedial reading techniques. If the resource room teacher is less skilled in the teaching of reading than the classroom teacher, placement in the resource room may not be helpful.

With the present emphasis on mainstreaming all types of special education students, most classroom teachers are now getting some training which will help them understand the diagnosis of the learning disabled student and carry out the recommended specialized instruction.

Distractibility

The distractible child often appears inattentive in the classroom, although, actually, his problem is one of attention to too many different things—a hyper-awareness of all stimuli, whether they be visual, auditory, or tactile. He is simply *so aware* that he is unable to sort out and ignore those stimuli which are irrelevant. Therefore, he is distracted by sounds, or movement, which may not even be noticed by the other children in the classroom who are concentrating on the task at hand.

Distractibility manifests itself in several ways. There are those children who simply appear to be inattentive. No matter what is happening, no matter how interested the child is in the book he is reading or in the discussion that is going on around him, he cannot help being distracted by any movement or noise around him.

Another form of distractibility is hyperactivity. The hyperactive child also reacts to every stimulus, but his reaction manifests itself through motion. He is unable to inhibit the muscular activity which results from every minor stimulus.

Another, although much less common, reaction of the distractible child is hypoactivity, the problem of the apparently lethargic, lazy daydreamer. Although this student may appear to be inattentive, his problem, in reality, may stem from over-attention. While he sits quietly at his desk and appears to be absorbed in his work, he is actually attracted by page numbers, marks on the page, a scratch in the desk, and other things which are not noticed by other busy students.

Another aspect of this same hyperattentiveness is perseveration—the inability to change activity. Perseveration and hyperactivity will be discussed separately, since they each may require special treatment, although most of the suggestions made for distractible children apply also to the hyperactive child.

In teaching the distractible child, the teacher will need to remove as many unnecessary stimuli as possible from the environment. There should be no extra materials in sight. The child should be away from any children carrying on other activities and in the quietest, least distracting part of the room—in a study cubicle if possible. Even distractions caused by such materials as bright pictures can interfere. Therefore, for some distractible children, the linguistic readers which have no pictures at all are appropriate.

Silence may be golden, but it is sometimes unattainable. In fact, a nearly quiet room may be more distracting for some children than a noisy one. When a quiet room is disrupted by an unexpected noise, even the "normal" child is distracted. Increased background noise and activity to reduce the effect of any one interference or soft background music work well for some children, although not at all for others, in reducing the effect of any one interference.

Total class oral reading, which was described in chapter 8 has been found to be very effective with distractible children, even though this may seem contradictory.

The teacher can use another contradictory method: Children are distracted from their work by objects and bright colors, but they also can be distracted from other stimuli to their work. One can try a strip of bright red construction paper down the left side of the page or give the child a brightly colored marker to use above the line of print.

Diagnostic and instructional procedures for work with the distractible child are summarized in Instructional Guide 12.1.

Hyperactivity

"Hyperactivity," or "hyperkinesis," is one manifestation of distractibility and is a very common learning disability in children. Hyperkinesis

INSTRUCTIONAL GUIDE 12.1

Distractibility

Characteristics	Diagnosis	Recommendations
Reacting to all stimuli; inability to screen out the unimportant. Distraction by sounds, movement, bright colors, sunlight. Dissociation.	Is low on arithmetic and digit span section of *WISC*. According to observation during testing and instruction is inattentive and has a short attention span for age. Has poor memory. Apparently is day dreaming. **Does more poorly on picture number 7 than other parts of** *Visual Memory Test.*	Do not make him exceed his attention span. Remove distractions. Break teaching into small parts. Give short assignments. Give one piece of work at a time. Use simple materials. Cut book—use one story at a time. Have student use marker—or finger—above line. Remove unnecessary stimuli. Make the classroom plain. Use no pictures. Have no materials in sight. Use cubicles. Have student face walls. Use calming music. Discourage an overabundance of activity. Use a metronome. Use colored paper on book. Use books without pictures. Bring student back to situation by reminder—use name, etc.

may also be termed "motor disinhibition." While it is natural for most children to be active, to move their arms and legs about, and to change position frequently, most children inhibit most of those actions which are aimless or which are not suitable to the situation. The hyperkinetic child is unable to inhibit these excessive motions. Consequently, he is often considered a disturbing influence in the room, and his teacher may interpret his aimless motions as intentional flaunting of the rules.

In some cases, the child is so hyperactive that he is unable to sit still and concentrate long enough to learn. Teaching in short units separated by activity often helps such a child. Teaching in a small space also helps. If the child is working in a walled-in four-by-four cubicle, he may lose his tendency toward impulsive activity almost completely.

Individual instruction in an absolutely quiet room with almost no outside stimulus is necessary for some extremely hyperactive children. Others react well in the opposite situation—an overcrowded room with a dozen different activities going on at once, so many stimuli that they simply cannot react to all of them.

Understanding and creating a lack of tension—relaxing and letting the child relax—are essential aspects of instruction for the hyperactive child. The touch of the teacher or parent may help the hyperkinetic child to gain control of his activity. Often, a calming hand on the shoulder is all that is needed.

Many children lose some of the tendency toward hyperkinesity when they reach puberty. Others learn to control their activity.

Some of the diagnostic and instructional procedures for working with the hyperactive child are summarized in Instructional Guide 12.2. Since this is really one aspect of distractibility, suggestions in Instructional Guide 12.1 are also applicable.

INSTRUCTIONAL GUIDE 12.2

Hyperkinesis

Characteristic	Diagnosis	Recommendations
Excessive activity.	Observation: Kicks, runs	Teach in small units.
Impulsiveness.	about, pushes other chil-	Reduce space.
Twitchings.	dren, waves arms.	Help child to relax.
Fidgeting.	Is in constant motion.	Decrease stimuli; do not
Inability to sit still.	Talks in disorganized tor-	use games and stimulat-
Inability to stay in seat.	rents.	ing activities.
Inability to stay with one	Responds to any object	Watch for frustration
activity.	which can be bent,	level and change activity.
Hands, legs, body always	twisted, pushed, pulled.	Use materials that re-

INSTRUCTIONAL GUIDE 12.2 *(continued)*

Characteristic	*Diagnosis*	*Recommendations*
moving. Excessive response to stimulation. Low tolerance for stress and frustration. Unpredictibility. Sudden letting off of stored-up energy when attempting to work quietly. Jumping from one activity to another. In older child, constant moving of leg, tapping of desk, talking too much without purpose.	or be inserted with fingers. Use a pedometer or actometer to measure student's activity. Can be identified earlier than any other learning disability—sometimes at age one month. Is hyperactive. Cries easily.	quire muscular activity. Find positive outlets for energy. Structure program so that it is simple and well planned. Be sure student knows what to do every minute. Try overstimulation. Use drug therapy if it is helpful. Caution: Do not scold or punish; they do not help. Realize that his movement cannot be inhibited consciously. Use special classes using behavioral modification techniques.
Little goal directed behavior. Begins many things, completes few. Inability to inhibit his impulsivity. Explosive, unpredictable behavior. Teacher and parents feel that child is always into things that don't concern him. Gets wound up and over-excited easily. Temper tantrums. Takes correction poorly. Accident prone. More vocal than other children. Comments often unrelated to subject being discussed. Restless sleep.	Scores on the following tests lower than other ability tests: *Goodenough Harris Draw-a-Person Test; Bender Visual-Motor Gestalt Test; Lincoln Oseretsky Motor Development Scale.*	Structure goals the child wants to reach. Accept child's goals. Keep emotions under control. Calm treatment. Extreme patience. Have time-out area available where child can go when needed. Use clear, simple instructions. Watch for pending tantrums and offer alternative distraction. Avoid rigid scheduling of fixed length activities. Help child control own activity through self-reminders such as loosely tied seat belt.

Perseveration

Perseveration is the inability to change from one activity to another. Although it appears to be the antithesis of distractibility and hyperactivity, it is really another aspect of the same disability—overattention to stimuli—and is often found in the hyperactive child. The child seems to "get hooked" by one stimulus and cannot change to another. It is as if he is "in a rut" and cannot get out of it.

Suggested diagnosis and treatment for perseveration are summarized in Instructional Guide 12.3.

INSTRUCTIONAL GUIDE 12.3

Perseveration

Characteristics	Diagnosis	Instruction
Inability to change activity. Continuing activity even though student is upset by it. Writing same error over and over. Repeating words or sentences over and over. Having trouble shifting from one idea to another. Inability to quit at end of song.	Study samples of school work: kind and number of errors made. Tries to correct spelling—spells same way. Use *Learning Potential Exam*—Visual Memory Test (Pictures 8, 10, and 11; type of errors made should be checked). *Bender-Gestalt* continues design.	Do not continue practice at time. Change activity. Change types of drill. Make work more meaningful. Eliminate repetitive drill. When repeating orally, say, "You said that. Now what else do you want to say?" Discontinue activity, then, at a later date, start again, making sure the task is done right the first time.
Talking incessantly about the same subject. Asking same questions repeatedly.	Disorganized but intense interest in one subject.	Have patience and do not react emotionally to talkativeness.

Drug Therapy

Drug therapy has become a much-used tool in the treatment of certain types of learning disabilities, particularly hyperkinesis. Drug therapy is based upon the discovery that changes in the body chemistry of the majority of hyperactive children will enable them to learn more effectively. There are three ways in which this body chemistry can be influenced: by the administration of drugs, by the administration of large doses of certain vitamins, and by dietary changes.

If treatment other than drugs is found to be effective for any individual child, the other treatment would usually be preferable. However, it is much better to treat the extremely hyperkinetic child with drug therapy than to fail to treat him at all until he has become both educationally and socially maladjusted.

Millichap (1968, p. 1527) states that: "Drugs are useful in the symptomatic treatment of hyperactive and perceptually handicapped children, but their administration should be preceded by a careful clinical evaluation. On the basis of present evidence, short-term trials of drugs are justified as an adjunct to remedial methods of education. . . ." The use of central nervous system stimulants and mood-modifying agents for prolonged periods should await further evaluation by long-term studies.

Drug therapy has been found to be effective in reducing hyperactivity in about two-thirds of the cases treated. The drugs found to be most effective for this purpose are the amphetamines or stimulants. Paradoxically, these drugs do not stimulate the hyperkinetic child as they would an adult. "Rather, they appear to mobilize and to increase the child's abilities to focus on meaningful stimuli and to organize his bodily movements more purposefully."[1] The stimulant drugs which, up to the present, have been found most effective are methylphenidate hydrochloride (Retalin) and dextroamphetamine (Dexedrine).

Other types of drugs which are sometimes used effectively with certain individual children with learning disabilities are anticonvulsants, antidepressants, and tranquilizers.

There are four possible problems in the use of drug therapy which should be of concern to those considering drug therapy for children:

1. *Psychological effects.* The physician knows of these possibilities and can alert parents and teachers, who can aid in detecting problems through careful observation.

2. *Faulty diagnosis.* Learning disabilities are difficult to diagnose, either for the neurologist or the educator. Close cooperation among the doctor, the teacher, and the parents is essential in both diagnosis and in determination of the effectiveness of the therapy.

---

[1] United States Department of Health, Education, and Welfare, *Report of the Conference on the Use of Stimulant Drugs in the Treatment of Behaviorally Disturbed Young School Children* (Washington: Government Printing Office, January 11-12, 1971), pp. 6–8.

3. *Possible addiction.* To prevent addiction, care in using only the required dosage is important. Drugs should not be prescribed for continuous use over long periods of time, and their use should be discontinued for short periods at intervals—of perhaps every six months—to determine their effectiveness and the need for continuation.

4. *Reliance on drugs instead of self-discipline.* Every individual must learn to regulate his own behavior. However, in some cases, it is impossible for a child to learn any self-control without medical assistance.

There are alternatives to drug therapy for some children. A New York group headed by Dr. Allan Cott, a psychiatrist, has had excellent results in controlling hyperactivity with massive doses of vitamins B_2, B_3, B_6, C, and E, along with high protein diets. The treatment requires more time to work than does drug therapy, but it is expected to have a long-lasting effect. An added bonus is that there is no danger of side effects or eventual addiction.[2]

Dietary changes can help a child who is hyperactive because of imbalances caused either by an imbalanced diet or by the inability of the particular child's system to assimilate certain foods effectively. The parents of the hyperactive child should check to see that the child's diet contains an adequate amount of protein and that there is not an excess of sweets in it. If there is any question regarding the child's diet, all sweets should be removed from the child's diet for a time.[3] Other diet items which may cause hyperactivity in certain children are carbonated beverages and wheat products.

Perceptual Problems

The world is perceived through the five senses, but reading is dependent upon only two of these, vision and hearing. Therefore, disability in the use of either of these senses results in great difficulty in learning to read.

Perception should not be confused with acuity. A person may have perfect visual and auditory acuity (that is, he may make perfect scores on vision tests and on the audiometer) yet have serious perception problems for "perception" is the ability to gain a *true* and *accurate* mental

---

[2] Frederick C. Klein, "New Techniques Help Pupils Who Can't Grasp Fundamental Concepts," *The Wall Street Journal,* 17 (November 1970): 1,20.

[3] "A Hyperactive Child Needs Nutrients, Not Drugs," *Prevention* 23, 4 (April 1971): 169–76.

picture of what is seen and heard. If there are abnormalities in the neural pathways which carry the information to the brain or process it once it is in the brain, the result may be in the form of inexact concepts. Many of the children who have learning disabilities in reading have difficulty because of problems in either auditory or visual perception.

Auditory Perception

Although it is more difficult to differentiate between different auditory perception problems than between problems in visual perception, auditory perception skills can be grouped under three headings:

1. Auditory acuity

2. Auditory conceptualization

   a. Auditory discrimination

   b. Auditory comprehension

3. Auditory sequential memory

   a. Auditory sequencing

   b. Auditory memorization

Although all of these skills are related, their effect upon learning can be quite different.

Auditory acuity. Auditory acuity is the ability to hear sounds of different tones and volumes. It is discussed in chapter 5.

Auditory conceptualization. Even though he hears all the sounds clearly, a child may not gain a clear mental image of what he has heard. The sounds may seem to come to him in a confused manner or their meaning may not be clear to him. This distortion of the message between the ear and the brain means that the child's concept of what he has heard will not be the same as that of others who hear the same sounds. To have good auditory conceptualization, a person must have both auditory discrimination and auditory comprehension, plus the ability to interpret these correctly.

Auditory discrimination. This is the ability to hear small differences in words. The child with auditory discrimination problems may be able to attain a perfect score on all tones of a hearing test yet not be able to recognize the small differences in words, such as the difference between the sounds of the letters *k* and *t* or between the words *pin* and *pen*.

Until the student can develop good auditory discrimination, he will have difficulty applying phonics. Therefore, if his visual memory is good, the teacher should place emphasis on the building of a sight vocabulary. However, phonetic instruction still should also have an important place in this child's program, for auditory discrimination usually can be improved. Instruction in phonics serves the double purpose of teaching the needed skills and also improving auditory discrimination. Auditory discrimination practice materials commonly used in beginning reading programs are also helpful.

Auditory comprehension.   A child with auditory comprehension problems may have trouble understanding what he has heard. Although he has heard all of the sounds distinctly, it is as if they have become jumbled and, therefore, do not have the expected meaning. He is simply unable to organize what he hears into something meaningful. In addition, he usually will have poor memory for spoken material, and his comprehension will vary greatly from day to day.

Poor auditory comprehension should not be confused with poor listening habits, although poor listening does lead to poor comprehension. It is very difficult, except by much careful observation, to determine which of these is the cause of the child's poor comprehension.

Auditory sequential memory.   Auditory sequential memory depends upon two skills, *auditory memorizing* and *auditory sequencing;* that is, it depends upon the ability to remember a group of sounds and the ability to recall the order in which they occurred (a sort of mental picturing of the pattern).

Many children who show few, if any, other signs of learning disability have difficulty in auditory sequential memory. For these children, the most obvious indication of difficulty is their great problem in learning to spell and in remembering names. If they are highly intelligent, they usually will learn to read well with good comprehension and very slow speed by fourth grade, although they still will be unable to spell well. Since they spell phonetically rather than by memory, they usually have particular difficulty with sounds which can be represented in several ways (e.g., *ow, au, aw, ough*). They often will go to any extent to avoid memorizing any material. They usually do well on tests of coordination and visual memory, except that they may reverse some symbols. Those who do well in visual memory will have no difficulty remembering or distinguishing letter shapes (choosing those that are alike, etc.) in beginning reading but will have trouble remembering the names of the letters.

Diagnostic and instructional methods for children with auditory perception problems are summarized in Instructional Guide 12.4.

INSTRUCTIONAL GUIDE 12.4

Auditory Perception

Characteristic	Diagnosis	Recommendations
Auditory Acuity		
Poor hearing. Monotone speech. See Instructional Guide 5.5 for other characteristics	Use audiometer test. Use articulation test.	Seat with best ear near teacher. Refer to physician. Always face child when speaking. Use visual methods and visual aids. See Instructional Guide 5.5.
Auditory Discrimination Inability to tell differences or similarities in similar words. Difficulty with phonics. Possible mild speech problems. Poor reproduction of tonal patterns. *Auditory Comprehension* Frequent misunderstanding. Inability to organize what he hears into something meaningful to him. Poor memory for spoken material. Little or no impairment in speech.	Use *Goldman-Fristoe-Woodcock Test of Auditory Discrimination.* Use *Wepman Test of Auditory Discrimination.* Use *Monroe Auditory Discrimination Test.* Use Listening Comprehension section *Durrell* or *Learning Potential* tests. Frequently asks, "What did you say?" Misquotes statements using similar sounds but different meaning. Use *Hearing of Speech Tests.* Use *Brown-Carlson Listening Comprehension Test* (grade 9 and up).	Emphasize visual learning when possible. Teach complete phonics. Improve auditory discrimination through: rhyming, readiness materials, phonetic instruction, music. If student is distractible, have him practice letters singly without distraction of pictures. Use tape recorder. Have him listen to story as he reads it. Have him record and then listen to his own reading. Use listening comprehension exercises, such as SRA. Have him listen for and identify sounds of cars, planes, animals, children in next room, recorded

Characteristics	*Diagnosis*	*Recommendations*
		sounds, food sounds, rhythmic patterns. Blindfold games for locating sounds. Seat where he can see best and use blackboard for explanation. When student doesn't understand, paraphrase, find new ways to explain, demonstrate.

Auditory Sequential Memory

Poor ability in oral memorizing, especially sequencing—both for long and short memory. Hatred of memorizing; preference for reasoning. Poor memory for names. Poor sight vocabulary. Reading phonetically. No difficulty distinguishing or remembering letters, only their names. Poor performance in following sequence of instructions.	Use *ITPA*—Auditory-vocal association. Use *WISC*—Digit Span-Backward. Use *Detroit Test of Memory Span.* Ask how many phone numbers he remembers. Has many reversals when under pressure. Omits sounds or syllables in speech. Use *Oliphant Auditory Discrimination Memory Test.* Use *Oliphant Auditory Synthesizing Test.* Use *Roswell-Chall Auditory Blending Test.*	Teach letter sounds and then teach student to read words phonetically. Hold interest; this is essential. Change activity often. Use activity. Teach word recognition through writing and spelling. Use interesting topics. Be enthusiastic.
Very poor performance in spelling; spells phonetically Comprehension high, but speed is low compared to total reading. If he is highly intelligent, he learns to read well slowly but still cannot spell. Oral language usually good.	Use a spelling test which includes words not spelled by rules. Ask if he spells phonetically? See if he has trouble with words in which spelling depends on meaning. Determine whether parents speak a foreign language.	Teach phonics and spelling rules. Build word recognition through experiences. Check his spelling to see if he spells words phonetically. Use plays—act them out. Do not hurry. Forget reading for speed until his other skills are good.

INSTRUCTIONAL GUIDE 12.4 *(continued)*

Characteristics	Diagnosis	Recommendations
Good ability in working with three-dimensional spatial relationships. Usually well co-ordinated in both hands.	Achievement tests which should be included are: reading comprehension, reading speed, spelling (He will be low on last two tests). Has good visual memory test except for reversals. Uses tools well.	Use many pictures, maps, and activities.

Visual Perception

Visual perception is the ability to see a thing and perceive it as it is. This is much more than mere visual acuity, or good vision. The visual perceptual skills which a child needs in learning to read effectively can be divided, for the sake of discussion, into eight areas: visual acuity, visual discrimination, visual imagery, figure-ground constancy, visual conceptualization, visual memory, time and space relationships, and visual-motor coordination.

It is important that deficiencies in visual perception be detected early so that a program can be planned to help the child adjust to those deficiencies. Some time should be spent attempting to help the child develop those visual skills which he lacks; however, the majority of the time should be spent in teaching his reading skills through auditory and other methods. In too many programs, the greater part of the time is spent trying to build missing perceptual skills unsuccessfully. Learning to read through the child's strengths should always receive more emphasis than trying to build up his weak areas.

Visual acuity.   Visual acuity is simply good vision or the ability to see clearly.

Visual discrimination.   Visual discrimination is the ability to see small differences in words. Many children with learning disabilities do not notice these small differences. They may recognize many words by the first letter only. As a result, they may leave off suffixes and endings such as *ed* and *ing.* Most good readiness tests have sections for evaluating visual discrimination; indeed, readiness materials may be used for practice for older children with visual discrimination problems. The more similar the material used in the visual discrimination practice is to reading material, the more carry-over there will be, and the more valuable the activity will be for developing reading ability.

Visual imagery. Visual imagery is the ability to form a clear and exact mental picture. This ability is sometimes referred to as "visual form perception" or as "visual form constancy." The child with a disability in this area has difficulty recognizing a letter as being the same letter when it is larger or smaller than what he has learned to expect. He cannot determine the size, shape, and texture of an object visually.

Manipulation of objects is necessary for the development of visual imagery. Most children learn visual imagery early in life through handling objects—a transfer of tactile imagery to visual imagery. Thus, visual imagery can be improved through handling materials, tracing around stencils, and using materials such as the "Perceptual Constancy" section of the Frostig Program.[4]

However, the majority of the time should be spent, not on attempting to build the visual skills which the child lacks, but on circumventing his deficiencies as much as possible by using auditory and kinesthetic methods. As Ackerman (1971) states, "It may well be that in many cases, remedial specialists are wasting their efforts teaching form perception skills, and that better remediation could be achieved by attacking verbal deficiencies straightforward." Harris (1976) reinforces this with the statement that "the limited time available can be spent more profitably in direct teaching of needed reading skills than in attempting to build up supposedly deficient abilities."

Visual memory. This is the ability to retain a visual image. Visual memory problems are quite common, and teaching methods must always be adjusted to compensate for them, if the child is to learn. If, after seeing a word, the child is not able to retain an exact mental image of that word, he will not be able to know which word he is seeing when he encounters a similar word.

Normal visual memory varies greatly. Each child is on a continuum—a normal curve somewhere between a photographic memory and an almost complete lack of visual memory. What methods of learning to read will work for him depend upon his position on that continuum.

Serious visual memory problems are usually easily identified by means of visual memory tests in which the subject looks at a design; the design is then covered, and he draws it from memory.

Two good visual memory tests are the "Visual Memory" section of the *Learning Potential Examination* and the Kendal-Graham *Memory for Designs Test.* The former was designed for identifying children with learning disabilities, including visual memory problems, distractibility, and perseveration. The latter was designed for identifying children with neurological problems and brain damage.

---

[4] Marianne Frostig and David Horne, *The Frostig Program for the Development of Visual Perception* (Chicago: Follett Publishing Company, 1964).

The child with visual memory problems should spend some time in learning recognition of some common nonphonetic words through kinesthetic tracing and in improvement of his visual memory. However, improvement in reading will be extremely slow by these processes. The majority of time should be spent in bypassing the visual memory problem and teaching reading through other channels, mostly phonetic.

The child with visual memory deficiencies will need to learn both consonants and vowels together so that he can sound out words completely. He also should become expert in the use of context.

Intelligent children whose visual memory was so poor that they could not learn to read, have been taught to read Braille. When they have become adept at reading and writing Braille, they have practiced reading identical content simultaneously in regular print and in Braille. In some cases they have learned to read regular print in this way.

Figure-ground constancy.   Figure-ground constancy is the ability to differentiate between the important and the unimportant. Many children are unable to distinguish between the main subject (the figure) and the extraneous material (the background) in a picture.

When a person looks at one particular item in a picture, he sees that item clearly and the rest of the items only vaguely. That item, then, becomes the figure and the rest become background. Until the child can do this—can choose which letters, words, or pictures, he will concentrate on and which he can more or less ignore—he has great difficulty in reading. He cannot concentrate on the word that needs to be recognized, and he is distracted by the pictures, the other words, and even marks on the paper.

Without the ability to differentiate figure from ground, the child cannot select the important elements in a complex situation and form a meaningful concept—a mental picture that will make sense to him and will help him to act upon the situation reasonably.

Figure-ground discrimination applies to auditory concepts as well as visual. When an individual is listening to one other person speak, he should be able to ignore all other sounds. The child with an auditory figure-ground disturbance cannot do this.

The relationship of figure-ground perception to distractibility is obvious. The distractible child is simply reacting to all the background stimuli as well as to the figure.

Figure-ground disturbance is closely associated with dissociation; (i.e., the inability to see the wholeness of a situation or thing—the ability to recognize each of the parts and integrate all of them into one meaningful whole). The ability to see the integrated wholeness of a thing is termed the Gestalt function. The child, then, whose problem is dissociation is unable to see the Gestalt of a situation or object—the way in which the parts form a completed whole. One test for dissociation, then, is to give the child incomplete pictures and see if he can complete them, to see whether he can visualize the figures as whole figures.

Visual conceptualization. Visual conceptualization refers to the ability to build clear concepts visually. Perception and thinking cannot be separated. Clear thinking requires exact perception. If a child does not see things as others see them and if he does not hear what others hear, then his concept of the world will be different from theirs.

In the regular classroom, there has been a tendency to shift away from arts and crafts and the use of three-dimensional objects for play and experimentation. However, these activities are very important if the child is to build the exact perceptions that lead to exact thinking. Visual conceptualization can also be improved through much discussion of pictures, experiments, observations, and experiences.

The building of true visual concepts is dependent upon all of the visual skills visual acuity, visual discrimination, visual imagery, figure-ground constancy, and visual memory. If a child has difficulty in any of these areas, his concepts will differ from those of other children.

Our concepts depend not only upon exact sensory perceptions, but also upon our background of experience, our cultural heritage, and the reactions of those around us to our previous expressions or concepts. Yet each individual is puzzled when other people's concepts do not agree with his because he assumes that others perceive the world as he does.

INSTRUCTIONAL GUIDE 12.5

Visual Perception

Characteristics	Diagnosis	Recommendations
Visual Acuity		
Near-sightedness. Far-sightedness. Strabismus, etc.	Use telebinocular test.	Refer student for glasses. Seat child in classroom according to his problem. Use easy sight materials.
Visual Discrimination		
Inability to see small differences in words, figures, or objects. Ignoring details of words. Confusion over letters.	Use *WISC*—Coding. Use *ITPA*. Use *Learning Potential*, Test 2—Symbolic Representation. Use *Developmental Survey of Basic Learning Abilities*.	Have child practice finding words that are alike or different. Use good readiness workbooks. Have child practice copying designs on pegboard.

Characteristics	Diagnosis	Recommendations
	Use Pegboard Test. Use Marbleboard Test. Use *Perceptual Forms Test.* Use *Contemporary School Readiness Test.* Use *Preschool Inventory.* Use *Minnesota Preschool Scale.* Use *Murphy-Durrell Reading Readiness Analysis.* Use any of most good readiness tests.	Have child match word cards for beginning letters. Have child underline words in story that begin alike. Have child match abstract figures. Begin with objects (only 2), have the child decide—alike or different. Have child sort sets of buttons by size, shape, color. Have child sort cut-out figures. Cut series of shapes, cut shapes in half. Have child match halves.

Visual Imagery

Inability to form a clear mental picture.	Use *Marianne Frostig Developmental Test of Visual Perception*—Part 3, Form Constancy test.	Teach letters kinesthetically; then emphasize phonics.
Inability to recognize a figure as being the same figure whether large or small. Difficulty reproducing symbols on paper—distortion of simple forms. Poor discrimination of size. Reversals. Poor spelling.	Use *WISC*—Object Assembly and Block Design. Use *Learning Potential*—Symbol Identification. Use *Weigl-Goldstein-Sheerer*—Color Form Sorting test. Copy squares, circles, triangles. Use *Developmental Test of Visual-Motor Integration.*	Teach subject matter through tapes. Improve visual imagery by: *Frostig program*—perceptual constancy, manipulation of objects, tracing letters and words with fingers, raised letters, tracing around templates. Have child build models from kits. Have child walk square, circles, etc., taped to floor. Use stencils and blocks. Have child copy block designs.

Characteristics	*Diagnosis*	*Recommendations*
		Have child assemble objects. Use Worksheets.

Visual Memory

Spelling errors—spelling is phonetic.	Give spelling test—Non-phonetic words will be spelled phonetically.	Teach phonics and spelling rules.
Inability to remember sight words. Inability to remember whole-word patterns. Confusion of similar letters. Poor memory of and reproduction of shapes. Difficulty in drawing. Consideration of jigsaw puzzles as being too difficult.	Use *Learning Potential*—Visual Memory. Use Kendal-Graham—*Memory for Designs*. Use Grace Arthur—*Stencil Design test*. Use *Benton Revised Visual Retention test*. Use *Ellis Visual Memory test*. Use *WISC*—Block Design, coding. Use *Bender Gestalt*. Use pegboard test. Use *Mills Learning Methods Test*. Use *Steinback Test of Reading Readiness—Memory for Word Forms*. Copy squares, triangles, circles. Use tachistoscopic test. Use *Spatial Orientation Memory Test*. Use *Word Discrimination Test*. Use *Benton Visual Retention Test*. Use *Primary Visual-Motor Test*.	Emphasize phonics. Emphasize auditory learning. Use a nonreading curriculum. Increase stimulus value of materials. Use oral impress method. Have child listen to taped story, following it with finger. Use Gillingham materials. Avoid use of sight vocabulary method. Use kinesthetic teaching. Use all the senses in teaching. Have child handle letter shapes with eyes closed. Use raised figures, beaded, felt, sandpaper. Have child write in hand, sand, clay, air. Have child make letters from clay and pipe cleaners. Help child make his body movement take shapes of letters. Have child draw around templates. Have child build models. Have child practice with pegboards.

Characteristics	*Diagnosis*	*Recommendations*
		Use jigsaw puzzles, form boards, stencils. Have child sort objects. Do Indian beadwork. Have child tell what is missing; start with two objects and keep adding. Have child identify parts missing from pictures. Use art projects. Have child practice with tachistoscope. Have him look at shapes, then draw with eyes closed. Have him look at word, cover, choose identical words from other word cards. Have child find a key word each time it is repeated in a paragraph. Have child determine if pair of words flashed are identical.
Inability to remember sequence of objects.	Use *WISC*–Picture Arrangement. Set up series cover; have child name series in order. Use *ITPA*–Visual Sequential Memory.	Have child string beads copying a pattern. Have child practice naming things in order. Cut comic strips apart and have child put them in order.
Figure-Ground Constancy		
Inability to distinguish important features. Inability to separate figure of interest from other parts. Dissociation; inability to see parts as parts and their relation to the whole Gestalt.	*Frostig*–Part I, "Figure-Ground Perception." *WISC*–"Picture Completion." *WISC*–"Object Assembly." *WISC*–"Block Design." Grace Arthur–*Stencil Design Test.*	In teaching words, instead of starting with the whole word, begin with parts and build to the whole. Use *Frostig*–Figure-Ground materials. Have child outline one figure among others.

304

Characteristics	*Diagnosis*	*Recommendations*
Seeing only parts and missing the whole. Inability to use small details meaningfully when there are also distracting stimuli. Difficulty in finding any object. Inattentive. disorganized. Appears disorganized or careless in approach to learning. Inability to find place in story. Confusion caused by crowded page. Inability to listen without noticing all background noise.	Gestalt Completion Test. Bender Visual Motor Gestalt Test. Use *Picture Interpretation Test.* Use *Learning Potential.* Part 6—"Picture Completion." Use *Syracuse Visual Figure-Background Test.* Is unable to pick out each figure in overlapping or superimposed figures. Use Strauss and Werner *Figure-Ground Discrimination* tests. Use Elking and Scott *Decentering of Perception* tests. Use Goldstein-Sheerer *Cube Test.* Use pegboard test. Use *Southern California Figure Ground Visual Perception Test.*	Have child outline one figure superimposed on others. Start with picture free of background and draw in background. Have child fill in missing parts in pictures, designs. signs. Use worksheets developed for purpose. Use three-dimensional objects. Have child outline or cut out one object from a magazine picture; gradually increase difficulty. Have child assemble two- and three-piece puzzles. Have child choose important items in a picture. Have child find hidden figure in a picture. Have child find a specific word on a page. Use anagrams.

Visual Conceptualization

All of the characteristics already listed in this guide. Indications in conversation that ideas of what he sees and hears are different. Difficulty with ideas of size and space. No problem with perception *per se,* but a problem with transferring perception into meaningful ideas.	Use *Learning Potential.* Part 3b—"Symbol Interpretation." Use *WISC*—"Picture Arrangement." Use *Ammons Full-Range Picture Vocabulary Test.* Describe an object and have child name it.	Have child handle concrete objects. Use arts and crafts. Use much discussion of pictures and observations. Use SRA *Lift Off to Reading.*

Time, Space, and Directional Concepts

A concept closely related to visual perception is the perception of space. A person who has difficulty in this area may have little concept of time, of location in space, or of direction. He may reverse a great many words in both reading and writing.

Time concepts develop later than most other perceptual concepts. Many children start to school with very little concept of time, although most children in our time-conscious society develop an understanding of time early in their school years, if not before. However, some do not. When discussing something that happened in the past, they are unable to tell whether it happened last week or last month. They may confuse first and last or make confusing statements like "after a while ago."

The reading teacher is concerned with time concepts only in their relation to sequential order and to understanding directional movement, which is also related to time. Many children with learning disabilities, especially the brain injured, have very little concept of location in space or of direction. Words such as "toward," "to the left of," and "under" have little meaning to them.

There are many tests which give indications of spatial orientation problems. The most obvious signs are mirror writing and rotations on visual memory tests. Ninty degree rotations (drawing a horizontal figure in a vertical position) are common with brain-damaged children.

In addition to the usual practice in drawing and in putting things in sequential order, practice in describing location and distance is helpful in developing concepts of both time and space. Going through mazes, tunnels, and monkey bars also helps.

A good sense of directional movement is essential for effective reading. Even though directional sense is not a natural skill for some people, it also can be a developed skill. The person who has much freedom of movement early, who walks a lot, and depends upon his sense of direction to get him where he is going develops both directional sense and understandings of time and space. These skills are helpful in developing the understanding of directional movement he needs for reading.

Reversals, both of letters and words, are natural in beginning reading, and since directional concepts develop later than many other concepts, children pushed into reading too early often make a great many reversals. There is nothing natural about going from right to left when looking at an object; nor is it natural to consider the letters *p* and *d* as being different. In fact, the child with a good sense of form constancy (recognition of a figure as being the same regardless of position or size) will have to be taught that letters are exceptions—that a letter turned the opposite way is not the same letter.

Reversals of words and letters usually are not consistent. If the child simply has not learned the difference between the two forms, he may give the name of either form. For example, he may say "was" when he sees either *was* or *saw* today, but since he has been taught both names for what seems to be the same symbol, he may call them both "saw" tomorrow—or he may happen to get both of them right. This inconsistency makes testing for reversals difficult. The fact that the child says all the words correctly today does not mean he will tomorrow.

There are many types of exercises which can be used to decrease reversals in reading by teaching directional sense. Kinesthetic tracing is a much-used method. When the kinesthetic method is used for teaching word recognition, it is done carefully and unhurriedly, with the words printed in manuscript to help the student get a clear picture of the word as he will see it in print, and the word is said, both before and after tracing. However, when it is used to eliminate reversals, the fingers should be moved over the letters very rapidly while the word is sounded, and the word may even be written in cursive form to give the feeling of left-to-right movement.

Practice in consonant substitution is useful for teaching directional orientation. For this purpose, it should always be the first letter that is changed, never the last. Likewise, word wheels when used for this purpose should have different beginnings only, not different endings.

The Controlled Reader, other similar machines, and the Iowa Reading Films are all used primarily to increase speed, but they are somewhat useful in developing left-to-right orientation in reading.

Other methods useful in improving directional attack are: dictionary and alphabetizing practice; writing dictated words phonetically; writing words in a column starting each word at the left edge of the chalkboard; and playing games such as "Consonant Lotto," the "Dog House Game," and other homemade games that call attention to the first letter of the word. Typing material with the first letter of each word in red sometimes helps, while another useful procedure is following with the finger while reading. For this purpose, the finger must move smoothly and steadily forward and not stop under each word.

Hand dominance has been greatly overemphasized in terms of its relationship to reading. There is very little research to indicate that the naturally right-handed child has any advantage over the naturally left-handed child. However, there is evidence that the child whose handedness has been changed and the one who has not established either the right or left hand as dominant is somewhat more apt to have problems in reading and speech.

Characteristics and methods of identifying deficiencies in time, space, and directional orientation are listed in Instructional Guide 12.6.

Time, Space, and Directional Orientation Problems

Characteristics	Diagnosis	Recommendations

Time

Little concept of time. Lack of understanding of days of week, time of day, months of year. Inability to relate time to distance.	Has poor reproduction of rhythmic patterns. Ask questions: What day is this? How long until Saturday?	Use questioning. Use discussion.
Difficulty carrying out activities in sequence.	Carry out written sequential instructions.	Have child build models following written instructions.
Difficulty remembering auditory sequence.	Use *WISC*—Digit Span.	Give oral directions to be carried out in order stated.

Space

Little understanding of position in space. Confusion in meaning of "toward," "away," "from," "ahead," "behind."	Use *ITPA*—Automatic Sequential Test. Use *Frostig* test, Part 5—Spatial Relationships. Check for rotations on *Visual Memory* test and *Bender Gestalt.* Use *WISC*—Picture Completion, Block Design, and Object Assembly.	Use *Frostig Program.* Have child practice putting things in, on, by, to the right of, etc. Have child imitate instructor's position. Use drawings and exercises that require moving hands across center line of body.

Direction

Confusion in meanings of "up," "down," "north," "south."	Use *Frostig Program,* Part 4—Position in Space. Reverses pictures on *Visual Memory Test.* Use Money—*Road Map Test of Directional Sense.* Use *WISC*—Picture Arrangement. Notice Difficulty with crossed commands: "Put	Use marching drills. Play games like "Looby Loo," "Oh! Johnny," and "Simon Says." Choose from pictures of right and left hand.

Characteristics	Diagnosis	Recommendations

your right hand on your left ear."

Reversals

Reversals in reading and writing.
Trying to start sounding a word with a letter other than the beginning letter, such as *o* in "done" and *th* in "mother."

Reversal of letters such as *b* for *d.*
Changing order of letter sounds.
Reversing entire word, as "was" for "saw."

Makes frequent reversals in reading, spelling, and writing.
Use *Test of Individual Needs*, Word Analysis Section—Reversals.
Use *Durrell Analysis of Reading Difficulty*—Word Analysis.
Listen to oral reading.

Use readiness materials to teach left-to-right movement.
Use kinesthetic teaching to emphasize direction.
Have child practice words in context with all of word blanked out except for beginning letter (cloze procedure with beginning letter on omitted words).
Have child start writing at the extreme left edge of the paper.
Have child trace words.
Have child use a typewriter.
Have child practice confusing words with flash cards and tachistoscope.
Have child practice consonant substitution, changing first letter of word.
Use *Frostig Program.*
Use the Controlled Reader.
Play games that call attention to the first letter.
Place orange paper down the left side of the page to be read.
Teach thoroughly one of words such as "was" and "saw" that are confused before teaching the other word.
Write letters on chalkboard. Have child circle

Characteristics	Diagnosis	Recommendations
		those that make a word, then write the word. Flash series of cards. Turn face down. Child enumerates cards from left to right. Draw series of shapes on chalkboard. Child looks, closes eyes, names from left to right. Have child sort word cards according to beginning letters.

Visual-Motor Coordination

Eye-hand coordination—the ability to guide highly coordinated muscular movement with the eyes—is important in both reading and writing. Many children who have learning disabilities have difficulty in this area. They may not be able to follow movement or a line of print easily with their eyes. They may not be able to coordinate their finger movements well enough to write legibly; they may be clumsy, always knocking things over or spilling things; they may be lacking in rhythm and balance. Some children have not learned to coordinate movement from one side of the body to the other so they cannot easily carry out any activity which crosses the center line of their body.

Usually it is fine muscular coordination rather than gross motor activity that is affected. Often the child who has difficulty with fine eye-hand coordination will be fond of sports such as football, swimming, and soccer, which require large-muscle activity, but will not enjoy table tennis, rope jumping, or jacks.

As it should with all learning disabilities, some time should be spent developing the ability, while most of the emphasis should be on instructional methods which circumvent the disability. If the child cannot follow a line of print easily with his eyes, a marker above the line, a card with a slot that exposes only one line, or material with each line a different color will help him. If he cannot write legibly on paper, he can print on the chalkboard or a slate.

310

Visual-motor control exercises can begin with physical education and with large arm motions. For example, write the alphabet, scattered so it covers the whole chalkboard. As letters are called, two children can race to see who can touch the letter faster. (Both children should be equal in ability; otherwise only one should practice at a time.) From this type of activity, move gradually to fine motor work with pencil and paper. There could be a little of each kind of activity each day. Instructional Guide 12.7 lists many ways of identifying visual-motor coordination problems, with suggestions for ways of improving them.

INSTRUCTIONAL GUIDE 12.7

Visual-Motor Coordination

Observations	Diagnosis	Recommendations
Difficulty following a line of print with the eyes. Poor ability at guiding fine motor activities.	Loses place on page. Facing child, move pencil in a circle, an "X," etc.; child follows with eyes and then with a pencil. Use *Frostig Test*, Part 2—"Hand-Eye Coordination." Use Eye movement camera. Child's writing is illegible. Child skips lines when reading.	Use marker above the line. Make alternate lines red. Slide a card with a slot which exposes part of one line along the line. For eye exercises, have child follow pencil or lines of print rapidly. Have child build with blocks, following a diagram. Use a Controlled Reader. Use dot to dot pictures. Use the *Frostig Program*.
Poor handwriting: slow, labored, immature, varying in slant and spacing.	Use *ITPA*—"Automatic-Sequential Level." Use *Purdue Perceptual Motor Survey*. Note coordination in handling pencil. Use *WISC*—"Coding."	Use SRA *Lift Off to Reading*. Have child draw circles and figure eights. Have child trace. Have child label pictures. Have child copy pictures.
Poor fine-motor coordination. Fine-motor skills vary from day to day.	Use *Lincoln-Oseretsky Motor Development Scale*.	Use art activities—painting, especially drawing people. Use mazes.

Observations	Diagnosis	Recommendations
Poor cutting, pasting, drawing, coloring.	Use *Moore Eye-Hand Coordination and Color Matching Test.*	Use a pegboard. Have child use a coloring book.
Difficulty crossing centerline of the body.	Draw diagonal line across chalkboard with one hand without turning body.	Have child place large circles and figure eights on chalkboard.
Difficulty catching balls, tying knots, drawing straight lines between points.	Have him touch separate fingertips rapidly, place finger to nose, heel to shin, alternate hand movements rapidly, catch a ball.	Use stencil work (cut circle, square, triangle from cardboard, trace inside of these holes with finger, pencil).
Poor coordination. Clumsiness. Knocking things over and spilling them. Poor ability at hopping.	Walk in a cross-pattern. Hop on one foot. Use *Osteretsky Test of Motor Proficiency.* Use *Southern California Perceptual Motor Tests.*	Use a basic physical education program. Use the *Vallett program.* Have the child jump rope, roll in a straight line, take tiny fast hops in place, do a series of fast leaps, walk balance beam, jump from beam to mark, crawl through barrel or hoops, play hopscotch, throw bean bags and balls. Have child copy instructor's movements. Use shop projects. Use sports materials emphasizing speed. Use *Delacato program* for extreme cases.
Poor rhythm. Lack of rhythm in movement.	Beat drum in different rhythms, copy instructor.	Play musical games. Do Indian dances. Have child bounce ball while walking. Form a rhythm band.
Abnormal posture. Poor balance.	Check ability to stand with eyes closed, feet together, arms extended horizontally before him.	Have child use a balance beam. Refer child for a physical examination.

Kinesthetic and Tactile Perception

It is through the tactile (sense of touch) and kinesthetic (sense of muscular movement) that auditory and visual perception are developed by the small child. It is also through these senses, through handling and feeling objects, that visual perception is built up in the child with visual perceptual problems.

Although problems in these areas are rare, occasionally a child does have poor tactile perception. If this is true, kinesthetic teaching and many of the procedures suggested for the development of visual

INSTRUCTIONAL GUIDE 12.8

Kinesthetic and Tactile Perception

Characteristics	Diagnosis	Instruction
Poor sense of touch and muscle movement. Failure to enjoy feeling shapes and textures. Failure to learn easily through touch. Failure to learn easily through kinesthetic methods.	Use Mills *Learning Methods Test.* Use Pinprick test locate pinpricks made with eyes closed. Touch object with one hand, close eyes and touch with other. Use *Southern California Kinesthetic and Tactile Perception Tests.*	Teach through visual, auditory, and other modalities.

perception will be ineffective. Except in the case of mentally retarded children, it is usually not necessary to check tactile and kinesthetic perception unless the child's reaction to other instructional procedures indicates there may be a problem in this area.

Self-Concept and Body Image

Because of their distortions in perceptions, children with learning disabilities often have distorted concepts of their own bodies and of themselves as persons. Body image may be described as an awareness of the parts and workings of a person's own body and of its position in time and space. It is derived not only from observation but also from internal feelings and from feedback from other people. This impression of the physical self seems to be-tied very closely to the child's impression of himself as a person. For example, the child with learning disabilities will often draw a picture of himself with arms misplaced or other distortions.

INSTRUCTIONAL GUIDE 12.9

Self-Concept and Body Image

Characteristic	Diagnosis	Recommendations
Unclear picture of own body. Insecure feelings of others' reaction to him. See Instructional Guide 9.1.	*Draw-a-Person* Test. Put hand on knee, ear, etc., with eyes closed as examiner names each body part.	Use physical activities with emphasis on body movement and pressures. See Instructional Guide 9.1.

Oral Language and Spelling

Because of their problems in visual and auditory perception, children with learning disabilities will, in general, have more problems than the average student in vocabulary, speech, and spelling. Problems in all three areas can be observed in nearly any group of children with learning disabilities.

As a group, children with learning disabilities will make more than five times as many spelling errors than their age-mates. A larger percentage of these errors will be reversals. Otherwise, the type of errors will not be significantly different in kind from those made by other children.

The reading teacher's main concern with the spelling of the pupils is seeing that they are not overly criticized for their spelling. If children with learning disabilities are made to correct every spelling error in their writing or if all their papers are always marked with red ink indicating spelling errors, most of them will refuse to write at all. If, instead, their ideas—the thoughts they express—receive the emphasis, their writing may surpass that of many other children. This fact alone provides a good reason for complementing them and building their self-concept instead of tearing it down!

Emphasizing Strengths

It has been stated repeatedly that the remedial reading teacher should emphasize strengths rather than weaknesses. A remedial reading program which puts most of the emphasis on improving, even more, those areas in which the child already does well is usually more successful in improving over-all reading ability than one which puts most of the emphasis on eliminating weaknesses. This is even more important in working with learning disabled children than with other remedial readers. There is often little chance of eliminating a learning deficit, but a good chance of helping the child learn to read through his strengths.

The teacher should try to determine initially what are the ways in which the child can learn most easily, and teach through these modalities.

The teacher can check each of the child's modes of learning through the methods suggested in the Instructional Guides throughout this chapter. However, it is difficult to make comparisons between the child's achievement of objectives which are tested through very different means.

One way of comparing a student's ability to learn through different instructional modalities is through controlled experimental teaching. Using the Dolch word list (if the child does not yet know those words) or a more difficult list for the more advanced child, go through the list letting the child read the words from sight until you have identified forty words which the child does not know. Selecting these words at random, divide them into four equal groups of ten words each. On Monday (or whatever day is convenient) spend exactly fifteen minutes teaching one group of words to the child as sight vocabulary, repeating them, using flash cards, discussing meanings, and so on, until the fifteen minutes is used. On Tuesday (the following day) test the child on these ten words to see how many he remembers. Then teach the next list auditorially, sounding them out, analyzing their structure, and so on, again using exactly fifteen minutes. On Wednesday, test the child on these and teach the next list kinesthetically. On Thursday, use a combination method, either combining all three, or the two methods which have been most effective. When the child is tested on these words on Friday, you should have a fairly accurate idea of which mode of instruction is the most effective way for this teacher to teach this child. You may find other ways of instruction that you will wish to compare also. For example, you might want to compare two different auditory instruction methods.

This type of informal testing should be an ongoing process during instruction as what is effective for a child today may no longer be the most effective method six weeks from now. Also, most children learn best through a multisensory approach which emphasizes their strengths but also includes the other modes and other senses. This allows them to select whatever cues are most helpful to them in learning the particular skill being taught.

The Interrelationship of Learning Disabilities

Although learning disabilities are manifested in many different ways, all are, in reality, different manifestations of the problems of perceptual inadequacy. Figure 2 is an attempt to show this interrelatedness.

1. *Perception.* Auditory and visual perception are shown in the figure as the starting point of learning disabilities.

2. *Figure-ground.* Visual and auditory perception influence figure-ground concepts—the ability to see relationships and to syn-

thesize the individual parts into a meaningful whole. The ability to see this Gestalt is necessary in both visual and auditory areas.

3. *Distractibility*. Poor perception and lack of figure-ground discrimination both cause or enhance distractibility. Poor perception makes concentration on either visual or auditory stimuli difficult. In addition, if the visual or auditory image cannot be distinguished as a whole, apart from its background, or if the individual cannot distinguish which factors are important and which are unimportant, he will react equally to both; he will react to the loudest noise, the brightest color, and the moving object—whether or not a lesser stimulus is more important. Distractibility is, then, closely related to the inability to automatically and subconsciously separate figure from ground.

4. *Hyperkinesis*. The inability to distinguish between important and unimportant stimuli leads to reaction to all stimuli and results in hyperkinesis.

5. *Perseveration*. The distractible child's overattention to certain stimuli leads to the inability to move away from a stimulus to new activities or to perseveration.

6. *Time, Space, and Body Concepts*. Poor visual perception, coupled with poor perception of figure and ground, causes confusion in the child's understanding of time, of direction, and of position in space. They also confuse his mental picture of his own body and its relation to the world about him.

7. *Visual-Motor Coordination*. Good visual-motor coordination requires muscular coordination controlled by good visual perception. It also requires that these be coordinated through a good understanding of time, of body movement, and of position in space. Inability to distinguish figure from ground, excessive activity, and distractibility will all make visual-motor control less effective. Therefore, a child with any of these five difficulties may be less well coordinated than his peer.

8. *Self-Concept*. Each of the disabilities listed will affect the child's mental concept of himself as a person.

Although all of the symptoms of learning disabilities are interrelated, each child will react differently to the original perceptual problem. Poor auditory perception also will have quite a different effect upon the other characteristics than will poor visual perception. Therefore, a child with one of the characteristics may or may not exhibit symptoms of any or all of the others.

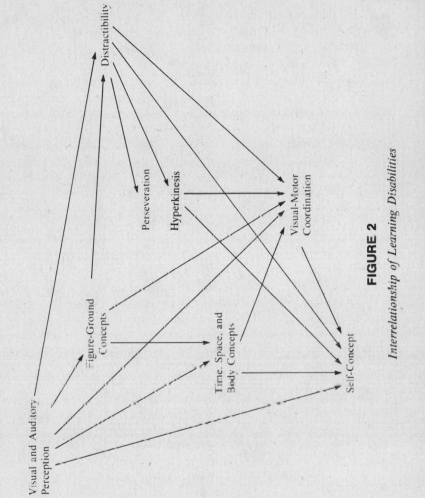

PERCEPTION   CONCEPTS   MOTOR CONTROL   DISTRACTIBILITY

Visual and Auditory Perception

Figure-Ground Concepts

Time, Space, and Body Concepts

Distractibility

Perseveration

Hyperkinesis

Visual-Motor Coordination

Self-Concept

FIGURE 2

Interrelationship of Learning Disabilities

317

Summary

A learning disability is a disorder, probably based in the central nervous system, which causes a person to have great difficulty in learning to read.

Most learning disabilities are in the areas of perception (visual perception, visual memory, or auditory perception) or distractibility (hyperactivity, perseveration, or short attention span). These disabilities lead to problems in motor coordination and in conceptualization.

A tendency toward learning disabilities may be inherited or the disability may result from brain injury before, during, or after birth. High fever and lack of oxygen to the brain are common causes.

Many of the more serious reading problems are caused by specific learning disabilities. Therefore, it is important that the remedial reading teacher be alert to such signs of learning disabilities as poor visual memory, poor visual perception, poor auditory perception, hyperactivity, distractibility, perseveration, directional disorientation, and poor visual motor coordination. If evidence of any type of learning disability is detected, she should arrange for special tests to identify the problem further. By identifying learning disabilities, the remedial teacher will be able to adjust instruction for each student accordingly.

Because of these factors, some children learn much more rapidly through one sensory modality than through another. The visually oriented child, for example, will not progress rapidly if instructional methods are auditorially oriented.

Instructional programs for children with learning disabilities must be individually planned according to the specific disabilities of each child. No one type of instruction is suitable to any large percentage of these children.

Instructional Guide 12.10 summarizes the symptoms, diagnostic procedures, and instructional methods for each type of learning disability. For more information on any one type of learning disability, the reader should refer to the more detailed guides found throughout this chapter.

INSTRUCTIONAL GUIDE 12.10

*Summary of Diagnostic and Instructional
Procedures for Learning Disabilities*

Characteristic	Diagnosis	Recommendations
Distractibility		
Distraction by sounds, movement, colors, light.	Is inattentive. Has short attention span	Teach in short spurts. Remove distractions.

Characteristic	*Diagnosis*	*Recommendations*
	for age.	Refer to Instructional Guide 12.1.
Hyperactivity		
Inability to sit still. Inability to stay with one activity.	Observe child closely. Pushes, kicks, hits. Is inconsistent.	Use drug therapy. Reduce space. Use positive outlets for energy. Refer to Instructional Guide 12.2.
Perseveration		
Inability to change activity. Repeating of errors.	Study samples of arithmetic and spelling. Administer *Visual Memory Test*.	Change activity. Use no repetitive drills. Refer to Instructional Guide 12.3.
Auditory Acuity		
Poor hearing.	Use audiometer test. Use articulation test.	Refer to physician. Refer to Instructional Guide 12.4.
Auditory Discrimination		
Confusion of similar words. Difficulty with phonics.	Use *Wepman Test*. Use *Monroe Test*. Use readiness tests.	Use visual learning. Use detailed phonics. Use readiness materials. Refer to Instructional Guide 12.4.
Auditory Comprehension		
Confusion while listening. Misquoting.	Use *Durrell Test*. Use *Learning Potential*. Ask child to paraphrase what he has heard.	Use a tape recorder and let child listen as he reads. Refer to Instructional Guide 12.4.
Auditory Memory		
Poor memorization ability. Forgetting of names. Very poor ability in spelling orally.	Use *ITPA*—Auditory. Use *WISC* Digit Span.	Teach to read visually. Emphasize interest. Refer to Instructional Guide 12.4.
Visual Acuity		
Poor vision.	Use telebinocular.	Refer to physician for glasses.

Characteristic	*Diagnosis*	*Recommendations*
		Refer to Instructional Guide 12.5.
Visual Discrimination		
Confusion of words and letters. Missing of details.	Use *WISC*—Coding. Use readiness tests.	Use readiness workbooks. Have child practice with pegboards. Have child match word cards. Refer to Instructional Guide 12.5.
Visual Imagery		
Inability to form mental picture. Difficulty in drawing.	Use *Frostig Test*—Form Constancy. Use *WISC*—Block Design. Copy figures.	Teach through tapes. Emphasize phonics. Use kinesthetic teaching. Refer to Instructional Guide 12.5.
Visual Memory		
Spelling phonetically. Forgetting sight words. Reversals.	Give spelling test. Use *Learning Potential* —Visual Memory. Give pegboard test.	Teach phonetically. Use non-reading curriculum. Use Oral Impress Method. Refer to Instructional Guide 12.5.
Figure-Ground Constancy		
Inability to distinguish figures from details. Losing things.	Give *Frostig Test*—Figure-ground. Outline overlapping figures.	Build letters to words. Use *Frostig Program*. Have child find hidden figures. Refer to Instructional Guide 12.5.
Visual Concepts		
Inability to translate perception into meaningful ideas.	Use *Learning Potential*—Symbol Interpretation. Use *WISC*—Picture Arrangement.	Use arts and crafts. Use written instructions. Use discussion. Refer to Instructional Guide 12.5.

Characteristic	Diagnosis	Recommendations
Time Concepts		
Little idea of time of day. Difficulty with sequencing.	Does not know time. Is poor with rhythms. Cannot do things in sequence.	Use *Frostig Program.* Use discussion. Use written instructions. Refer to Instructional Guide 12.6.
Space Concepts		
Confusion of meanings of "by," "past," "to the left of."	Use *ITPA*—Automatic Sequential Level. Use *Frostig*—Spatial Relationships.	Use *Frostig Program.* Draw maps. Use written instructions. See Instructional Guide 12.6.
Directional Concepts		
Reversal of letters and words. Lack of knowledge of left from right.	Use *Frostig*—Position Test of Individual Reversals.	Use *Frostig Program.* Play first-letter games. Play marching games. Refer to Instructional Guide 12.6.
Visual-Motor Coordination		
Poor handwriting. Poor coordination. Clumsiness.	Has illegible writing. Skips lines in reading. Use *Frostig*—Hand-Eye Coordination.	Use marker above the line. Encourage drawing and coloring. Refer to Instructional Guide 12.7.
Kinesthetic and Tactile Perception		
Poor sense of touch.	Give Mills *Learning Methods Test.* See Instructional Guide 12.8.	Teach through vision and hearing.
Self-Concept		
Unclear ideas of own body. Lack of self-confidence.	Use *Draw-A-Person Test.* Give *Rorschach Test.* Give *Vineland Scale of Social Maturity.*	Emphasize physical activity. Emphasize success. Create a relaxed atmosphere.

Recommended Related Reading

The following list is long because we have tried to include articles on each area discussed in this chapter, so that the person wanting additional information on any one type of learning disability will find at least two or three sources listed here.

Ackerman, Peggy T. "Children with Specific Learning Disabilities, *WISC* Profiles," *Journal of Learning Disabilities* 4 (March 1971): 150–66.

Shows relationships between *WISC* profile scores and specific learning disabilities.

Aliberto, Charles A. "Assessing Perceptual-Motor Competence." *Academic Therapy* (Spring 1975): 255–59.

Suggests ways of evaluating a child's ability to use time, space, and directional concepts.

Anderson, Robert, Charles Holcomb, William Gordon, Jr., and Delmer A. A. Azolias. "Measurement of Attention Distractibility in LD Children." *Academic Therapy* 9 (Spring 1974): 261–66.

Report on experiment to determine ways of testing for distractibility.

Bussell, C. "Positive Reinforcers for Modifications of Auditory Processing Skills in LD and EMR Children." *Journal of Learning Disabilities* 8 (June/July 1975): 373–76.

Study indicates that listening skills can be improved but only through positive effort with teacher reinforcement.

Carrier, James T. "Techniques for Controlling Distractibility within the Classroom." *The Slow Learner Workshop* (April 1976): 3–4.

Lists six principles for working with distractible children.

Harris, Albert J. "Practical Applications of Reading Research." *Reading Teacher* 29 (March 1976): 559–65.

Harris reviews the research on teaching modalities and concludes that combination approaches and those that focus on reading skills rather than perceptual skills are most effective.

Katz, Jack. "The Use of Staggered Spondiac Words for Assessing the Integrity of the Central Auditory Nervous System." *Journal of Auditory Research* 2 (October 1962): 327–37.

Recommends a testing system in which different words are presented to the right and left ear simultaneously. A good basis for a research project testing this as a means of diagnosing auditory figure-ground perception.

Kottler, Sylvia B. "The Identification and Remediation of Auditory Problems." *Academic Therapy* 8 (Fall, 1972): 73–86.

Describes characteristics which help to identify child with auditory perceptual problems.

Kronick, Doreen. "Visual-Motor Skill and Eye-Hand Coordination," in *They Too Can Succeed.* Academic Therapy Publications, 1969, pp. 101–3.

Describes the use of templates for developing visual-motor coordination.

Mayer, Colleen. *Understanding Young Children: Emotional and Behavioral Development and Disabilities.* Anchorage, Alaska: Alaska Treatment Center for Crippled Children and Adults, Inc., 1974, ERIC ED 092–258.

A good review of instructional methods for distractible children.

Millichap, J. Gordan. "Drugs in Management of Hyperkinetic and Perceptually Handicapped Children." *Journal of the American Medical Association* 206 (November 11, 1968): 15–27.

Expresses opinion that drug control of hyperactivity is useful and essential in some cases, but should be used with caution.

Nobler, Linda W., and E. Harris Nobler. "Auditory Discrimination of Learning Disabled Children in Quiet and Classroom Noise." *Journal of Learning Disabilities* (December 1976): 57–60.

Suggestions for identifying and teaching children with problems in auditory perception.

Ricks, Nancy L., and Allen F. Mirsky. "Sustained Attention and the Effects of Distraction in Underachieving Second Grade Children." *Journal of Education* 156 (November 1976): 4–17.

Ideas for working with distractible children in the primary grades.

Reger, Roger. "What does 'Mainstreaming' Mean?" *Journal of Learning Disabilities* 7 (October 1974): 513–15.

Reviews various arrangements for teaching learning disabled children, and gives basic principles for their instruction.

Rukeyser, Leah S. "Finding the Crocodile." *Learning Disabilities Guide* (January 1976): 5–6.

Suggests methods for increasing ability to differentiate and screen out extraneous sounds for child with auditory figure-ground problems.

_____. "Strawberry Short Cake," in *Learning Disabilities Guide.* New London, Conn.: NEI Croft Publications, May 1976, pp. 5–6.

Suggests ways of assessing and developing visual-motor coordination.

Sartain, Harry W. "Who Shall Teach the Learning Disabilities Child?" *Journal of Learning Disabilities* 9 (October 1976): 489–97.

Discusses importance of having Learning Disabilities classes taught by reading specialists.

Schoenrade, Joyce L. "Help Means Hope for Laurie." *Journal of Learning Disabilities* 7 (August/September 1974): 23–25.

Ideas for teaching the hyperactive child.

Simpson, D. Dwayne and Arnold E. Nelson. "Attention Training Through Breathing Control to Modify Hyperactivity." *Journal of Learning Disabilities* 7 (May 1974): 274–82.

Suggestions for helping the child control his own hyperactivity.

Tarver, Sara G., and Daniel P. Hallahan. "Attention Deficits in Children with Learning Disabilities: A Review." *Journal of Learning Disabilities* 7 (October 1974): 517–18.

Discusses characteristics and identification of the distractible child.

Throne, John M. "Learning Disabilities: A Radical Behaviorist Point of View." *Journal of Learning Disabilities* 6 (November 1973): 14–17.

This article emphasizes the potential for learning of every child. The environment must be altered to fit the child.

Threshour, Frank W. "Dyslexia: A Sure Cure." *Educational Digest* 40 (November 1974): 34–35.

Emphasizes the need for differential instruction for each child with reading problems. There is no one type of instruction appropriate to all.

Vance, Hubert Booney, and Norman E. Hankins. "Teaching Interventions for Defective Auditory Reception." *Academic Therapy* 11 (Fall 1975): 68–78.

Describes different auditory perception skills and methods of teaching to compensate for deficits.

Volkmar, Cara B., and Anne L. Langstaff. "Developing Visual Perception Abilities." *Teaching Exceptional Children* (Fall 1971): 29–32.

Recommends specific exercises for improving recognition of shapes, figures, etc.

Wallin, Kenneth, Kenneth U. Gutsch, and John C. Koeppel. "The Impact of Two Behavioral Treatments on Highly Distractible 5th and 6th Grade Students." *Southern Journal of Educational Research* 8 (Winter 1974): 182–91.

Experiment which indicated that help from another child in learning to concentrate was more effective than control methods used by teacher.

Waugh, Kenneth W., and Wilma Jo Bush. *Diagnosing Learning Disorders.* Columbus, Ohio: Charles E. Merrill Publishing Co., 1971, 182 pp.

Thorough coverage of diagnosis and interpretation. Includes 91 pages of case studies.

Whisler, Nancy G. "Visual-Memory Training in First Grade. Effects on Visual Discrimination and Reading Ability." *Elementary School Journal* 7 (October 1974): 51–54.

Suggests ways in which visual discrimination and visual memory can be developed in primary grade children.

Wilson, Robert M. *Diagnostic and Remedial Reading,* Columbus, Ohio: Charles E. Merrill Publishing Co., 1972, pp. 66–68 and 164–66.

Discusses auditory perceptual problems, their identification, and ways of teaching both in regular and special classes.

Zukow, Arnold H., M.D. "Helping the Hyperkinetic Child." *Today's Education* 64 (November–December 1975): 39–41.

A good discussion of the treatment and education of the hyperactive child from a physician's viewpoint.

13

Using Remedial
Reading Materials

If the remedial reading teacher is to meet the needs and interests of the pupils, an adequate supply of good materials must be available to her. Every teacher must develop some of her own materials in order to meet the special needs of individual pupils; however, with the proliferation of materials now available, the teacher should not expect to use a great portion of her valuable time developing materials which are already available commercially.

If the reading materials available to the teacher cover a variety of interest areas and all of the reading levels with which she must deal, she will be able to choose those materials which will meet every individual student's needs as determined through diagnosis.

If a variety of other types of materials is available in addition to books, the teacher will find it easier to maintain student interest. Tape recorders, projected materials, games, charts, cards, word wheels, kinesthetic materials—all have a place in the reading program. Several companies are producing packaged reading programs which use several of these media in combination.

One caution should be extended here though. Merely using a multitude of interesting-looking materials and equipment does not necessarily insure a good reading program. Often, the more complex and elaborate the program, the more inflexible it is, thus making it more difficult for the teacher to adjust the use of the material to the individual needs of each student. However, if used properly, a good variety of materials can be a real aid in adding interest and meeting individual needs. Nonetheless, the first essential is an adequate supply of good books, and this necessity should not be sacrificed in order to purchase expensive gadgets.

Selection of Materials

Because schools, communities, and pupils are not all alike and because teaching methods differ, the same materials will not meet the needs of all schools. The reading program should be carefully planned first; then materials should be selected with specific instructional techniques in mind.

The selection of materials obviously should be made by the teacher who is going to use those materials. If there is a reading supervisor, he or she should assist the teacher, but the final decision as to which materials will be ordered should be the teacher's alone. She can best determine which items will probably benefit the most students in her type of instruction. A great many expensive materials sit unused on the shelves of classrooms and in storage closets because a salesman convinced a superintendent that they would benefit his reading program without consulting the teacher who would have to use the materials.

All materials and equipment must be easily accessible to the teacher and the students, and teachers should have training in their use. Materials "preserved in good condition" represent wasted money and needs not met. The materials used are not as important as creativity and flexibility in their use.

Several criteria should be kept in mind in the selection of materials to be purchased for the remedial reading program:

1. *What is the readability level?* Are the readability levels clearly distinguished and consistent throughout the material? If it is intended to provide reading at a variety of levels, is the reading level of each part clearly marked? If at one level (such as a book), does it supplement other materials available to help provide material at all levels at which students in the program may be reading?

2. *Is it highly interesting?* Will most students be motivated by this material? When possible, materials should be tried out with students before purchasing them.

3. *Does it provide variety?* It should not be too similar to either the material in the classroom reading program or to other materials already available in the remedial reading program.

4. *Do skills materials zero in on a specific skill?* Unless you can identify and use those parts which teach the specific skill in which a student needs help, without using other parts, the material is not appropriate for remedial reading.

5. *Can students use the material independently with a minimum of teacher assistance?* It is rare that a group of remedial reading students all need the same skill and can be taught as a group for much of the time. The teacher must supervise several students working on different skills with different materials. After the teacher helps students start work with a particular material, they must be able to go ahead on their own.

6. *Is the cost reasonable?* The answer to this question must be decided in relation to the durability of the material, the number of skills to be taught, and the number of students who will work with the material at the same time.

Books

Good books are the one essential material for every reading program. There should be a plentiful supply at all grade levels and interest areas. The teacher buying books should remember that approximately four times as many paperback books as casebound books can be purchased with the same amount of money. In addition, one should keep in mind that paperback books do not seem so formidable to many remedial students. Of course, in a large school, in which all books get a good deal of wear and tear, the durability of those books, which will be used most, is a factor to be considered.

Choosing Books for the Remedial Reader

Vocabulary or reading level.   The importance of using material that is easy enough to guarantee success was discussed in Chapter Six.

Interest.   Interest in reading is hard to promote among any readers unless the material to be read is, in itself, interesting. If the material is fiction, it should be short, fast-starting, and full of action. If the action and the plot do not both start on the first page, forget it!

Most children like fiction, but some feel that reading fiction is a waste of time. They do not want to use their time reading unless they will learn something new from it. It is important that whatever the preferences of the child, they should be respected.

When there are news events of importance—an election or an earthquake—the teacher should listen for indications of the children's interest in them and then bring in stories and articles that are related to the events.

Small children often like best the stories that they have been told before, and most enjoy fantasy.

Older students who have seen a good movie may enjoy reading the book from which it was made. Others may reject this approach completely because they already know the plot and want something completely new.

Many studies have been made to determine the reading interests of specific groups of children. Eight of these studies are included in the recommended readings at the end of this chapter. When ordering reading books, it is important that the remedial reading teacher know the general reading preferences of the age and ethnic groups with which she works. Individual discussion will then help in identifying the reading interests of individual students.

Since the majority of remedial readers are boys, and since it remains a fact that girls usually like boys' stories while boys will seldom read girls' stories, the remedial reading teacher should concentrate mainly on obtaining good stories with boys' interests. Adventure, suspense, and mystery are the most popular subjects. Remedial students, especially those from disadvantaged backgrounds, usually have a definite preference for the plot of the underdog who triumphs in the end.

Mature content is essential if reading is to interest older children. Although the material should be easy for the student to read, it should not have the appearance of primary material or be written for much younger children. For this reason, basic readers are not suitable for most remedial students. First graders enjoy first-grade books, but sixth graders reading at first-grade level usually detest them. They need material written for sixth-grade interests with a first-grade vocabulary level. There should be no grade level designations on any books or other materials used in the remedial reading program, although some type of code should be used which will enable the teacher to know immediately the reading level of all available materials.

The student's individual interests must receive prime consideration in the selection of materials, for high interest in a subject may overcome a great many other problems.

Length. Few students who have real difficulty in reading can be encouraged to even begin a novel because they know from past experience that they will never complete it. However, books with a number of short stories may be accepted if the student understands that he will not be expected to read *all* the stories. Still other students, however, can be encouraged only by short booklets or folders of one or two pages. Many remedial reading teachers tear their anthologies of short stories apart and bind each story in a separate colorful cover to reduce the threat their students feel from long books.

Variety Anything that adds variety to the reading material or the program will help maintain interest. Books with unusual format, such as Bill Martin's *Sounds of Language* books and the Dr. Seuss books, will add interest. Comic books, stories on films and plays, and stories written by the children themselves will accomplish the same purpose.

Availability. A successful program can be conducted with a minimum number of books, but a broad selection will make it easier to meet the needs and interests of every student. In addition to using books purchased by the school, the children can take a survey of the community which may turn up a great many useful books which can be donated to the program.

All books and equipment in the remedial reading room should be available to the students and the teacher at all times. A rack of children's paperback books, such as those available through school book clubs to which the children can go for recreational reading and from which they can borrow books for outside reading without the formalities of a library may do a great deal to promote independent reading and, thereby, improve reading skills. One school in a poverty area has such a book rack from which children are encouraged to borrow books and, if they like the book well enough, to keep it; they do not need to bring it back. The feeling in this program is that the success of each year's program can be judged by the number of books the school must purchase. Another school, located in a more affluent neighborhood, has increased its supply of paperbacks by offering to trade one book for any two that the students bring in. A program called "Reading is *Fun*damental" for promoting reading by supplying each child with his own paperback **books has been started in many locations, and is proving very successful.**[1]

Regardless of what else is available, a good supply of interesting, easy to read books is the most essential requirement for a successful remedial reading program—next to the teacher.

Source of books.   Space cannot be allotted here for listing specific books, workbooks, and other materials which may be useful in remedial reading programs. However, several annotated lists of good books for poor readers are available. The remedial reading teacher should go over these lists carefully before ordering books for the remedial reading program in order to select those books which are most appropriate to the pupils and the reading program for the particular school. The following lists should provide adequate information on available books and materials:

Berridge, Wayne E. and Siedrow, Mary D. *Guide to Materials for Reading Instruction.* Bloomington: ERIC Clearinghouse on Reading, Indiana University, 1971.

Della-Piana, Gabriel M. *Reading Diagnosis and Prescription.* New York: Holt, Rinehart & Winston, 1968, pp. 194–208.

Listing of over 500 books with reading level and interest level.

Ekwall, Eldon E. "Evaluation and Use of Materials," in *Diagnosis and Remediation of the Disabled Reader.* Boston, Mass.: Allyn & Bacon, 1976, pp. 386–410.

Ekwall gives criteria for evaluating reading materials, lists many books appropriate for remedial reading, and makes suggestions regarding homemade materials.

Gilliland, Hap. *Indian Children's Books.* Will be available in 1978 from Montana Council for Indian Education, 517 Rimrock Road, Billings, Montana. Con-

---

[1] For information on this program, contact "Reading is *Fun*damental," Smithsonian Institution, Washington, D.C.

tains three chapters on the selection of books for or about Indian children, and evaluations by Indians of 600 children's books about Indians. Organized for easy location of materials by subject, reading level, or interest level.

_____. *Materials for Remedial Reading and Their Use,* 5th ed. Billings: Montana Reading Publications, 1808 3rd Ave. North, 1976.

Comprehensive annotated list of books grouped according to reading level and interest area. Also lists films, games, recordings, kits and other reading materials with suggestions for their proper use in the remedial reading program. Revised frequently.

Keblitz, Minnie W. *The Negro in Schoolroom Literature.* New York: Center for Urban Education, 1968.

Annotations on about 250 elementary level books on Negro heritage.

A Preliminary Bibliography of Selected Children's Books about American Indians. New York: Association on American Indian Affairs, 1969.

Listing of 188 books rated according to readability and children's interests.

Schubert & Torgerson. "Multilevel Materials and Devices," in *Improving the Reading Program.* 4th ed. Dubuque, Iowa: William C. Brown Co., 1976, pp. 306–53.

Lists a variety of kits, workbooks, films, machines, and devices useful in teaching remedial reading.

Spache, George D. *Good Reading for Poor Readers.* Champaign, Ill.: Garrard Publishing Co., 1968.

Comprehensive list of printed materials, plus information on book selection.

Stauffer, Hilda. "New Materials on the Market," *The Reading Teacher* 29 (February 1976): 474–89.

A list of reading materials published in 1974 and 1975. Some of them would be appropriate for remedial students.

Choosing Books for the Disadvantaged

For disadvantaged students, high interest-low vocabulary materials with short, fast-starting stories are even more important than for other remedial students. Even the top students in a group of disadvantaged students will often state that they are "turned off" by thick books and small print. Materials should be relevant to the needs and interests of the particular individual or group, and these needs and interests are often very different from those of students with a middle class background.

Culture and values. If possible, at least part of the reading materials used with disadvantaged students should portray the child's own culture. Those that do not, should not be in direct conflict with the child's culture.

If the reading materials portray the teacher's middle-class culture and values the teacher should ask herself if they imply that the culture and values of other groups are wrong or even less worthwhile. If so, they may do great harm to the child's self-concept in addition to causing him to develop a dislike for reading and reading materials.

Interest areas.   The student's background also affects his interests. He cannot be greatly interested in an area of which he has little or no knowledge. For example, the middle-class child lives in a world of things; things are important to him. His conversations center around the past and the future. The disadvantaged student lives in a world of people. He has few possessions, and they are of little importance to him. His interest is in the present, and his goals center around people rather than things. This fact should be reflected in the plots of the stories he is expected to read. Children from upper economic levels may be more interested in history, geography, and science, but those in the lower economic levels are interested in reading about people.

Experiential background.   The majority of the stories in most basic readers and other available reading materials are based on an upper middle-class background and presuppose that the reader has had similar experiences through which he can understand the story. However, the life of the reservation Indian or the inner-city black child may be so different from that which is portrayed in such a story that he may get little or no understanding from the story and will develop neither good comprehension nor an interest in reading from it.

Stories of distant and unusual places are excellent reading material for the good reader who has built a background for understanding them through broad reading and experience. They should not be the steady diet of the student who has had neither of these and for whom the suburb itself is a strange and distant place. Films and other audiovisual materials may be useful for building background for reading some materials, but some of the materials should still relate to the child's own background.

Present-day basic readers are greatly improved over those published ten or more years ago. The stories have better plots, are portrayed more realistically; some really portray a variety of cultural backgrounds. However, many of those which purport to be multi-ethnic have really only changed the illustrations and, sometimes, the settings. The characters still portray the roles they would play in the middle-class urban home and continue with their middle-class activities and goals. The teacher should check all material which is culturally oriented to be sure that it gives a true portrayal of the life of the people.

Attitudes of writers. The student who comes from a different cultural background is usually very sensitive to the small innuendos which betray the writer's hidden attitudes toward particular groups of people. Sometimes, the writer's prejudices are obvious (like the author who said, "He was a Mexican, but he was just as smart as you or me"), but, more often, they are hidden and seem obvious only to a sensitive person from that cultural group. The teacher needs to become particularly aware of these hidden prejudices and make sure that books portray an acceptance of the equal worth of each individual regardless of race, occupation, or social position.

In most of the available trade books, there is no inter-mixing of cultures; there are no black or Mexican people unless they are in positions of serving the more important characters; there are no good Indians, except those who have become traitors to their people.

Ethnic readers. Some basic readers have been written with specific groups in mind. Unfortunately, like other basic readers, they may be inappropriate for the older child who is reading at a low level. Some examples of the materials developed for specific groups are: the Bank Street Readers, written for children in New York City, with language taken from those children's speech; the Skyline Series about urban life in St. Louis; the Indian Culture Series, written for American Indian children; the Chandler Language Experience Readers about San Francisco, and the Alaskan Readers, written for Alaskan Indian and Eskimo children.

Worksheets and Workbooks

Special exercises through which the student can get additional practice on skills in which he is receiving instruction must be available to the remedial reading program. It is not possible for any teacher to take the necessary time to make all of the needed material. It should be made by the teacher only if she cannot get the needed material from another source.

If used properly, a variety of good workbooks emphasizing different areas of reading can be one of the most valuable resources in the school's reading center. However, if a child is assigned a workbook to go through page by page, as is done in some basic reading classrooms, then the workbook may very well do more harm than good. No child should be asked to complete a worksheet or a page in a workbook unless that page was selected to meet his specific needs.

A great deal of teacher time can be wasted in thumbing through stacks of workbooks trying to find a page that will give a student the specific practice he needs on a particular skill. Therefore, an efficient filing system for all workbook material and all teacher-made worksheets is needed. This filing is commonly done in three different ways.

A workbook index. Some teachers keep an alphabetically indexed notebook with a page for each skill. As she acquires each new workbook the teacher lists each of the skills covered in this notebook with the name of the workbook and the page. Thus, a glance in the notebook will locate any needed material quickly.

A File of Pages. A more efficient method of filing is to take all workbooks apart and file all of the pages in manila folders labeled with the skill practiced on that particular page. Teacher-made worksheets are filed in the same file.

Homemade kits. The method found most efficient in the writer's reading center is making all workbooks into homemade reading kits. Each workbook is taken apart, and each page is attached to a nine-by-twelve sheet of tagboard with masking tape. Two copies of the workbook are needed so that the odd numbered pages can be used from one and the even numbered pages from the other, as one side of each page will be covered when they are attached to the tagboard. A color code has been worked out indicating each skill area, (e.g., red for beginning consonant sounds, yellow for short vowel sounds, and black for comprehension). A piece of colored plastic tape representing the skill taught is placed over the top of each sheet so that by looking at the top of the sheets in the box in which they are filed, the teacher can pick out quickly all of the sheets dealing with any general area of instruction.

A plastic cover is slipped over the workbook page when it is to be used, and the child writes his answers on this plastic sheet. After he has checked his answers, the writing can be wiped off with a cloth and the same plastic sheet used again.

Multi-Level Kits of Reading Materials

In addition to the homemade kits made from workbooks, there are a great many commercially produced kits or "reading laboratories" available. When used in the remedial reading program, these kits can be beneficial to the students only if they are used strictly to meet individual needs. Each selection should be chosen to meet a specific need of an individual child.

Programmed Reading Materials

Programmed materials can be very useful in the teaching of remedial reading. They have the advantages of small steps in teaching, active participation of the reader, immediate reinforcement, and assurance that the student will get most of his answers right.

An example of programmed material follows. In reading it, place your right hand over the right half of the page. This half contains the answers. Read each question, decide on the correct answer to fill the blank, then slide your hand down and check the answer before going on to the next question.

The first basic principle of programmed material is that the material to be taught is broken down into small steps. Each step is based upon an understanding of the previous _____.

STEP

Each step is in the form of a question for which the reader must given an _____.

ANSWER

The second principle is that the steps must be arranged in logical order. This means that each question is based upon the previous _____.

STEP or QUESTION

If the student has thought carefully and understood each of the previous steps, then he should know the correct answer to the following _____.

QUESTION or STEP

The third principle is that the student takes an active part in learning. He is being active when he writes the answer to a _____.

QUESTION

Information will be remembered longer and will be more meaningful if the student takes an _____ part in learning.   ACTIVE

The fourth basic principle is that the student knows immediately whether his answers are right or _____.   WRONG

If he has gotten a wrong impression, he does not have to wait until this impression has caused more confusion; instead, he has his answer corrected _____.   IMMEDIATELY

Fifth, since each student works through the program independently, he does not have to wait for the others but can move at his own _____.   RATE or SPEED

These five principles indicate the advantages that can be gained in teaching some reading skills through _____ materials.   PROGRAMMED

A few really good programmed materials for reading improvement are now on the market, and more work is being done in this field. If teachers learned to apply these five principles to all teaching of information and skills, this might well be the greatest contribution that programmed materials could make to remedial reading instruction.

Newspapers

Newspapers have several advantages over all other reading materials used in the classroom.

1. Newspapers are the reading material most likely to be available in the student's own home. If he sees only one kind of material being read outside of school, that kind of material is more likely to be a newspaper than any other.

2. The student already knows the importance of reading the newspaper, and looks upon it as adult reading.

3. The newspaper is up-to-date and is about the things familiar to the student in his daily life.

4. The newspaper has a greater variety of reading material to offer than any other single source.

5. The newspaper is adaptable to the teaching of a great variety of skills.

6. Newspaper reading develops critical reading skills more easily than any other material.

There are several specific reading skills for which the newspaper is a particularly appropriate instructional medium.

1. Vocabulary improvement can be more interesting when taught through the newspaper because reporters intentionally use picturesque and creative words. Students can look for unusual words in different sections of the paper and note the differences.

2. *Locating the main idea* of a story and answering the questions of "who," "what," "where," "when," and "how" are easier in the news story than in other material because all of these points are usually stated in the first paragraph.

3. Literal comprehension is as easily taught through the newspaper as through any other material.

4. Instruction in differentiation between statements of fact and of opinion is an excellent use of the newspaper. Students should read through items and attempt to identify those words, phrases, and arrangements which identify statements which are intended to be opinion.

5. Propaganda devices—name calling, association, and all the rest—can be found in the newspaper. This is the most appropriate material to use in teaching students about such devices, for it is largely in the newspaper and other news media that the informed citizen will encounter and must recognize such devices for what they are.

6. The newspaper is an excellent source material for the study of charts, graphs, and political cartoons.

7. The newspaper editorial page is the ideal material for teaching critical reading. There are many facets to critical reading, but

one that can be studied by even remedial readers is the identification of "slanted" articles—and editorials are, by their very definition, a statement of opinion and, therefore, slanted in some way.

Since most daily papers are written at about the fifth or sixth grade level, they are appropriate reading material for remedial readers in junior and senior high school classes. They are, however, too difficult for elementary children with reading problems.

Classroom newspapers—those published for use in schools—are not appropriate for children several years older than the intended audience because of the immature level of the content. For the upper grade and secondary student who is reading at a level too low to read the daily paper, the most appropriate newspapers are those published for use in adult basic education classes.

The teacher desiring additional ideas for the use of the newspaper should refer to Piercey (1970) who had many excellent suggestions, and Johnson (1969) and (1975) who describes a high school remedial reading program based almost entirely on the newspaper for students who had been hostile to school and reading. Hallenbeck (1976) tells how she teaches reading to learning disabled children using comic strips as the medium for teaching.

The local newspaper could well become one of the most important materials of instruction in any junior high or high school reading program.

Tape Recordings

The tape recorder can be one of the most useful and versatile pieces of equipment in the classroom. It has four main uses in the remedial reading program:

1. In an individualized program, the tape recorder can be used for teaching skills and giving instructions. If cassette recorders are available, the teacher can have a cassette for each student. As each student works independently, the teacher moves from one to another, giving individual help or teaching skills to two or three students at a time. If there are workbook pages or similar materials on which the teacher wants individuals to work, the instructions for this work can be prerecorded. In this way, when a student completes the work he is doing, he does not have to interrupt the teacher to get help or sit and wait for additional instructions. Instead, he puts his cassette in a recorder and listens to the instructions. If additional instructions are needed as he

goes through the material, he can turn the recorder off, do part of the work, turn the recorder on, listen to the next set of instructions, and then go ahead with the work.

2. The tape recorder is also an effective tool for improving oral reading and speech. The student can read into the recorder, listen to his own reading, and then decide for himself what reading problems he wants to work on to improve his own oral reading. The teacher can work with him in outlining a program for improvement based on his decision. This method is usually much more effective than the same program would be if the teacher simply tells the student what skills he needs to work on.

   A group of students can record their reading of a play or of poems used for choral reading, listen to the tape, and then decide together how they can improve the reading.

3. Tapes which the student has recorded for analyzing his own reading can be saved and used for evaluation of progress. After the student has worked several days or weeks on those phases of oral reading which he felt needed improvement, he can record another passage similar to the first one and of the same difficulty. The student and the teacher can then listen to the two tapes and make a comparison.

4. Stories which the student is going to read can be recorded on tape; then the student can listen to the tape as he reads the same material aloud. In this way, any word on which he is hesitant is said for him while he looks at the word. Since he will be trying to stay with the tape and read as much like it as possible, he also will improve his expression, fluency, and phrasing; since he also will adopt characteristics of the taped reading, the prerecorded tape must be recorded by a very good oral reader.

Recorded Word Cards

Another type of recorder, the Language Master, is also of value in teaching reading. The Language Master and similar machines produced by other companies records material on cards, along the bottom edge of which is a strip of recording tape.

To use this machine in remedial reading, the teacher should print one word in large letters on each of the cards. These should be words from the student's word box or other words which he has failed to recognize while reading. The teacher places the card in the Language Master and records the word on the tape. The student can then practice on the words in this way: He takes a card and says the word as he thinks it is printed on the card. He then puts the card in the Language Master and hears the correct pronunciation of the word as it was recorded by the teacher. He can go through all the cards in this manner, checking his own recognition of the words. If there are any that he does not know, he puts those words aside and goes over them again. He repeats this process until he knows all the words. This type of activity makes the student much more independent in the use of the word box.

If a student has difficulty with the correct pronunciation of certain words or sounds, he can practice these in the same manner. In this case, he listens to the teacher's pronunciation, records his own, and then listens to both and compares them. He continues to practice and to rerecord the word until he is satisfied with his pronunciation.

The Language Master thus provides an excellent means of letting a pupil improve his sight recognition of words independently.

Projected Reading Materials

There are five types of projected materials designed for teaching reading: tachistoscopes, which flash words on the screen to teach quick recognition; motion pictures, which may teach reading skills, build background for reading comprehension, or motivate pupils to read a particular piece of literature; film strips, which also may be used for background or for teaching skills; stories, which are projected on the screen a few words at a time, going across the screen from left to right to promote good eye movement and increase speed; and transparencies projected on the overhead projector.

Each of these materials has a specific place in the remedial reading program, though the chief value of all of them may be motivation. Machines are used more commonly in remedial reading than in the regular classroom, not because they are more specifically related to remedial reading than to developmental reading, but because variety and motivation must receive more emphasis in remedial reading.

Overhead Projectors

The overhead projector is one of the most versatile of all the "machines" used by the reading teacher. The teacher can make material to be projected, or she can use its unique feature of being the only projector which allows the students to watch *as* the teacher writes or marks on the copy.

In the reading program, the overhead projector is used for five main purposes.

1. Word lists or other material which the teacher would ordinarily write on the chalkboard can be written on a transparency before class and projected later as needed.

2. When the teacher wants a group of students to read from the same material and discuss it together, she can project the material on the screen, and all students can read it at the same time. This material may range from an item in this morning's newspaper that is being used for critical reading, to a page from a workbook or any other material. For this purpose, the material must be copied from the original onto a transparency by use of a heat-operated copying machine. These copying machines are now available in most school offices, and the process of making a transparency takes only a few seconds.

3. If the teacher wants a group to work together on an exercise, such as a page from a workbook, the material can be projected onto the chalkboard instead of the screen. As the group discusses the material, individuals can write in answers, fill in blanks, or do whatever is needed by simply writing these on the chalkboard.

4. A technique for using the overhead projector in teaching word recognition was suggested in a lecture by Dorothy McGinnis. A group of pictures is projected on the chalkboard with the overhead projector. The children then suggest labels which are written on the chalkboard under each of the pictures. After the children have read the labels a time or two, the projector lamp is turned off and they again try to read the labels without the pictures to aid them. If needed, the light may be turned on again to identify the words. These words should be used immediately in other ways for reinforcement—in experience stories, perhaps.

5. The overhead projector also can be used as a tachistoscope.

Opaque Projectors

The opaque projector is not as versatile as the overhead projector; however, material to be projected does not have to be copied onto a transparency before projection with this machine. The opaque projector is particularly useful to the reading teacher in projecting pages of workbooks on the chalkboard when filling them in is to be a group project.

Films and Film Strips

Films come in two main forms—motion picture films and film strips. In each of these forms, there are two main types of films used in the reading program: those which are intended to motivate and build background for reading and those which are intended to teach specific reading skills.

Motivational Films.   Films and film strips which give factual information or which tell stories can be used for several purposes. They may be used to create an interest in reading. This may be accomplished by telling about something—a group of people, a geographical region, an area of science—in such a way that the person watching will want to read in order to learn more about the subject. Or the film may tell a story, in whole or part, and thereby motivate the student to want to read the story.

Films also can build background and give vicarious experience so that the pupil who reads certain material will have a better understanding of the material he reads. This aids both in developing comprehension and in promoting interest in reading.

Vocabulary needed for reading about a subject can be acquired by watching films which deal with that subject. This viewing also may increase comprehension and decrease the tendency toward word-by-word repetition of words which are not understood clearly.

Reading the subscripts on film strips which have pictures accompanied by printed information can give the student a different kind of practice in either oral or silent reading.

Before using the motivational type film, the teacher should always preview the film in advance in order to use the presentation of the film to best advantage and to determine whether the film is worthwhile in terms of meeting planned objectives. Immediately before showing the film, the teacher should give the students some background on it and clarify the purposes for its presentation. If a student is to get full benefit from a film, he should know what to look for, just as he should know what his objectives are before reading a selection.

After the presentation, a few minutes should always be used to clarify concepts, answer questions, and summarize those learnings related to the objectives for using the film.

Instructional films.   A number of films are available which teach specific reading skills. There are series of motion pictures on study skills as well as film strips which present letter sounds and other phonetic information. A good introduction and summarization is even more important in the use of these films than in the use of motivational films. The films are usually of little value unless the teacher helps the students to apply the skill presented in the film to his own reading, immediately after seeing the film. They should be used only when the students who are to use them need instruction in the specific skills for which the film was intended.

Directional Control Projectors

A number of devices have been invented which are intended to control both the eye movement of the reader and the rate at which he reads. The first materials developed for this purpose were motion picture films which projected printed material on the screen a few words at a time. These were followed by filmstrip projectors such as the "Controlled Reader." These devices can be useful in improving the reading of some students who have a great many regressions in their eye movement when reading. They also can be useful for increasing gradually the reading rate of those students whose other reading skills are adequate, but whose rate is slower than necessary; they also can help the student develop the habit of concentrating on his reading, for he knows that he cannot go back to reread a paragraph if he lets his mind wander.

A great deal of improvement in reading rate is often seen while a student is using "controlled reader" techniques. However, how much of this improvement will carry over to the regular reading of books varies greatly between individuals.

In using any device for increasing speed, it is important that the teacher check the students' comprehension frequently. Otherwise, the effort to develop speed may result in a significant loss in comprehension. If a drop in comprehension occurs, the speed setting should not be increased until adequate comprehension is again achieved.

Better carry-over of reading techniques developed through projected materials to the reading of books can sometimes be promoted through the use of an accelerator, a device with a shield which moves down over the page of print at a set rate.

Tachistoscopes

The tachistoscope is a mechanical device which allows a student to glimpse a letter, word, or phrase for a fraction of a second. There are two main types of tachistoscopes—a projector with a flash attachment that permits the operator to flash an image on the screen for a very short time and a small device to be held in the hand which uncovers a word and covers it again.

A number of both types of tachistoscopes are available on the market, and a small tagboard hand tachistoscope can easily be made by the teacher or pupils.[1] Several teachers have given the instructions for making the hand tachistoscope to junior high or upper elementary students and had them make their own tachistoscopes as an exercise in reading and following directions.

The overhead projector can be easily converted into a tachistoscope by placing a sheet of tagboard with a slot in it on the stage of the projector so that only one word of the transparency is projected at a time. Another sheet of tagboard held between the stage of the projector and the lens acts as a shutter. By moving this "shutter" back and forth quickly, the teacher can flash the word on the screen.

The purpose of the tachistoscope is to promote quick recognition of letters, words, or phrases, and to act as a motivational device. Seventy percent of primary reading and almost half of adult reading consists of a little over 200 basic words. If a person can recognize each of these basic words instantly, he will be able to read all material at a much higher speed than if he has to stop to analyze these words each time he comes to one of them in reading. The tachistoscope provides one method of practicing for this quick recognition, and also furnishes an incentive for this practice.

If the overhead projector is used as a tachistoscope, any list of words on which a student needs practice can be copied onto a transparency and practiced tachistoscopically.

Tachistoscopic practice loses its value if it is continued for more than a few minutes each day.

Reading Games

Games are very effective in providing practice on certain reading skills, for they can serve the same purposes as other drill and do it more effectively. Where drill is often monotonous and causes a loss of interest, the games can be highly motivating. However, time in the remedial reading class is too valuable to be used just for fun. A reading

---

[1] Complete instructions for making the hand tachistoscope can be found in Hap Gilliland, *Materials for Remedial Reading and Their Use,* Stapleton Building (Billings: Montana Reading Publications, 1976), pp. 131–41.

game should be used only if it will teach or reinforce a specific skill needed by the particular students who play it.

Most games are—or can be made—flexible enough to meet a variety of needs. A "rummy" game which today is used to give practice on beginning consonants may be used tomorrow with a different group of students to teach the short vowel sounds.

There are many good commercially produced reading games available. However, in too many classrooms, those games are used just as the directions are printed, even though the students using them may not need practice on the particular skill for which they were intended. With a little ingenuity on the part of teacher and students, these same games can be used to provide practice on a variety of other skills.

It often is profitable for the teacher to make up new games to meet the need for practice on a specific skill. Most card games—"rummy," "pig," "author," "poker," "black jack," "old maid"—can be revised to teach reading skills. "Auto race" games are always popular with children and can be varied to reach a variety of objectives. If the teacher will plan the basic game to give the required practice, the pupils will usually have good ideas for those added innovations that make the game exciting and fun.

Although reading games can be very useful as teaching devices, too-frequent use will cause them to lose their motivational advantage. The reading room should not become just a "game room."

Nonetheless, games are excellent devices to give pupils needed practice while the teacher instructs others, even though they are seldom as effective in teaching as direct instruction on a one-to-one basis. After a game has been taught to a group of pupils, they should be able to carry on with it and gain the benefit of the game without the teacher's assistance, thus freeing the teacher to work individually with other children.

In creating new reading games, or selecting games to be purchased, two items should be kept in mind. Although the student uses reading skills in playing the game, winning must be almost entirely a matter of chance so that the poor reader can win from the better reader; players should never be eliminated from the game for making errors. This policy would just give the practice to those who need it least.

Summary

The essentials of a good remedial reading program are—in order of importance:

1. A well-trained, interested, inspiring teacher

2. A variety of interesting, low vocabulary books

3. Other printed materials to meet specific needs

4. Other types of materials to add interest

Criteria for selection of remedial reading materials are:

1. Readability (The material must be easy enough to assure success.)

2. Subject areas of interest to the students

3. Skills material geared to specific needs of students

4. Material capable of being used independently by students

5. Cost in proportion to durability and usefulness

6. Writing must be for the age level of the students

7. Stories which are short, fast action, quick starting

8. A format appropriate to the age of the students

9. Variety

Effective use of materials is facilitated when:

1. All materials and equipment are stored in the reading room.

2. Workbook pages and worksheets are made into kits or filed according to skills taught.

Multi-level kits or "reading laboratories" can aid in:

1. Individualizing instruction

2. Teaching specific skills

Programmed reading materials follow five principles which the teacher can apply to all skills teaching:

1. The material to be taught is broken into small steps.

2. The steps are organized in logical order.

3. The student takes an active part in learning.

4. The student knows immediately if his answers are right or wrong.

5. The student learns at his own rate.

Newspapers have two advantages over other reading materials: They are more easily available and are better known to most students than other nonschool reading materials, and they are also the most easily accessible material appropriate for teaching such skills as interpretation of cartoons, recognition of propaganda techniques, and critical thinking.

The tape recorder is valuable for giving instructions on routine work to one group while the teacher works with another, for giving a student an opportunity for self-evaluation of his reading, for evaluating progress, and for improving fluency in oral reading.

The Language Master can help teach sight vocabulary and improve pronunciation.

The overhead projector can be used as a more effective chalkboard, for group reading of materials, for group discussion and completion of worksheets, and as a tachistoscope.

Opaque projectors can be used for projecting pages for group reading and as aids in copying materials on charts.

Film strips and motion picture films can be used to teach specific reading skills. They also can be used to build background and to motivate reading. Videotapes can be used for similar purposes.

Controlled reading projectors can be useful for developing good left-to-right eye movement, for breaking habits of regression, and for increasing the rate of reading. An accelerator may aid in getting a carryover and application of skills taught with these projected materials to the reading of books.

Tachistoscopes help to motivate the learning of quick recognition of words.

Many different kinds of games can be adapted to the teaching of phonics and other reading skills. These games give effective, highly motivated practice which can be carried on independently by one or more students.

Using a variety of materials makes it possible to adapt the remedial reading program more easily to the needs of each student. However, good materials do not necessarily insure a good reading program. It is the teacher's knowledge of the individual needs of each pupil and her innovative use of materials to meet those needs that makes the materials valuable. Nothing is as important as a well-informed teacher with an understanding of children and a real desire to help each individual child.

Recommended Related Reading

Beta Upsilon Chapter, Pi Lambda Theta. "Children's Reading Interests Classified by Age Level." *Reading Teacher* 27 (April 1974): 694–700.

Study covering grades 2 through 6.

Bleil, Gordon. "Evaluating Educational Materials." *Journal of Learning Disabilities* 8 (January 1975): 12–19.

Bleil states that "Teachers are less and less dispensers of narrow areas of knowledge and more and more managers of materials and systems created by technicians and specialists." He gives criteria for selecting materials to be purchased.

Carlsen, G. Robert. *Books and the Teenage Reader.* New York: Bantam Books, 1972.

Reading interests of children from grades five through college level.

Hagen, Mary and Barbara Selfermeser. "Surveying a Community for Reading Materials." *The Reading Teacher* 22 (December 1968): 228–29.

Suggestions on obtaining reading materials from the community.

Hallenbeck, Phyllis N. "Remediating with Comic Strips." *Journal of Learning Disabilities* 9 (January 1976): 11–15.

Tells of the advantages of using comic strips for teaching reading skills.

Hunt, Lynn C. "The Effect of Self-Selection, Interest, and Motivation upon Independent, Instructional, and Frustrational Levels." *The Reading Teacher* 24 (November 1970): 146–51.

Discusses ways in which self-selection of materials promotes motivation and motivation raises the child's reading level.

Johns, Jerry L. "What do Inner City Children Prefer to Read?" *The Reading Teacher* 26 (February 1973): 462–67.

Covers inner city children in grades 4–6.

Johnson, Laura S. "The Newspaper: A New Textbook Every Day." *Journal of Reading* 13 (November 1969): 107–12.

Describes a high school reading program based on the newspaper.

King, Ethel. "Critical Appraisal of Research on Children's Reading Habits." *Canadian Education and Research Digest* 7 (December 1967): 312–26.

A summary of information on children's reading interests gleaned from 300 different studies.

Kirsch, Dorothy, Robert S. V. Pehrsson, and H. Alan Robinson. "Expressed Reading Interests of Young Children: An International Study," in *New Horizons in Reading.* Newark, Del.: International Reading Association, 1976, p. 302.

A significant study of reading interests of children in ten countries.

Liebler, Roberta. "Reading Interests of Black and Puerto Rican, Inner-City, High School Students." *Graduate Research in Education and Related Disciplines* (Spring-Summer 1973): 23–43.

Studies interests of academic and college bound eleventh and twelfth grades. These may be quite different from those of remedial students from the same groups.

Palmatier, Robert A. "The Role of Machines in the Reading Program," in *The Quest for Competency in Teaching Reading,* ed. Howard A. Klein. Newark, Del.: International Reading Association, 1972, pp. 269–79.

Emphasizes the importance of making materials readily available to teachers, and of training teachers in their use.

Piercy, Dorothy. *A Daily Text for Thinking—Newspaper in the Classroom.* Phoenix: The Arizona Republic, 1970.

An excellent guide to the use of the newspaper in the reading program.

Robinson, Helen M. and Samuel Weintraub. "Research Related to Children's Interests and to Developmental Values of Reading." *Library Trends* 22 (October 1973): 81–108.

Reading interests of children from pre-school through high school.

Witty, Paul A. "Roll of Interest." *National Society for the Study of Education Yearbook, Part I.* Vol. 60, 1969, pp. 127–43.

Lists interests of different ages of children.

Tests Referred to in This Book and Their Publishers

Ammons Full Range Picture Vocabulary Test—Psychological Test Specialists

Analysis of Reading Difficulty—Harcourt Brace Jovanovich, Inc.

Arthur Point Scale of Performance Tests—C. H. Stoelting Company

Auditory Discrimination—see Wepman, Monroe, Templin

Bender Visual Motor Gestalt Test—American Orthopsychiatric Association, Inc.

Botel Reading Inventory—Follett Publishing Company

California Phonics Survey—California Test Bureau

California Reading Test—California Test Bureau

California Study Habits Survey—California Test Bureau

California Test of Mental Maturity—California Test Bureau

California Test of Personality—California Test Bureau

Classroom Reading Inventory, Silvaroli—William C. Brown Publishing Company

Clymer Barrett Prereading Battery—Personnel Press

Contemporary School Readiness Test—Montana Reading Publications

Detroit Test of Learning Aptitudes—Public School Publishing Co. Division of Bobbs-Merrill Company, Inc.

Detroit Test of Memory Span—Bobbs-Merrill Publishing Company, Inc.

Developmental Survey of Basic Learning Abilities—Consulting Psychologists Press, Inc.

Developmental Test of Visual Motor Integration—Follett Educational Corporation

Diagnostic Reading Scales—California Test Bureau

Diagnostic Reading Test—Scholastic Testing Service, Inc.

Draw-A-Person Test—Harcourt Brace Jovanovich, Inc.

Durrell Analysis of Reading Difficulty—Harcourt Brace Jovanovich, Inc.

Durrell Listening-Reading Series—Harcourt Brace Jovanovich, Inc.

Durrell-Sullivan Reading Capacity Test—Harcourt Brace Jovanovich, Inc.

Eames Eye Test—Harcourt Brace Jovanovich, Inc.

Eisenson's Examining for Aphasia—Psychological Corporation

Frostig Developmental Test of Visual Perception, 3rd ed.—Psychological Corporation

Full-Range Picture Vocabulary Test—Psychological Test Specialists

Gates-MacGinitie Readiness Skills Test—Teachers College, Columbia University

Gates-McKillop Reading Diagnostic Tests—Bureau of Publications, Teachers College, Columbia University

Gates Basic Reading Tests—Bureau of Publications, Teachers College, Columbia University

Gestalt Completion Test—Industrial Relations Center

Gilliland Learning Potential Examination—Montana Council for Indian Education

Gilliland Test of Individual Needs—Montana Reading Publications

Gilmore Oral Reading Test—Harcourt Brace Jovanovich, Inc.

Goldman-Fristoe-Woodcock Test of Auditory Discrimination—American Guidance Service

Goldstein Sheerer Cube Test—Psychological Corporation

Goodenough-Harris Draw-a-Man Test—Harcourt Brace Jovanovich, Inc.

Harrison-Stroud Reading Readiness Profile—Houghton-Mifflin Co.

Hearing of Speech Tests—Pennsylvania State University

Illinois Test of Psycho-linguistic Abilities (ITPA)—University of Illinois Press

Iowa Every-Pupil Test of Basic Skills—Houghton Mifflin Company

Kendal-Graham Memory for Designs Test—Psychological Test Specialists

Keystone Telebinocular—Keystone View Company

Learning Potential Examination—Montana Reading Publications

Lincoln-Oseretsky Motor Development Scale—C. H. Stoelting Company

Lorge Thorndike Intelligence Test—Houghton Mifflin Company

Macmillan Reading Readiness Test—Macmillan Publishing Company

McKee Inventory of Phonetic Skill—Houghton Mifflin Company

Memory for Designs Test—Psychological Test Specialists

Metropolitan Readiness Tests—Harcourt Brace Jovanovich, Inc.

Metropolitan Reading Test—Harcourt Brace Jovanovich, Inc.

Minnesota Pre-School Scale—Educational Test Bureau, American Guidance Service, Inc.

Money Road-Map Test of Directional Sense—The John Hopkins University Press

Monroe Auditory Discrimination Test in *Children Who Cannot Read* by Marion Monroe—University of Chicago Press

Moore Eye-Hand Coordination and Color-Matching Test—Joseph E. Moore & Associates

Murphy-Durrell Reading Readiness Analysis—Harcourt Brace Jovanovich, Inc.

Oliphant Auditory Discrimination Memory Test—Educators Publishing Service

Oliphant Auditory Synthesizing Test—Educators Publishing Service

Ophthalmograph—see *Reading Eye* camera

Peabody Picture Vocabulary Test—Educational Test Bureau American Guidance Service, Inc.

Perceptual Forms Test—Winter Haven Lions Research Foundation

Picture Vocabulary Test—Psychological Test Specialists

Pre-Reading Inventory—Houghton-Mifflin Company

Primary Visual Motor Test—Grune & Straton

Purdue Perceptual-Motor Survey—Charles E. Merrill Publishing Company

Reader's Digest Skill Builders (used for testing speed and comprehension)—Reader's Digest Association

Reading Diagnosis Kit, Miller—Center for Applied Research in Education

Reading Eye (Eye Movement Camera)—Educational Developmental Laboratories, Inc.

Rorschach Test—Harcourt Brace Jovanovich, Inc.

SIT (Slosson Intelligence Test)—Slosson Educational Publications

Slingerland Test—Educator's Publishing Service

Slosson Intelligence Test (SIT)—Slosson Educational Publications

Southern California Figure-Ground Visual Perception Test—Western Psychological Services

Southern California Kinesthetic and Tactile Perception Tests—Western Psychological Services

Southern California Perceptual-Motor Tests—Western Psychological Services

Spache Orientation Memory Test—Language Research Associates

Spatial Orientation Memory Test—Language Research Associates

Standard Reading Inventory, McCracken—Klamath Printing Company

SRA Reading Record—Science Research Associates, Inc.

Stanford-Binet Intelligence Scale—Houghton Mifflin Company

Stanford Diagnostic Reading Test—Harcourt Brace Jovanovich, Inc.

Stencil Design Test (from *Arthur Point Scale of Performance Tests)*—C. H. Stoelting Company

STS Diagnostic Reading Test—Scholastic Testing Service, Inc.

Survey of Study Habits and Attitudes—Psychological Corporation

Syracuse Visual Figure-Background Test—Syracuse University Press

Telebinocular—Keystone View Company

"Templin Auditory Discrimination Test" in *Certain Language Skills in Children* by M. C. Templin—University of Minnesota Press

Test of Individual Needs in Reading—Montana Reading Publications

Vineland Scale of Social Maturity—Educational Test Bureau

WAIS (Wechsler Adult Intelligence Scale)—Psychological Corporation

Weigl Goldstein Sheerer Color Form Sorting Test—Psychological Corporation

Wechsler Adult Intelligence Scale (WAIS)—Psychological Corporation

Wechsler Intelligence Scale for Children (WISC)—Psychological Corporation

WISC (Wechsler Intelligence Scale for Children)—Psychological Corporation

Woodcock Reading Mastery Tests—American Guidance Service

Publishers of Tests

American Guidance Service, Inc.
Publisher's Building
Circle Pines, Minnesota 55014

American Orthopsychiatric
   Association, Inc.
1775 Broadway
New York, New York 10019

The Bobbs-Merrill Company, Inc.
4300 West 62 Street
Indianapolis, Indiana 46268

William C. Brown Publishing
   Company
2460 Kerper Blvd.
Dubuque, Iowa 52003

California Test Bureau
Del Monte Research Park
Monterey, California 93940
Center for Applied Research in
   Education, Inc.
521 Fifth Avenue
New York, New York 10017

Consulting Psychologists Press, Inc.
577 College Avenue
Palo Alto, California 94306

Educational Developmental
   Laboratories, Inc.
1221 Avenue of the Americas
New York, New York 10020

Educational Test Bureau
American Guidance Service, Inc.
Publishers Building
Circle Pines, Minnesota 55014

Educational Test Bureau
Philadelphia, Pennsylvania 19103

Educator's Publishing Service
75 Moulton Street
Cambridge, Massachusetts 02138

Follett Publishing Company
1010 West Washington Boulevard
Chicago, Illinois 60607

Grune and Straton, Inc.
111 Fifth Avenue
New York, New York 10003

Harcourt Brace Jovanovich, Inc.
757 Third Avenue
New York, New York 10017

Houghton-Mifflin Company
2 Park Street
Boston, Massachusetts 02107

Industrial Relations Center
University of Chicago
Chicago, Illinois 60637

The Johns Hopkins University
   Press
Baltimore, Maryland 21218

Keystone View Company
2212 East Davenport
Davenport, Iowa 52803

Klamath Printing Company
320 Lowell Street
Klamath Falls, Oregon 97601

Language Research Associates, Inc.
175 East Delaware Place
Chicago, Illinois 60611

Macmillan Publishing Company
866 Third Avenue
New York, New York 10022

Charles E. Merrill Publishing
   Company
1300 Alum Creek Drive
Columbus, Ohio 43216

Miami University Alumni
   Association
Murstein Alumni Center
Miami University
Oxford, Ohio 45056

Montana Council for Indian
   Education
517 Rimrock Road
Billings, Montana 59102

Montana Reading Publications
1810 3rd Avenue, North
Billings, Montana 59101

Joseph E. Moore & Associates
4406 Jett Road, N W
Atlanta, Georgia 30327

Pennsylvania State University
6 Willard Building
University Park, Pennsylvania
    16802

Personnel Press
191 Spring Street
Lexington, Massachusetts 02173

Public School Publishing Company
Division of Bobbs-Merrill
    Company, Inc.
4300 West 62 Street
Indianapolis, Indiana 46268

Psychological Corporation
304 East 45th Street
New York, New York 10017

Psychological Test Specialists
Box 1441
Missoula, Montana 59801

Reader's Digest Association
Pleasantville, New York 10570

Slosson Educational Publications
140 Pine Street
East Aurora, New York 14052

Science Research Associates, Inc.
259 East Erie Street
Chicago, Illinois 60611

Scholastic Testing Service, Inc.
480 Meyer Road
Bensenville, Illinois 60106

C. H. Stoelting Company
1350 South Kostner Avenue
Chicago, Illinois 60623

Syracuse University Press
Box 8
University Station
Syracuse, New York 13210

Bureau of Publications
Teachers College, Columbia
    University
1234 Amsterdam Avenue
New York, New York 10027

University of Chicago Press
5801 Ellis Avenue
Chicago, Illinois 60637

University of Illinois Press
Urbana, Illinois 61801

University of Minnesota Press
2037 University Avenue, S E
Minneapolis, Minnesota 55455

Western Psychological Services
12031 Wilshire Blvd.
Los Angeles, California 90025

Winter Haven Lions Research
    Foundation, Inc.
Box 111
Winter Haven, Florida 33880

Index